Donna Malcolm 04/93 VAN GOGH MUSEUM, Amsterdam.
8.26
cost 49.50

KU-452-178

‘A Great Artist is Dead’

Letters of Condolence on Vincent van Gogh’s Death

CAHIER VINCENT 4

Rijksmuseum Vincent van Gogh
in cooperation with the Vincent van Gogh Foundation

Ronald Pickvance

'A GREAT ARTIST IS DEAD'

Letters of Condolence on Vincent van Gogh's death

Edited by Sjraar van Heugten and Fieke Pabst

Waanders Publishers, Zwolle

Contents

Foreword

One of the apparently indestructible myths surrounding Vincent Van Gogh is that his contemporaries failed to recognize his genius. While there is no denying that Van Gogh struggled hard for his very survival from the moment he decided to become an artist at the beginning of the 1880s, these circumstances should be seen in their proper perspective. As Alan Bowness recently observed in his Walther Neurath Memorial Lecture (*The Conditions of Success: How the Modern Artist Rises to Fame*, London 1989), Van Gogh's career differed little from that of any other talented avant-garde artist. One might even say that the completely unknown Dutch artist who went to Paris in 1886 to revitalize his hitherto old-fashioned manner of painting, had little cause for complaint when he was invited a mere three years later to take part in the exciting exhibitions held by the Indépendants in Paris and Les XX in Brussels. Shortly before his death, Van Gogh enjoyed the recognition of a select group of artists, while leading critics such as Albert Aurier had shown interest in his work. Notwithstanding this unequivocal success, the prevailing view of his career continues to be defined in terms of his tragic personal life and his untimely death.

The letters of condolence which Theo and his family received after the announcement of Vincent's death attest to the fact that Van Gogh – far from lacking recognition or affection – died precisely when he was making his breakthrough as an artist. Not only had he established a reputation among the avant-garde, to which he himself belonged, but older artists, too, had demonstrated their appreciation of his work. And even some of his relatives had finally come to realize that Vincent's career as an artist could no longer be written off as yet another of his failures.

This interesting set of letters belongs to the Vincent van Gogh Foundation. The museum was fortunate enough to enlist the expertise of Ronald Pickvance, who prepared the letters for publication. The project was supervised and coordinated by Sjraar van Heugten, research curator of the Van Gogh Research Project. For the complex editorial work, we are also greatly indebted to our documentalist Fieke Pabst.

Ronald de Leeuw
Director

Preface

I should like to thank many people who helped me realize this publication. First of all, Johan van Gogh, President of the Vincent van Gogh Foundation and Ronald de Leeuw, Director of the Van Gogh Museum, both of whom responded warmly to my initial suggestion of a publication of the letters of condolence on Vincent's death.

Within the Van Gogh Museum, I owe a great debt to two old friends whose track record in unearthing documents and references is impeccable: I'm referring to Han van Crimpen and Fieke Pabst. Han has given freely of his time on many occasions; and I for one look forward impatiently to his publication of the letters exchanged by Theo and Jo. Fieke has tracked down the identities of several, and the dates of other, Dutch friends of Vincent's. Louis van Tilborgh began as the editor and gave much early encouragement. His mantle has been efficiently and good-humouredly taken over by Sjraar van Heugten: I'm grateful to him for gently reminding me that deadlines do exist, even for condolences. Anita Vriend has swiftly answered many calls in the library. I'm extremely grateful to Martha Op de Coul for providing the necessary biographical skeleton for the Roos family in The Hague.

Yvette Rosenberg has produced an efficient rendering of the unruly nineteenth century Dutch, and the appropriately simple layout is by Marjo Starink.

In Paris, I have received much help in decoding the odd recalcitrant word of French, and in preparing much of my medievally written manuscript for the modern computer from the three resident magicians of the Institut Van Gogh – Dominique Janssens, Yves Schwarzbach and Martine Villemot.

As always, my wife has acted as a critical collaborator; and, as always, the debt goes beyond mere words.

I know that everyone will join me in dedicating this small opus to the memory of a very dear and indomitable spirit whose remorselessly high standards and relentless search for the truth about Van Gogh, shedding the dross of accumulated legend, insinuation and false innuendo, made her a constantly stimulating companion on the trail of *her* beloved Vincent. Sadly, Artemis Karagheusian died in January 1990: one of fate's nastier blows, preventing her from seeing the Centenary Exhibition in Amsterdam and Otterlo. Nor will she read this; but I like to think that her spirit informs it, and that she would approve of it.

Ronald Pickvance

Introduction
'A Great Artist is Dead'.

Letters of condolence have an ephemeral and private quality, as well as a contrived and artificial element in their make-up. They respond to certain rituals of social behaviour and operate within certain established conventions. There is seemingly little scope for totally honest appraisal – that is more the province of an obituary notice; nor is it always appropriate to express deeply felt grief. Such constraints do not seem to provide the stuff of biographical and artistic *aperçus*.

Why, then, publish the letters of condolence received by Theo van Gogh, his wife and his mother on the death of Vincent van Gogh on 29 July 1890? Does it reflect nothing more than a morbid interest in every little aspect of Van Gogh's existence – and his immediate 'existence' after death? And of what value can they be when we are led to believe that Van Gogh was unappreciated and virtually friendless during his lifetime, the very epitome of the *peintre maudit* who didn't sell any paintings? Here is the popular Romantic myth on which to hang the parasitical roster of cumulative misery and inevitable martyrdom. And such an image is further heightened by the legend that only eight people attended his funeral.

So how many letters of condolence might there to be to satisfy the accepted legends? Eight also? Ten perhaps? A dozen at most? Apart from members of his family – some thirteen letters – there are thirty-seven letters. Eleven came from Dutch artists and acquaintances; twenty-six from French, Australian, Belgian, Danish, English and Italian. In all, some fifty letters.

It's not just the quantity that surprises one and upsets the accepted legends; nor that among those who wrote were Monet and Pissarro, Guillaumin and Vignon, Gauguin and Toulouse-Lautrec, Aurier and Fénéon, Comte Doria and Henri Rouart, Breitner and Isaac Israëls, Gausson and Dr Gachet. It's the quality of what they said. These letters reveal a great deal about his friends' view of him *as friend*. As for their view of him *as artist*, the marks of appreciation of his talent, significance and stature are quite remarkable, whether from Monet, Pissarro, Aurier, Fénéon, Van Rappard, Mourier Petersen, Dr Gachet and the Belgian artist Eugène Boch who assured Theo: 'a great artist is dead'.

Those who had never met Vincent but who had seen his work in Paris at Theo's, in exhibitions, or in dealers' shops, wrote admiringly of his work. The Dutch artist Meijer de Haan, friend of Theo and painting partner of Gauguin in Brittany, for instance; or the Italian Vittorio Corcos who knew only the paintings from the Dutch period, especially those from Nuenen, and thought they 'showed an extremely well observed and intensely felt vision of nature'.

The Neo-Impressionist Léo Gausson often went to Tanguy's shop just to see

Vincent's paintings, and hoped that even without knowing him, Vincent would agree to exchange a picture with one of his own. While Monet had already told Theo in April 1890 that the ten paintings he had seen by Vincent at the Salon des Indépendants were the best in the show; so all he needed to say in his letter of condolence was 'I have already told you of my feelings for your brother'.

As for the quality of Vincent's friendship, one has only to read the letters from Toulouse-Lautrec, the Australian John Russell, Quost, Van Rappard and the Dane Mourier Petersen to gain some notion of how highly it was valued. And Gauguin, too, affirms that for him Vincent was 'a sincere friend'; and 'an *artist* a rare thing in our epoch'.

So much for the myth of the friendless artist, unappreciated and unrecognized. Of course, some friends were brief – Koning and Breitner, Guillaumin and Vignon. And Camille Pissarro, writing in haste, was unable to expand his thoughts and feelings. His son Lucien attended the funeral at Auvers, and therefore did not write to Theo. But another Neo-Impressionist, Louis Hayet, did write. Indeed, with Gaussons's outstandingly appreciative letter, the Neo-Impressionist network functions well. And, as so often in the years from 1886 to 1890, that network was activated by the art critic Félix Fénéon.

One has to remember that by the end of July many artists had already left Paris for their summer painting campaigns. And it was Fénéon, still in Paris, who told Signac in Saint-Briac, Brittany, of Vincent's death. Signac in turn then wrote to Seurat, who was working at Gravelines on the Channel coast. Seurat in turn then relayed the news back to Paris in his famous letter of 28 August 1890 to the art critic Maurice Beaubourg. And Beaubourg incorporated much of what Seurat wrote about Vincent in his obituary notice that appeared in the *Revue Indépendante* of September.

But there are additional side-products for the historian that add point and sometimes a note of mystery. Take the questions of family appreciation of Vincent's work, and that of lost paintings.

It would be wrong to think that no one in the family appreciated Vincent's achievement. Certainly his sister Wil did: she was, after all, something of his pupil by proxy in the appreciation of 'modern' painting as well as in the appreciation of the 'modern' novel. But another sister can now be added: Lies. Three days after Vincent's death, Lies told Theo of two paintings that she had and how much she admired them. Eventually, Lies had the largest collection of Van Gogh's work of all the family (except Jo of course); its true extent, its mode of acquisition, and its eventual dispersal all need defining. For the moment, her letter to Theo is by far the most interesting of all the family letters.

As for the question of lost paintings, the point arises in the letter of Léo Gausson. He pressed Theo hard for an exchange; and it is virtually certain that Gausson's painting *Le clocher de Bussy-Saint Georges* (Van Gogh Museum), represented his side of the exchange. But what of Vincent's painting? Gausson continued to paint (and sculpt) until 1901 when he suddenly abandoned his métier and went to Guinea (French West Africa) where he lived on and off until 1908, occupying minor government posts. Was it there that he took Van Gogh's painting? And left it, so that it is now lost and destroyed?

There are three lost Arles paintings: an upright version of the park or garden in the Place Lamartine, a 'pendant' to the well-known and happily still existing horizontal version (F 428). This upright version is recorded in one of Vincent's twelve drawings after his paintings that he sent to Russell in early August 1888 (F 1449). The next lost painting is one of *Thistles*, described in a letter of August 1888 (LT 522). And the third is fully documented in a long letter description (LT 541) as well as in two drawings (F 1465 and LT 553b). Could one of these have been the exchange with Gausson? And lost in West Africa between 1901 and 1908?

One has strayed from the straight-and-narrow path of documents to seemingly wild and improbable hypotheses. Returning to the letters and disclosures that emerge from them, there is one whose correct dating has biographical and psychologically significant consequences. Theo's letter to Jo after Vincent's death was quoted in part in the 1914 Introduction, but without giving a date. This omission has led some writers to assume that the letter was written on Tuesday 29 July, the very day of Vincent's death. In fact it is dated Friday 1 August. Why should this two-day difference be so important? First, it makes clear that Theo allowed four days to elapse without writing a word to Jo – from Monday 28 July to Friday 1 August. Nor, as has been claimed, did he send a telegram to his mother. He avoided doing so for quite deliberate reasons. It would have been too cruelly abrupt, and all the more so after the family had come to believe that Vincent was now calmly and happily settled in Auvers-sur-Oise, cared for by Dr Gachet, enjoying the picturesque ambience of the village, and only one hour by rail from Theo and Jo in Paris. Theo could not break the news of Vincent's death so abruptly to the womenfolk in Leiden and Amsterdam. He chose to remain silent with his wife. And he chose a different stratagem for his mother. Theo wrote one letter only on Tuesday 29 July: to his brother-in-law, J.M. van Houten, who lived just outside Leiden, and who broke the news by word of mouth, gently, the day after Vincent's burial. And only on Friday 1 August, when Theo was back in Paris, did he write both to his mother and to Jo. By then, of course, the whole family knew.

More serious innuendos can now be dismissed. In particular, that which suggested that Gachet's letter to Theo of 27 July telling of Vincent's attempted suicide, had been arbitrarily cut in two places by Jo to conceal the fact that Gachet and Vincent had bitterly quarrelled. The 'offending' letter is reproduced here, transcribed and translated, and no such passage exists. Gachet and Jo are vindicated.

Gachet, indeed, becomes the hero and very much the lead actor. And the major revelation of these fifty letters has to be his of mid-August 1890, so long hibernating à la Rip van Winkle, and here rescued and given the full spotlight. It is an astonishing letter; and rendered more astonishing by its being unique. No other written assessment of Vincent by Gachet exists: it is his sole testimony. Without disclosing its date, without knowing that it responded to Theo's letter of 12 August to Gachet, Jo took from it its most assertive value-judgement: Giant-Colossus and Philosopher – Martyr à la Seneca. While this has occasionally been repeated by later writers, its significance has never been discussed or dissected. And using the metaphor of Seneca's suicide, Gachet develops the argument further. Antonin Artaud, whose vividly violent and wilfully wrong-headed, yet often amazingly acute, exegesis of Vincent's suicide, would surely now be forced to modify his view of Gachet, *pace* doctor, as murderer of Vincent. He might now have saluted the letter, however reluctantly, if not Gachet himself.

The Gachet letter was lost by Theo's mother in September 1890. But it was eventually found and Jo had access to it for her 1914 Introduction. Since then, it has been lost again. Its re-emergence gives one hope that another letter that Jo cited liberally at three different prints in that same 1914 Introduction could also be resurrected – Van Rappard's letter to Vincent's mother. For the moment, one can only regret its disappearance.

And another note of hope: that someone reading this small opus might come up with firm and incontrovertible evidence that will identify beyond doubt the mysterious writer of the letter published here as Dutch 10. Is he Van Teijn or is he not?

The material is plentiful: some 50 letters of condolence. How could it best be handled? A chronologically unfolding sequence was certainly possible, but it would have separated like from like. A division into three groups is preferable, each having some unity in itself. Thus, a family group of 13 letters is followed by a Dutch group of 11 letters, with, finally, a group of 26 French and Others, the 'others' being, with one exception, very much artists, friends, and admirers with definite French connections.

Preceding the letters of condolence is a prologue of four letters that describes the events from Sunday 27 July, when Vincent shot himself, to Wednesday 30 July, the day of his funeral.

To provide the larger historical perspective – and also as a document in its own right – Johanna van Gogh-Bonger's account of Vincent's Auvers period, written in December 1913, is reprinted. This was the concluding part to her long Introduction to the first collected edition of Vincent's letters published in spring 1914. There, Jo often chose passages from letters that are published here in full.

Van Gogh in Auvers-sur-Oise
by Johanna van Gogh-Bonger, 1913*

To set the scene for the letters of condolence, it seems useful to publish Johanna van Gogh-Bonger's account of Vincent's stay in Auvers-sur-Oise, written in December 1913. This was published, in the spring of 1914, as the final part of her biographical memoir that introduced the first edition of Vincent's letters.

Johanna Gesina Bonger, known as Jo, was born in Amsterdam on 4 October 1862, the fifth child of a family of seven. Her father, Hendrik Christiaan Bonger (1828-1904), was an insurance broker who enjoyed music. Jo was well-educated, spending some time in London to improve her English and study English literature. In 1884, she taught English at Elburg and later in Utrecht. She married Theo van Gogh in April 1889; their only child, Vincent Willem, was born on 31 January 1890. After Theo's death in January 1891, she devoted herself to the task of preparing Vincent's letters for publication.

She herself was very much a participant in the unfolding tragedy of the summer of 1890. No longer a recently married woman receiving letters from a brother-in-law some 730 kilometres away in Provence, no longer a somewhat perplexed admirer of the many paintings her husband received, Jo now knew Vincent, talked with him, observed him. She knew, too, Auvers-sur-Oise and Dr Gachet, especially after her day's visit on Sunday 8 June. She would have seen there Vincent's recently completed paintings, including the portrait of Dr Gachet (F 753). In Paris, she met Vincent's and Theo's friends and admirers: the artist's colourman 'Père' Tanguy, the art critic G. Albert Aurier, the artists Pissarro (father and son), Guillaumin and Toulouse-Lautrec.

She was subsumed into Vincent's world – and directly involved in such ways that *her* decisions could crucially affect Vincent's life. All this is disguised in her Memoir, where she sees herself as recorder and observer, allowing others to speak for themselves. In particular, she often quotes Dr Gachet and Theo, allowing their words to provide her with a great deal of primary evidence: for the most part without editorial comment. Whatever parti-pris or interpretive angle she adopts is confined to the thesis that Vincent's death was self-generated (determined, that is, within the confines of his own 'illness' and the fear of another 'attack'), and that Theo, together with Dr Gachet, did everything possible to ease his burden. This is arguably too simple an explanation; but in a Cahier essentially devoted to the publication of documents, it is inappropriate to argue at length the tenability of such a position.

Jo told the story simply and movingly. Elaborate questioning of motivation and questions of guilt and remorse were left to later commentators. (And how they have grasped the nettle!).

For some time Theo had been looking around for a suitable place – near Paris and yet in the country – where Vincent could live under the care of a physician who would at the same time be a friend to him. On Pissarro's recommendation he finally found this at Auvers-sur-Oise, an hour by train from Paris; Dr Gachet, who in his youth had been a friend of Cézanne, Pissarro and the other impressionists, lived there.[1] Vincent returned from the South on May 17, 1890. First he was going to spend a few days with us in Paris. A telegram from Tarascon informed us that he was going to travel that night and would arrive at ten in the morning. That night Theo could not sleep for anxiety lest something happen to Vincent on the way; he had only just recovered from a long and serious attack, and had refused to be accompanied by anyone.[2]

How thankful we were when it was at last time for Theo to go to the station![3] It was a long way from the Cité Pigalle to the Gare de Lyon; it seemed an eternity before they came back. I was beginning to be afraid that something had happened when at last I saw an open fiacre enter the Cité; two merry faces nodded to me, two hands waved – a moment later Vincent stood before me. I had expected a sick man, but here was a sturdy, broad-shouldered man, with a healthy colour, a smile on his face, and a very resolute appearance; of all the self-portraits, the one before the easel is most like him in that period.[4] Apparently there had again come the sudden puzzling change in his condition that the Reverend Mr. Salles had already observed to his great surprise in Arles.[5]

'He seems perfectly well; he looks much stronger than Theo', was my first thought.

Then Theo drew him into the room where our little boy's cradle was; he had been named after Vincent.[6] Silently the two brothers looked at the baby sleeping quietly – both had tears in their eyes. Then Vincent turned to me smiling and said, pointing to the simple crocheted cover on the cradle, 'Do not cover him with too much lace, little sister'.

He stayed with us three days, and was cheerful and lively all the time. Saint-Rémy was not mentioned. He went out by himself to buy olives, which he used to eat every day and which he insisted on our eating too. The first morning he was up very early and was standing in his shirtsleeves looking at his pictures, which filled our apartment. The walls were covered with them – in the bedroom,the orchards in bloom; in the dining room over the mantelpiece, the Potato Eaters; in the sitting room (salon was too grand a name for that cosy little room), the great landscape from Arles and the night view on the Rhône. Besides, to the great despair of our *femme de ménage*, there were under the bed, under the sofa, under the cupboards in the litle spare room, huge piles of unframed canvases; they were now spread out on the ground and studied with great attention.[7] We also had many visitors,[8] but Vincent soon perceived that the bustle of Paris did him no good, and he longed to set to work again. So on May 21 he started for Auvers, with an introduction to Dr Gachet,[9] whose faithful friendship was to become his greatest support during the short time he spent at Auvers. We promised to come and see him soon, and he also wanted to come back to us in a few weeks to paint our portraits. In Auvers he lodged at an inn and went to work immediately.[10] The hilly landscape with the sloping fields and thatched roofs of the village pleased him, but what he enjoyed most was having models and again painting figures. One of the first portraits he painted was of Dr Gachet,[11] who immediately felt great sympathy for Vincent. They spent most of their time together and became great friends – a friendship not ended by death, for Dr Gachet and his children continued to honour Vincent's memory with rare piety, which became a form of worship, touching in its simplicity and sincerity.[12]

'The more I think of it, the more I regard Vincent as *a giant*. Not a day goes by without my looking at his canvases. I always find a new idea in them, something different from the day before, and I return by the mental phenomenon of thought to the man himself whom I think of as a Colossus... He was, moreover, a philosopher [...]', Gachet wrote to Theo shortly after Vincent's death. Speaking of the latter's love for art, he said, 'The word *love* of art is not right – *Faith* is the proper word. Faith to the point of martyrdom!!!!'[13] None of his contemporaries had understood him better.

It was curious to note that Dr Gachet himself somewhat resembled Vincent physically (he was much older), and his son Paul – then a boy of fifteen – looked somewhat like Theo.[14]

The Gachet house, built on a hill, was full of pictures and antiques, which received but scant daylight through the small windows; in front of the house there was a splendid terraced flower garden, at the back a large yard where all kinds of ducks, hens, turkeys and peacocks walked about in the company of four or five cats. It was the home of an eccentric, but an eccentric of great taste. The doctor no longer practiced in Auvers, but had an office in Paris where he held consultations several days a week; the rest of the time he painted and etched in his room, which looked like the workshop of a medieval alchemist.[15]

Soon after, on June 10, we received an invitation from him to spend a whole day in Auvers and bring the baby. Vincent came to meet us at the train, and he brought a bird's nest as a plaything for his little nephew and namesake. He insisted upon carrying the baby himself and had no rest until he had shown him all the animals in the yard. A cock crowing too loudly made the baby flushed with fear and made him cry; Vincent laughed, 'The cock says *cocorico*', and was very proud that he had introduced his little namesake to the animal world.

We lunched in the open air, and afterwards took a long walk; the day was so peacefully quiet, so happy that nobody would have suspected how tragically our happiness was to be destroyed a few weeks later.[16]

Early in July, Vincent visited us once more in Paris.[17] We were exhausted by the baby, who was seriously ill; Theo was again considering the old plan of leaving Goupil and setting up in business for himself; Vincent was not satisfied with the place where the pictures were kept, and our move to a larger apartment was discussed – so those were days of much worry and anxiety.[18]

Many friends came to visit Vincent – among them Aurier, who had recently written his famous article about Vincent, and now came again to look at the pictures with the painter himself.[19] Toulouse-Lautrec stayed for lunch and made many jokes with Vincent about a pallbearer they had met on the stairs.[20] Guillaumin was also expected,[21] but it became too much for Vincent, so he did not wait for this visit but hurried back to Auvers – overtired and excited, as his last letters and pictures show, in which the threatening catastrophe seems approaching like the ominous black birds that dart through the storm over the wheatfields.

'I hope he is not getting melancholy or that a new attack is threatening again, everything has gone so well lately', Theo wrote to me on July 20, after he had taken the baby and me to Holland and returned to Paris for a short time until he also could take a vacation.[22] On July 25 he wrote to me, 'I have a letter from Vincent which seems quite incomprehensible; when will there come a happy time for him? He is so thoroughly good'.[23] That happy time was never to come for Vincent; fear of an impending attack or the attack itself drove him to his death. On the evening of July 27 he shot himself with a revolver. Dr Gachet wrote to Theo that same evening: 'It is with the utmost regret that I intrude on your privacy, however I regard it as my duty to write to you immediately, today, Sunday, at nine o'clock in the evening I was sent for by your brother Vincent, who wanted to see me at once. I went there and found him very ill. He has wounded himself... Not having your address which he refused to give me, this letter will reach you through Goupil'.[24] Consequently, the letter did not reach Theo until the next morning; he immediately started for Auvers. He wrote to me from there the same day, July 28, 'This morning a Dutch painter who is also in Auvers came to bring me a letter from Dr Gachet who had bad news about Vincent and requested me to come. Abandoning everything I went at once and found him better than I had thought, although he is very very ill. I shan't enter into detail, it is all too sad, but know my love that his life might be in danger. [...] He was pleased that I had come and we are together almost constantly. [...] Poor fellow, he was not granted much happiness, he cherishes no more illusions. It is sometimes too much for him, he feels so alone. [...] He talks to me so agreeably & inquired after you and the boy & said that you had not imagined such sadness in life, how I wish we could give him faith in life. [...] Don't worry, things have been as hopeless before & the doctors were surprised by his strong constitution'.[25]

This hope proved idle. Early on the morning of July 29 Vincent passed away.[26]

Theo wrote to me, 'One of his last words was I wanted it to end like this & so it was for a few moments & it was over & he found the peace he could not find on earth [...] the following morning 8 friends came from Paris & elsewhere and hung his paintings that looked so beautiful on the walls of the room that the coffin was in. There were masses of bouquets and wreaths. Dr Gachet was the first to bring a magnificent bouquet of sunflowers because he loved them so dearly. [...] He is buried in a sunny spot in the middle of the cornfields'.[27]

From a letter of Theo's to his mother: 'One cannot write how sad one is nor find solace in pouring out one's heart on paper. [...] It is a sadness which will weigh upon me for a long time and will certainly not leave my thoughts as long as I live, but if one should want to say anything it is that he himself has found the rest he so much longed for. [...] Life weighed so heavily upon him, but as happens more often everyone is now full of praise for his talent too. [...] Oh Mother, he was so very much my own brother'.[28]

* The translation of Jo's Memoir has been taken from the English edition of the letters from 1958, with amendments and corrections. Passages quoted by Jo from letters which appear in this cahier are published in the new translation.

1. Vincent had been living at the asylum of Saint-Paul-de-Mausole at Saint-Rémy-de-Provence since May 1889. Already in September 1889, he had intimated to Theo that he wished to leave the asylum and return to the North (LT 607). Vincent suggested he might share a studio in the country with Victor Vignon. But it was Pissarro who suggested Dr Gachet at Auvers-sur-Oise (T 18, 4 October 1889). Several months passed before Theo eventually met Dr Gachet - towards the end of March 1890 (T 31, 29 March 1890). Dr Paul-Ferdinand Gachet (1828-1909), homeopathic doctor, collector, etcher and eccentric, had lived in Auvers-sur-Oise since 1872. Cézanne, Pissarro and Guillaumin worked there. See Gachet's letters to Theo (Prologue 1 and French 21).

2. The 'long and serious attack' had lasted two months – from 22 February to 24 April 1890. Yet Vincent's recovery was astonishingly rapid and complete. During his last three weeks in Saint-Rémy, his output was phenomenal. He insisted to Theo that he should travel alone from Tarascon to Paris.

3. Theo and Jo had moved to a fourth-floor apartment at 8 Cité Pigalle after their marriage in April 1889. Jo described the apartment, its outlook, its furnishing and the hanging of Vincent's pictures, in what was her first letter to him of 8 May 1889 (T 8).

4. The self-portrait is F 522.

5. The Reverend Fréderic Salles was the Protestant Pastor who befriended Vincent in Arles after his hospitalization in December 1888 and who accompanied him to Saint-Rémy in May 1889.

6. Vincent Willem was born on 31 January 1890.

7. Vincent stayed three days at 8 Cité Pigalle, from Saturday 17 to Tuesday 20 May. The paintings referred to by Jo can be identified as the triptych of Orchards (F 555, F 404, F 403), *The Potato Eaters* (F 82), the 'great landscape from Arles' is *The Harvest (La Moisson)* (F 412), and the *Starry Night over the Rhône* (F 474).

8. It is pity that Jo doesn't name any of the visitors. One friendship was renewed - with her brother Andries Bonger (1861-1936), whom Vincent had first met in Nuenen in August 1885, but whom he knew best during his two-year stay in Paris. Vincent visited Tanguy's shop, and the Salon du Champ de Mars where he greatly admired a painting by Puvis de Chavannes (1824-1898). But he did not meet Gauguin or Emile Bernard, though he may well have met Aurier (see note 19).

9. Vincent actually left Paris for Auvers-sur-Oise on Tuesday 20 May, not 21 May as Jo wrote, followed by many later writers. The date was first correctly identified by Jan Hulsker ('Van Gogh's bedreigde leven in St. Rémy en Auvers', *Maatstaf* 8 (1961), pp. 639-664, on p. 654). According to Gachet's son, Dr Gachet wrote in his notebook for 20 May: 'M. Van Gogh – A (Auvers)'. Theo's letter of introduction to Dr Gachet is dated (Sunday), 19 May 1890 (see Paul Gachet, *Deux Amis des Impressionnistes: le Docteur Gachet et Murer*, [Paris] 1956, p. 110).

10. Vincent took an attic room in the Café de la Mairie, opposite the town hall, run by Arthur Gustave Ravoux (1848-1914).

11. Vincent painted the *Portrait of Dr Gachet* (F 753) in early June (see LT 638).

12. Jo maintained the friendship with Dr Gachet until his death in 1909, when she wrote a touching letter of condolence to his two

children, Marguerite Clémentine (1869-1949) and Paul Louis Lucien (1873-1962). See Paul Gachet, *Lettres Impressionnistes au Dr Gachet et à Murer*, [Paris] 1957, pp. 156-158.

13. This long quotation is taken from Gachet's letter to Theo of mid-August 1890 which is here published in its entirety for the first time. See French 21, and note 5 there.

14. Gachet's resemblance to Vincent was noted by Theo after his first meeting with the doctor: 'Physically he is a little like you' (T 31). And Vincent himself remarked to his sister Wil on 4 June: 'And then I have found a true friend in Dr Gachet, something like a new brother, so much do we resemble each other physically and also mentally' (W 22). Gachet's son – whom Jo said looked somewhat like Theo – was then 17, not 15, years old.

15. Gachet's house was described by Vincent in several letters (LT 635, LT 641a), and Jo knew its idiosyncratic character from her visit on Sunday 8 June 1890. She also returned in June 1905.

16. The visit on Sunday 8 (not 10, as Jo wrote) June was a happy one, recollected by Vincent in letters to Theo (LT 640), his mother (LT 641a) and his sister Wil (W 23).

17. Vincent's visit to Theo's and Jo's apartment at 8 Cité Pigalle took place on Sunday 6 July.

18. Jo has succinctly listed the problems that beset the family – reflecting what Theo wrote to Vincent in his letter of 30 June/1 July (T 39).

19. As with her account of Vincent's three-day stay with them in May, Jo refers to 'many friends'. There, she did not name any: here, she names Aurier and Toulouse-Lautrec. But it is possible that Vincent met Aurier in May (see note 8).

20. Henri de Toulouse-Lautrec (1864-1901) had known Vincent well during his two-year stay in Paris. See French 3.

21. Vincent wrote that he was 'sorry not to have seen Guillaumin again, but I am glad that he has seen my canvases' (LT 649). See French 4.

22. Theo had planned to visit Monet at Giverny with Monsieur Valadon on 14 July. But in a letter to Theo of 10 July, Monet postponed the visit – in favour of Berthe Morisot and Mallarmé (See Pickvance in exhib. cat. *Monet in Holland*, Amsterdam (Rijksmuseum Vincent van Gogh) 1986, pp. 183-84). Theo had also evolved the plan of visiting Pissarro at Eragny the same day – with Vincent and Andries Bonger. Because of Monet's cancellation, Theo took Jo and the baby to Leiden to introduce the five-month old Vincent Willem to his mother. Theo left Leiden on Thursday 17 July for business visits to The Hague, Antwerp and Brussels, eventually arriving back in Paris on Saturday 19 July.

23. Theo is referring to Vincent's last letter to him of 23 July (LT 652). It seems somewhat incomprehensible why Theo found this letter 'quite incomprehensible'.

24. Dr Gachet's letter of 27 July is here published in its entirety for the first time. See Prologue 1.

25. Theo's letter to Jo of 28 July is here published in its entirety for the first time. See Prologue 3.

26. Vincent died in his attic room at Ravoux's inn at 1.30 a.m. on Tuesday 29 July.

27. Theo's letter to Jo of 1 August is here published in its entirety for the first time. See Prologue 4.

The Letters of Condolence

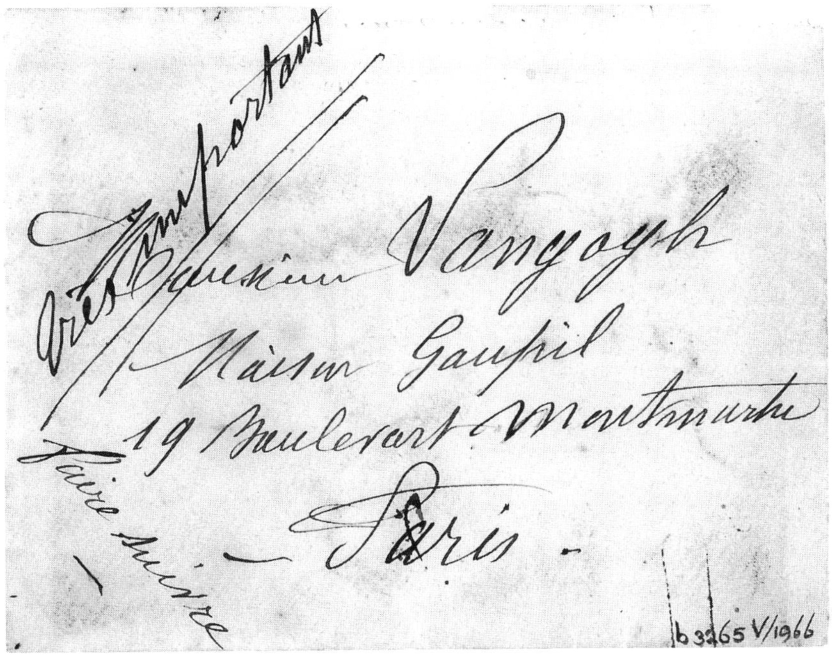
Très important
Monsieur Vangogh
Maison Goupil
19 Boulevart Montmartre
Paris
Faire suivre
b 3265 V/1966

Note to the reader

The letters of condolence are divided into the following categories: Prologue, Family, Dutch and French. Each section opens with a brief introduction which contains additional explanatory notes. Wherever possible a literal transcription of the letter has been published together with the English translation and annotations. Two letters (Family 11a and French 21a) are based on printed sources rather than original correspondence or earlier transcriptions. Unless otherwise stated, the letters have not been published previously.

The translated versions reflect the original texts as closely as possible. For the sake of clarity, however, certain liberties have been taken with the punctuation. Upper case letters have occasionally been used, for instance, where the writer in fact used lower case, and vice versa. Paragraphs, too, are all indented for the reader's convenience. The editor's insertions are in square brackets.

Almost every letter is accompanied by a portrait of its author, while the provenance of these portraits can be found in the photograph credits.

The nicknames or pet names by which members of the Van Gogh family were known to the authors of these letters, and by which they were addressed or referred to, have been left unchanged. Vincent van Gogh is called Vincent, his sisters Willemien and Elisabeth were known as Wil and Lies, his brother is Theo, and their mother is simply Mother. Theo's wife, Johanna Bonger, is generally referred to as Jo. Citations from Vincent van Gogh's correspondence are followed by the abbreviations:

- LT Letter to Theo
- W Letter to Wil
- T Letter from Theo

The numbers following citations refer to the *Verzamelde brieven van Vincent van Gogh*, 4 vols., Amsterdam & Antwerpen 1973, and the English edition, *The Complete Letters of Vincent van Gogh*, 3 vols., Greenwich (Conn.) 1958. The most recent edition, *De brieven van Vincent van Gogh*, edited by Han van Crimpen and Monique Berends-Albert, 4 vols., 's-Gravenhage 1990, is referred to as '1990 Letters'.

Other abbreviations:
– Cooper 1983: followed by a number refers to the corresponding letter in Douglas Gooper, *Paul Gauguin: 45 lettres à Vincent, Theo et Jo van Gogh. Collection Rijksmuseum Vincent van Gogh. Amsterdam*, 's-Gravenhage & Lausanne 1983.

– F: followed by a number refers to the corresponding catalogue number in J.-B. de la Faille, *The Works of Vincent van Gogh. His Paintings and Drawings*, revised, augmented and annotated edition. Amsterdam 1970.
– FF Oeuvres: Félix Fénéon, *Oeuvres plus que complètes*, vol. I, ed. Joan U. Halperin, Genève 1970.
– 1914 Introduction: J. van Gogh-Bonger, 'Inleiding', *Verzamelde brieven van Vincent van Gogh*, 4 vols., Amsterdam & Antwerpen 1973, vol. I, pp. II-XLIX; English translation: idem, 'Memoir of Vincent van Gogh by his sister-in-law', *The Complete Letters of Vincent van Gogh*, 3 vols., Greenwich (Conn.) 1958, vol. I, pp. XV-LVIII.
– exhib. cat. Paris 1988: exhib. cat. *Van Gogh à Paris*, Paris (Musée d'Orsay) 1988.
– Pabst no.: refers to the corresponding address in Ronald de Leeuw et Fieke Pabst, 'Le carnet d'adresses de Theo van Gogh', in exhib. cat. Paris 1988, Annexe 2, pp. 348-369.
– cat. Amsterdam 1987: E. van Uitert and M. Hoyle (ed.), *The Rijksmuseum Vincent van Gogh*, Amsterdam 1987.
– Stein 1986: Susan Alyson Stein (ed.), *Van Gogh: a Retrospective*, New York 1986.

Prologue

In her 1914 Introduction, Jo quoted from Dr Gachet's letter to Theo of 27 July 1890, and from two letters from Theo to herself, only the first of which she provided a date for – 28 July. All three letters are published here in full for the first time. And to add another – and extremely valuable – voice to this trio, Emile Bernard's letter to Aurier of 31 July is interleaved with them. This quartet of letters provides us with first-hand and contemporary accounts of what happened between Sunday 27 July, when Vincent shot himself, and Wednesday 30 July, the day of his funeral. These accounts are supplemented by Theo's letter to his mother of 1 August (Family 6) and to his sister Lies of 5 August (Family 11a).

The most unexpected revelation concerns Theo's four days silence. The letter that Jo left undated and which some later commentators have thought to be 29 July, is in fact dated 1 August. Theo wrote nothing to Jo between Monday 28 July, when he arrived in Auvers-sur-Oise, and Friday 1 August. Dr Gachet warned him to be tactful with regard to Jo who was still nursing her baby; but such a degree of taciturnity, whether due to unbearable stress, numbed silence, or paralysis of will, is quite remarkable.

The effects of Theo's delay, the strategy he used to disclose the news of Vincent's death, not only to Jo, then in Amsterdam, but also to his mother in Leiden, will be seen in the next section devoted to family letters of condolence.

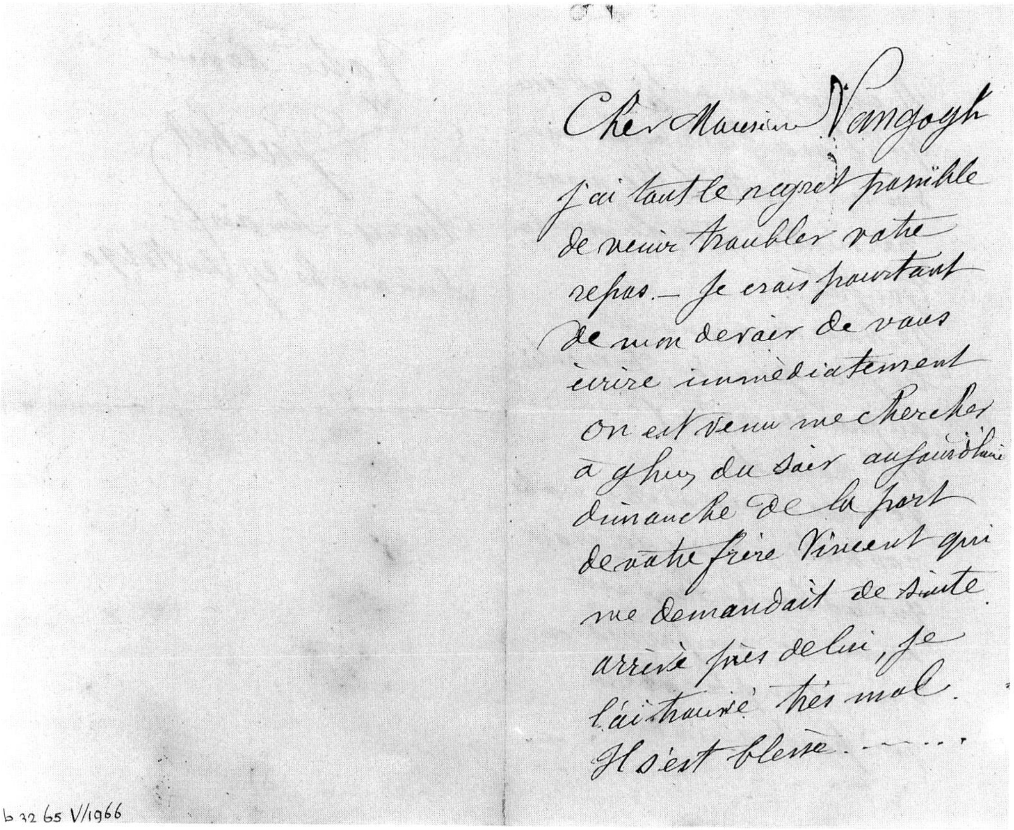

Cher Monsieur Vangogh

J'ai tout le regret possible de venir troubler votre repos. — Je crois pourtant de mon devoir de vous écrire immédiatement. On est venu me chercher à 9 heures du soir aujourd'hui dimanche de la part de votre frère Vincent qui me demandait de suite. Arrivé près de lui, je l'ai trouvé très mal. Il s'est blessé......

b 32 65 V/1966

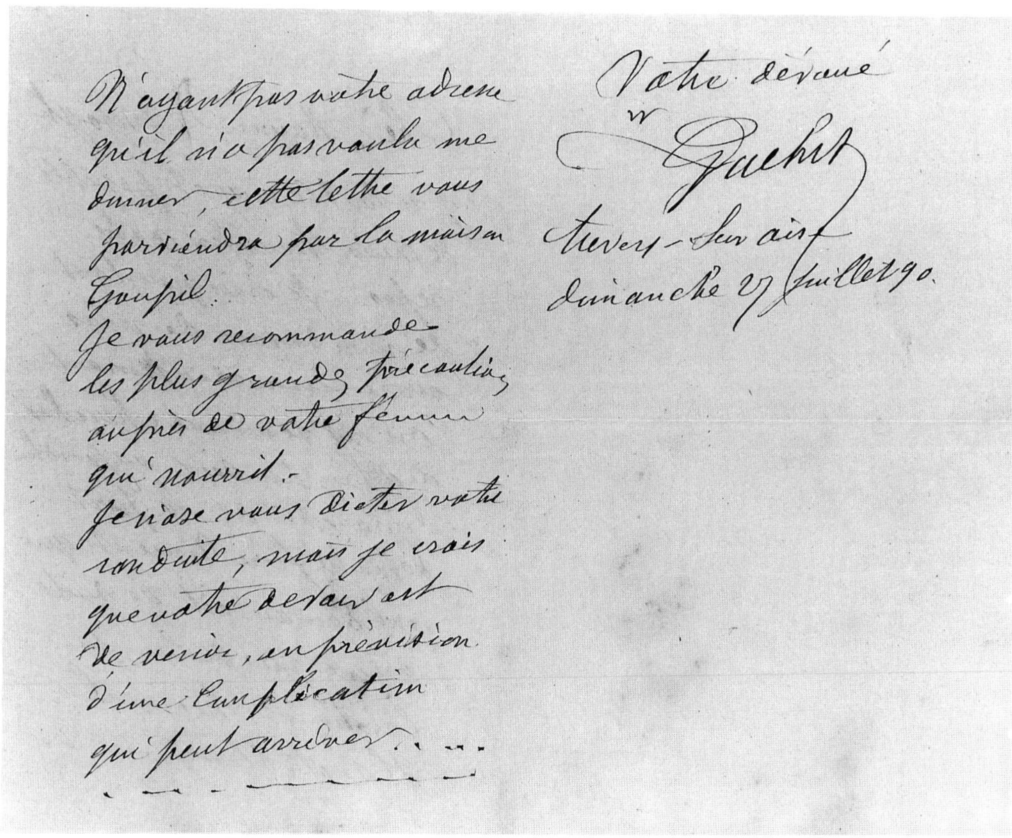

N'ayant pas votre adresse qu'il n'a pas voulu me donner, cette lettre vous parviendra par la maison Goupil.
Je vous recommande les plus grandes précautions auprès de votre femme qui nourrit.
Je n'ose vous dicter votre conduite, mais je crois que votre devoir est de venir, en prévision d'une complication qui peut arriver.......

Votre dévoué
Gachet

Auvers-sur-Oise
dimanche 27 juillet 90.

Cher Monsieur Vangogh,

J'ai tout le regret possible de venir troubler votre repos, je crois pourtant de mon devoir de vous écrire immédiatement, on est venu me chercher à 9 heur du soir aujourd'hui dimanche de la part de votre frère Vincent, qui me demandait de suites. Arrivé près de lui, je l'ai trouvé très mal. Il s'est blessé...

N'ayant pas votre adresse qu'il n'a pas voulu me donner, cette lettre vous parviendra par la maison Goupil.

Je vous recommande les plus grandes précautions auprès de votre femme qui nourrit.

Je n'ose vous dicter votre conduis, mais je crois que votre devoir est de venir, en prévision d'une complication, qui peut arriver...

votre dévoué
Gachet

Auvers-Sur Oise
dimanche 27 juillet 90

Dear Monsieur Vangogh,[1]

It is with the utmost regret that I intrude on your privacy, however I regard it as my duty to write to you immediately, today, Sunday, at nine o'clock in the evening I was sent for by your brother Vincent, who wanted to see me at once.[2] I went there and found him very ill. He has wounded himself...

Not having your address which he refused to give me,[3] this letter will reach you through Goupil.

I would advise you to take the greatest precautions with your wife who is still breast feeding.

I would not presume to tell you what to do, but I believe that it is your duty to come, in case of any complications that might occur...[4]

ever yours
Gachet

Auvers-Sur Oise
sunday 27 July 90

Dr Paul-Ferdinand Gachet to Theo, Sunday 27 July 1890.
Inv. no. b. 3265 V/1966
First published by Johanna van Gogh-Bonger in 1914, omitting only the last two sentences about herself and Theo. The only error in the printed edition was 'demanda' instead of 'demandait'. This has been perpetuated in all subsequent Dutch editions. Ironically, the letter appeared to have been lost, and was uncatalogued until I discovered it in 1988 in a grey folder among the Gustave Coquiot material. Its museum accession number was then given to it retrospectively. It is published here for the first time in its entirety, together with its accompanying envelope. The envelope is addressed to: 'Monsieur Vangogh / Maison Goupil / 19 Boulevart Montmartre / Paris', and marked 'très important' and 'faire suivre'(reproduced on p. 21). It bears no stamp because it was delivered by hand to Theo by the Dutch painter Anton Hirschig (1867-1939).

1. This relatively formal address shows that Dr Gachet and Theo, while being fairly well acquainted, were not yet close friends.

2. Since Gachet was summoned at 9 p.m., Vincent must have shot himself in the evening, probably between 7 and 8 p.m., rather than in the afternoon, as often asserted. This is surely confirmed by Bernard's reference to 'the evening' in his letter of 31 July (see Prologue 3, note 3).

3. That Vincent refused to give Theo's address was not a sign of his antipathy towards Gachet; rather it argues that Vincent did not want to have his brother disturbed, preferring to die quietly and quickly.

4. These last two sentences were omitted by Jo. Louis Anfray read this as a sinister subterfuge, plotted by the Van Gogh family to hide revealing evidence of the antipathy that allegedly existed between Vincent and Dr Gachet ('Pèlerinage à Auvers-sur-Oise sur la tombe de VincenThéo Van Gogh', *Art-Documents* 51 (December 1954), pp. 4-5). This is clearly nonsense. Dr Gachet's recommendation regarding Jo could well have been one of the causes of Theo's silence between 28 July and 1 August. See Prologue 4.

Auvers 28 Juli 1890

Lieve beste Vrouwtje,

Het is een moeilijken tijd voor ons lieveling en telkens weer wat waar men niet op gerekend had. Van morgen kwam er een hollandsche schilder die ook in Auvers is mij een brief brengen van Dr Gachet die slechte berichten van Vincent gaf en mij verzocht te komen. Ik ging er dadelijk heen alles in den steek latend en vond hem nog beter dan ik gedacht had hoewel hij erg erg ziek is. Ik zal maar niet in bizonderheden treden die zijn al te triest, maar weet het lieveling dat zijn leven wel eens in gevaar kon zijn. Wat moeten wij ervan zeggen of voor hem hoopen. Hij vond goed dat ik gekomen was en wij zitten bijna aldoor bij elkaar. Als de nacht wat beter is ga ik morgen vroeg weer naar Parijs terug, maar anders blijf ik nog hier. Arme kerel, hem werd het geluk niet in groote mate toegedeeld en illusies blijven hem niet over. Het wordt hem soms te zwaar hij gevoeld zich zoo alleen. Wijfjelief wees niet te bedroefd hoor je weet wel ik zie de zaken dikwijls te zwart in, misschien wordt hij weer beter en komt er nog een beteren tijd voor hem. Ik was juist aan een brief voor je bezig toen Tanguy mij van morgen op kwam houden. Ik vertelde je erin hoe heerlijk ik gisteren met Dries & Annie naar het bosch van Medon ging, o lieveling ik dacht zoo dikwijls aan je & ik was wel een beetje onder de impressie van de brief die je mij schreef over t'huis. Dries die ik

Auvers 28 July 1890

My dearest, sweet wife,

This is a difficult time for us my love and time and again things we had not expected. This morning a Dutch painter who is also in Auvers came to bring me a letter from Dr Gachet who had bad news about Vincent and requested me to come.[1] Abandoning everything I went at once and found him better than I had thought, although he is very very ill.[2] I shan't enter into detail, it is all too sad, but know my love that his life might be in danger. What can we say or what ought we to hope for him? He was pleased that I had come and we are together almost constantly. If the night passes somewhat more smoothly I shall return to Paris early tomorrow, but otherwise I shall remain here. Poor fellow, he was not granted much happiness, he cherishes no more illusions. It is sometimes too much for him, he feels so alone. My dearest wife don't be too upset, will you, you know I am often unduly pessimistic, perhaps he will recover and live to see better times. I was just writing a letter to you this morning, when Tanguy arrived and I was detained.[3] I was telling you that I went to the woods of Medon with Dries & Annie yesterday, how wonderful it was,[4] oh darling, I thought of you so much & the letter you wrote to me about home was on my mind.[5]

er over sprak zei o, die heeft ze onder den indruk van het ogenblik geschreven. Ik was al van plan om Moe een standje te maken als ik in Amsterdam kwam, maar toen ik je tweede brief las begreep ik het wel, het zal zijn zooals van de winter toen de jongen kwam & Moe uit goedigheid mij bijna omverliep. Lieve schat als er eens wat met Vincent mocht gebeuren dan is het toch beter voor je om in Holland te zijn & ik zal sterk zijn. Wat vreemd niet waar dat ik verleden week den heelen tijd zoo zenuwachtig & onrustig ben geweest, het was alsof ik een voorgevoelen had er iets gebeuren zou. Hij kan zoo lief met mij praten & vroeg zoo naar jou en den jongen & zei dat jij die droefheid in het leven niet vermoed had, och konden wij hem toch maar wat moed in t'leven geven. Nog eens trek je dit niet te veel aan want het zou soms ook niet goed voor jezelf zijn. Denk erom wat er ook gebeure ik zal moedig zijn want ik heb immers jou om voor te leven; ik blijf niet alleen over, maar ik heb mijn vrouw & mijn jongentje. Wij kunnen bedroefd zijn maar wij verliezen den moed niet. Nu lieveling ik moet mij wat met den zieken bemoeien en anders schiet deze er bij in dus adieu mijn lieve schat. In gedachten druk ik je aan mijn hart en noem je mijn eenige eenige troost. Maak je niet al te ongerust het was vroeger ook al zo hopeloos & zijn sterk gestel bedroog de dokters. Adieu lieveling kus mijn jongen & wees omhelst duizend & duizend maal door je altijd & altijd het meest liefhebbende

Theo.

Dries, whom I spoke to about it said well, she wrote it in the heat of the moment. I had been intending to have a word with Mother when I got to Amsterdam, but upon reading your second letter I realized it would be like last winter when the baby came and Mother, out of kindness, all but knocked me off my feet.[6] My dearest, should anything happen to Vincent, it is better for you to be in Holland & I shall be strong. Curious, is it not, that I was so nervous & restless all of last week, as though I had a premonition that something would happen.[7] He talks to me so agreeably & inquired after you and the boy & said that you had not imagined such sadness in life, how I wish we could give him faith in life. Once again, do not take this too much to heart for it will do you no good. Come what may, remember that I shall face it bravely since I have you to live for; I shan't be left alone, but I have my wife and my little son. We might be sad but we shall not despair. Now, my darling, I must attend to the patient or he will be wanting, so adieu my dear love. In my thoughts I draw you close to my heart and call you my only only comfort. Don't worry, things have been as hopeless before & the doctors were surprised by his strong constitution.[8] Adieu darling & kiss my son, I embrace you a thousand thousand times your ever & ever most loving

Theo.

Theo to Jo, Monday 28 July 1890.
Inv. no. b 2066 VF/1982
Several passages from this letter were quoted by Johanna van Gogh-Bonger in her 1914 Introduction. These passages have often been quoted by later authors.

1. This is referring to Anton Hirschig (1867-1939), the young Dutch painter who had been living in Auvers since 16 June. For Gachet's letter, see Prologue 1.

2. Theo most probably caught the 11.25 a.m. train from the Gare du Nord, enabling him to arrive at Ravoux's inn by 12.45 p.m. In order not to alarm Jo unduly, Theo only says that Vincent is 'very very ill' (this was omitted in the 1914 Introduction), without mentioning that he had shot and wounded himself. Theo probably wrote this letter in the late afternoon or early evening of Monday; but Jo did not receive it in Amsterdam until Wednesday, the day of the funeral.

3. Theo was probably discussing with Julien Tanguy (1825-1894) Vincent's recent order (LT 652) for paints for himself and Hirschig, though Vincent intended the order to go to Tasset.

4. Theo visited Meudon, to the south-west of Paris, in the company of Jo's brother Dries – Andries Bonger (1861-1936) – and his wife Annie – Anne Marie Louise van der Linden (1859-1931).

5. Theo is referring to a letter from Jo of 25 July (information from Han van Crimpen, who is preparing the publication of the correspondence between Theo and Jo).

6. Vincent Willem was born 31 January 1890. Both Theo's sister Wil and Jo's mother, Hermine Louise Bonger (1831-1905), came to stay in Paris to help at the time of the birth.

7. Such a premonition was already expressed by Theo in his letter to Jo of 25 July, quoted in the 1914 Introduction.

8. The doctors Theo is referring to are Félix Rey (1867-1932) at Arles and Théophile Peyron (1827-1895) at Saint-Rémy.

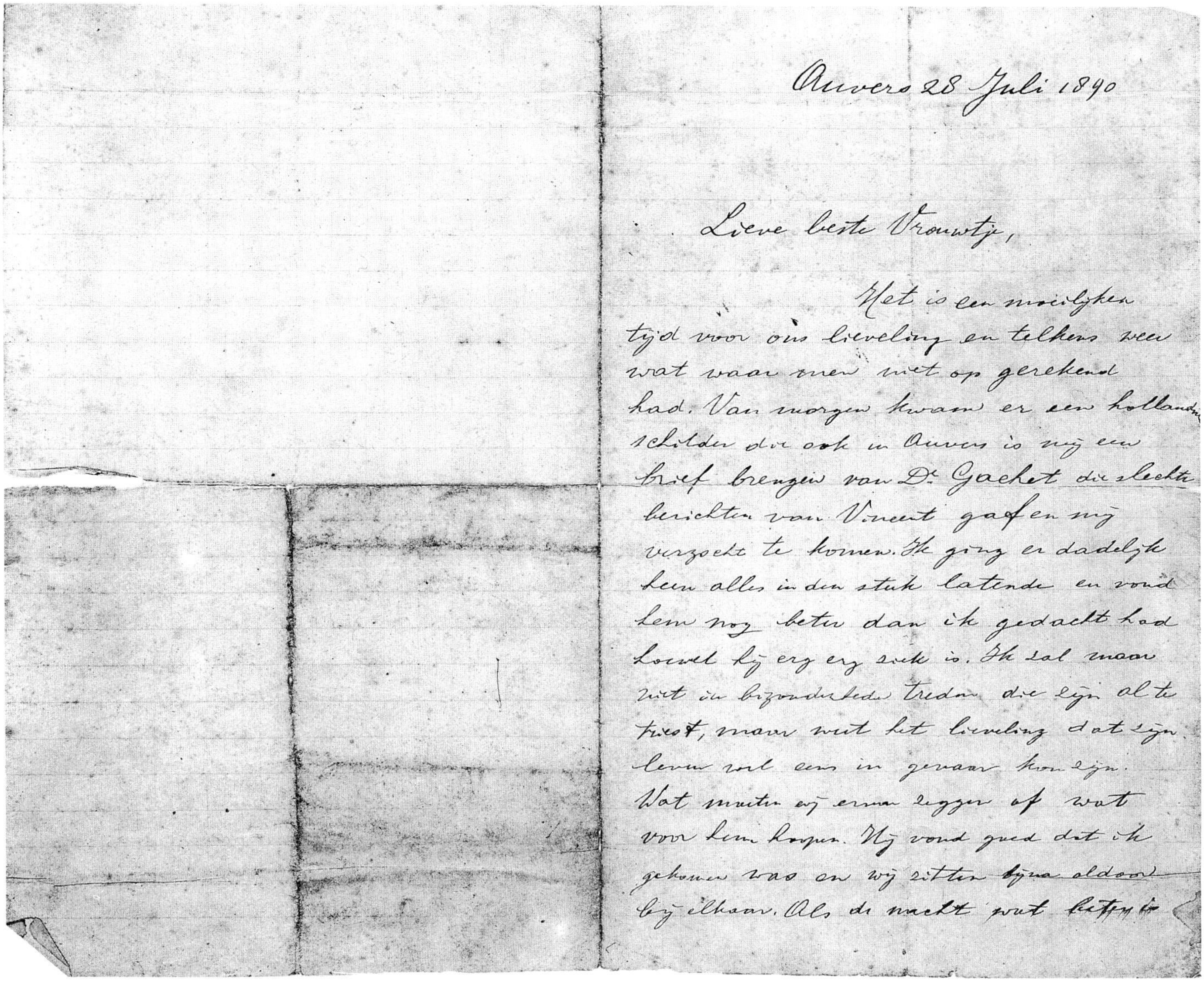
Auvers 28 Juli 1890

Lieve beste Vrouwtje,

Het is een moeilijken tijd voor ons lieveling en telkens weer wat waar men niet op gerekend had. Van morgen kwam er een hollandsch schilder die ook in Auvers is mij een brief brengen van Dr Gachet die slechte berichten van Vincent gaf en mij verzocht te komen. Ik ging er dadelijk heen alles in den steek latende en vond hem nog beter dan ik gedacht had hoewel hij erg erg ziek is. Ik zal maar niet in bijzonderheden treden die zijn al te triest, maar weet het lieveling dat zijn leven wel eens in gevaar kon zijn. Wat moeten wij ervan zeggen of wat voor hem hopen. Hij vond goed dat ik gekomen was en wij zitten bijna aldoor bij elkaar. Als de nacht wat beter is

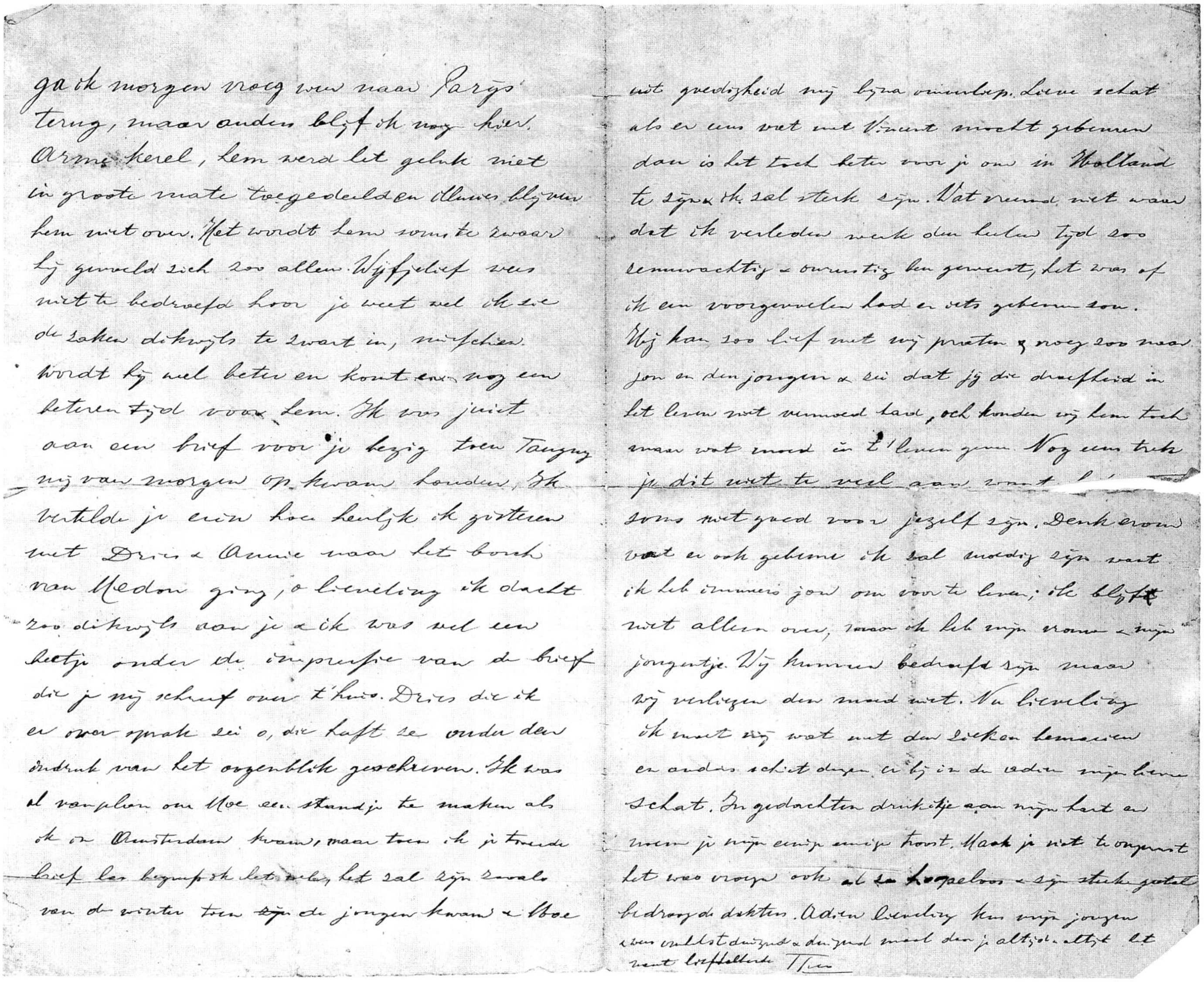

ga ik morgen nog even naar Parijs
terug, maar anders blijf ik nog hier.
Arme kerel, hem werd het geluk niet
in groote mate toegedeeld en illusies blijven
hem niet over. Het wordt hem soms te zwaar
hij gevoeld zich zoo alleen. Wijfjelief wees
niet te bedroefd hoor je weet wel ik zie
de zaken dikwijls te zwart in, misschien
wordt hij wel beter en komt er nog een
beteren tijd voor hem. Ik was juist
aan een brief voor je bezig toen Tanguy
mij van morgen op kwam houden. Ik
vertelde je even hoe heerlijk ik gisteren
met Dries & Annie naar het bosch
van Meudon ging, o lieveling ik dacht
zoo dikwijls aan je & ik was wel een
beetje onder de impressie van de brief
die je mij schreef over t'huis. Dries die ik
er over sprak zei o, die heeft ze onder den
indruk van het oogenblik geschreven. Ik was
al van plan om Moe een standje te maken als
ik in Amsterdam kwam, maar toen ik je tweede
brief las begreep ik het beter, het zal zijn zooals
van de winter toen ~~zijn~~ de jongen kwam & Moe

uit goedigheid mij bijna omverliep. Lieve schat
als er eens iets met Vincent mocht gebeuren
dan is het toch beter voor je om in Holland
te zijn & ik zal sterk zijn. Wat vreemd niet waar
dat ik verleden week den heelen tijd zoo
zenuwachtig & onrustig ben geweest, het was of
ik een voorgevoelen had er iets gebeuren zou.
Hij kan zoo lief met mij praten & nog zoo mooi
over den jongen & zei dat jij die droefheid in
het leven niet vermoed hadt, och konden wij hem toch
maar wat moed in 't leven geven. Nog eens trek
je dit niet te veel aan want [illegible]
soms niet goed voor jezelf zijn. Denk erom
wat er ook gebeure ik zal moedig zijn want
ik heb immers jou om voor te leven; ik blijf
niet alleen over, maar ik heb mijn vrouw & mijn
jongentje. Wij kunnen bedroefd zijn maar
wij verliezen den moed niet. Nu lieveling
ik moet nog wat met den dokter bemoeien
en anders schiet deze er bij in de verdere mijn lieve
schat. In gedachten druk ik je aan mijn hart en
noem je mijn eenige eenige troost. Maak je niet te ongerust
het was vroeger ook al zoo hopeloos & zijn sterk gestel
bedroog de dokters. Adieu lieveling kus mijn jongen
eens omhelst duizend & duizend maal door je altijd & altijd het
meest liefhebbende Theo

PROLOGUE 2

Mon cher Aurier

Votre absence de Paris a du vous priver d'une affreuse nouvelle que je ne puis différer pourtant de vous apprendre:

Notre cher ami Vincent est mort depuis quatre jours.

Je pense que vous avez deviné déjà qu'il s'est tué lui même.

En effet Dimanche soir il est parti dans la campagne d'Auvers, il a deposé son chevalet contre une meule et il est allé se tirer un coup de revolver derrière le château. Sous la violence du choc (la balle avait passé sous le coeur) il est tombé, mais il s'est relevé, et consecutivement trois fois, pour rentrer a l'auberge où il habitait (Ravoux, place de la mairie) sans rien dire à

My dear Aurier

Your absence from Paris[1] means that you have not heard the appalling piece of news which however I am obliged to tell you without delay:

Our dear friend Vincent died four days ago.[2]

I suspect that you will have already guessed the fact that he killed himself.

On Sunday evening he went out into the countryside around Auvers, placed his easel against a haystack and went behind the château and fired a revolver shot at himself.[3] The violence of the blow (the bullet entered his body under the heart) felled him, but he got up and fell again three times, before he got back to the inn where he was lodging (Ravoux, place de la Mairie) without telling anybody about

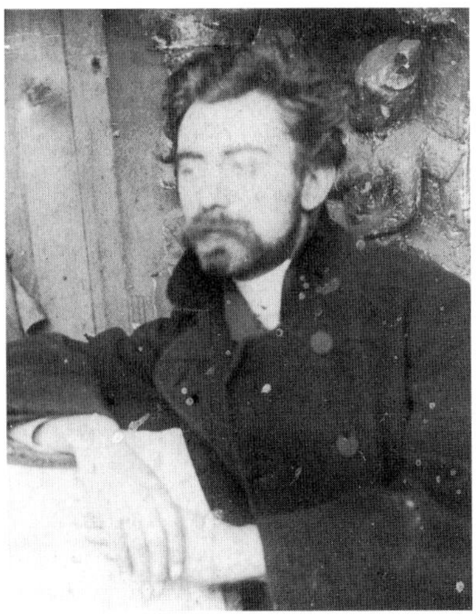

Emile Bernard to Gustave-Albert Aurier, Thursday 31 July 1890. Inv. no. b 3052 V/1985
First published in 'Un Document sensationnel et inédit: L'enterrement de Vincent Van Gogh, par le peintre Emile Bernard', *Art-Documents* 29 (February 1953), pp. 1-2. Parts of the letter were translated in John Rewald, *Post-Impressionism: from Van Gogh to Gauguin*, New York 1956, pp. 411-412; and in idem, *Le post-impressionnisme*, Paris 1961, pp. 247-248. Translated parts were also published in Ronald Pickvance, exhib. cat. *Van Gogh in Saint-Rémy and Auvers*, New York (The Metropolitan Museum of Art) 1986-87, pp. 217-219, and one page (the first) illustrated, p. 218. The first full translation in English was printed in Stein 1986, pp. 219-222. Two pages were illustrated in the catalogue of the exhibition *Les Amis de Van Gogh*, Paris (Institut Néerlandais) 1960, pp. 54-55, when the letter was first exhibited (without catalogue number).

The letter, written on three pages, with a schematic drawing on the fourth page, was sold at Nouveau Drouot, Paris, 29 March 1985, lot 49, where it was purchased by the Van Gogh Museum. Aurier's reply, dated 29 August 1890, was also first published in no. 29 of *Art-Documents* (February 1953), p. 2. Translated in part in Rewald, *Post-Impressionism*, op. cit., p. 412; translated in Stein 1986, pp. 234-235.

1. Emile Bernard's friendship with the Symbolist poet and art critic, G. Albert Aurier (1865-1892) began in Saint-Briac, Brittany, in July-August 1888. Their friendship was cemented by their common admiration for Van Gogh. Following Van Gogh's self-mutilation in Arles in December 1888, Bernard gathered some elements of the episode from Gauguin on his return to Paris and then related this information in a long letter to Aurier on 1 January 1889. This letter was also sold at the Nouveau Drouot, Paris, on 29 March 1985, lot 48. Both Bernard and Gauguin contributed articles to Aurier's short-lived magazine, *Le Moderniste*, in 1889. And Bernard strongly encouraged Aurier to write on Van Gogh, sending him biographical data to urge him on. The ensuing article, 'Les Isolés: Vincent van

qui que ce soit de son mal. Enfin Lundi soir il expirait en fumant sa pipe qu'il n'avait pas voulu quitter et en expliquant que son suicide était absolument calculé *et voulu en toute lucidité. Un fait assez caracteristique que l'on m'a rapporté touchant sa volonté de disparaitre est: 'C'est à refaire alors' quand le docteur Gachet lui disait qu'il esperait encor le sauver. Mais ce n'était hélas plus possible...*

Hier, Mercredi 30 Juillet j'arrivai a Auvers vers 10 heures. Theodore Van ghohg son frère etait là avec le docteur Gachet. Tanguy aussi (il etait là depuis 9 heures.) Laval Charles m'accompagnait. Déjà la bière était close j'arrivais trop tard pour le revoir lui qui m'avait quitté il y quatre ans si plein d'espoirs de toutes sortes... L'aubergiste nous raconta tous les détails de

his injury.[4] He finally died on Monday evening[5] still smoking his pipe which he refused to let go of explaining that his suicide had been absolutely deliberate and that he had done it in complete lucidity. A typical detail that I was told about his wish to die was that when doctor Gachet told him that he still hoped to save his life,[6] he said, 'Then I'll have to do it over again'. But, alas, it was no longer possible to save him...

On Wednesday 30 July, yesterday that is, I arrived in Auvers at about 10 o'clock.[7] His brother, Theodore Van ghohg,[8] was there together with doctor Gachet. Also Tanguy (he had been there since 9 o'clock). Charles Laval accompanied me.[9] The coffin was already closed I arrived too late to see the man again who had left me four years ago so full of expectations of all kinds...[10] The innkeeper told us all the details of the accident, the offensive visit of the gendarmes

Gogh', appeared in the first number of *Le Mercure de France*, January 1890, pp. 24-29. By late July 1890, Aurier had left Paris for a summer break in his birthplace, the town of Châteauroux in the Indre, some 280 kilometres south of Paris. He remained there until 2 September. Presumably, Bernard wrote from his parents' house in Asnières, a northern suburb of Paris, but without giving his address.

2. Taken literally, four days ago means that Bernard was writing on 1 August, since Vincent died on Tuesday, 29 July. But, as it transpires later in the letter, Bernard believed that Vincent had died on Monday 28 July; therefore, a date of 31 July is correct. In any case, such a date is confirmed by the sentence beginning, 'Hier, Mercredi 30 Juillet'. So Bernard's letter was written the day after the funeral; and Aurier must have received it in Châteauroux on 1 August, the same day that he wrote his letter of condolence to Theo (see French 7). On the other hand, he did not reply to Bernard's letter until 29 August, four weeks later.

3. Interestingly, Bernard speaks of Sunday *evening*, not afternoon, as many later accounts state. Compare Prologue 1, note 2.

4. Most of this information must have been gathered from the innkeeper, Arthur Gustave Ravoux (1848-1910), in whose Café de la Mairie, situated in the square opposite the Town Hall, Vincent had taken an attic room on his arrival in Auvers-sur-Oise on Tuesday 20 May. Ravoux told Bernard and Charles Laval (1862-1894), 'all the details of the accident' on the morning of the funeral, and probably related more details on their return to the inn after the burial. These details have the mark of authenticity, without elaboration in the retelling.

5. A serious lacuna in Bernard's narrative is any mention of the Dutch artist Anton Hirschig (1867-1939) who delivered Dr Gachet's letter to Theo in Paris on Monday, 28 July, or of Theo's arrival in Auvers that same day. Technically, Bernard is inexact in saying that Vincent died 'on Monday evening': although 1.30 a.m. Tuesday morning is only shortly after midnight.

6. The disclosure about Vincent's calculated and 'voulu' decision to commit (or attempt) suicide, carried out 'in complete lucidity', and with the rider that, if he were to recover, he would do it again, must clearly come from Dr Gachet. Continuous smoking of his pipe is common to all accounts.

7. 'Wednesday 30 July, yesterday that is' establishes the date of the letter as 31 July, rather than 1 August.

8. Like many Frenchmen, Bernard had difficulty in spelling Van Gogh's surname. In this letter, he twice calls Theo 'Van ghohg', and on a third occasion, 'Van ghog'.

9. Julien Tanguy (1825-1894) was artists' colourman, art dealer, anarchist, and friend of many avant-garde artists from Cézanne, Pissarro and Monet to Gauguin, Signac, and especially Van Gogh, who three times painted his portrait (F 263, F 363, F 364). Tanguy was with Theo when Hirschig arrived in Paris with Dr Gachet's letter (Prologue 1) on Monday, 28 July. On the day of the funeral, Tanguy must have caught the 7.25 a.m. train from the Gare du Nord, enabling him to be at Ravoux's inn by 9 a.m.

10. Again, Bernard miscalculates. It was not four, but only two-and-a-half years since Vincent had left Paris for Arles (February 1888). The two artists had corresponded; especially during Vincent's first seven months in Arles; but only twice in Saint-Rémy. And Bernard's letter confirms that he did not meet Vincent during the latter's three day stay in Paris (17-20 May), nor on his brief return on Sunday 6 July. Coquiot was the first mistakenly to suggest that Bernard met Vincent on this last visit.

l'accident, la visite impudente des gendarmes qui sont venus jusqu'à son lit lui faire des reproches d'un acte dont il était seul responsable .. etc ...

Sur les murs de la salle où le corps etait exposé toutes ses toiles dernières etaient clouées lui faisant comme une aureole et rendant par l'eclat du genie qui s'en degageait cette mort plus penible encore aux artistes. Sur la bière un simple drap blanc puis des fleurs en quantité, des soleils qu'il amait tant, des dahlias jaunes, des fleurs jaunes partout. C'etait sa couleur favorite s'il vous en souvient, symbole de la lumiére qu'il revait dans les coeurs comme dans les oeuvres.

Près de la aussi – son chevalet son pliant, et ses pinceaux avaient eté posés devant le cercueil à terre.

Beaucoup de personnes arrivaient des artistes surtout parmi lesquels je reconnais Lucien Pissarro et Lauzet les autres me sont inconnus, viennent aussi des personnes du pays qui l'avaient un peu connu vu une ou deux fois et qui l'aimaient car il etait si bon si humain..

Nous voila réunis autour de cette bière qui cache un ami dans le plus grand silence. Je regarde les études: une très belle page souffrante interprétee d'après Delacroix La vierge et Jesus. Des galeriens qui tournent dans une haute prison, toile d'après Doré d'une ferocité terrible de symbole pour sa fin. Pour lui la vie n'etait elle pas cette prison haute de murs si hauts – si hauts.. et ces gens tournant sans cesse dans cette cave n'étaient-ils pas les pauvres artistes, les pauvres maudits marchant sous le fouet du Destin ...

a trois heures on lève le corps, ce sont des amis qui le portent jusqu'au corbillard, quelques personnes pleurent dans l'assemblee. Theodore Van ghohg qui adorait son frère, qui l'avait toujours soutenu dans sa lutte pour l'art et l'indépendance ne cessait de sangloter douloureusement...

Dehors il faisait un soleil atroce nous montions les cotes d'Auvers en parlant de lui, de la poussée hardie

who even went up to his bedside to reproach him for an act for which he alone was responsible .. etc ...[11]

On the walls of the room where his body was laid out all his last canvases were hung making a sort of halo for him and the brilliance of the genius that radiated from them made this death even more painful for us artists who were there. The coffin was covered with a simple white cloth and surrounded with masses of flowers, the sunflowers that he loved so much, yellow dahlias, yellow flowers everywhere.[12] It was, you will remember, his favourite colour, the symbol of the light that he dreamed of as being in people's hearts as well as in works of art.

Near him also on the floor in front of his coffin were his were his easel, his folding stool and his brushes.

Many people arrived, mainly artists, among whom I recognized Lucien Pissarro and Lauzet I did not know the others,[13] also some local people who had known him a little, seen him once or twice and who liked him because he was so good-hearted, so human...

There we were, completely silent all of us together around this coffin that held our friend. I looked at the studies; a very beautiful and sad one based on Delacroix's La vierge et Jésus. Convicts walking in a circle surrounded by high prison walls, a canvas inspired by Doré of a terrifying ferocity and which is also symbolic of his end.[14] Wasn't life like that for him, a high prison like this with such high walls – so high .. and these people walking endlessly round this pit, weren't they the poor artists, the poor damned souls walking past under the whip of Destiny? ...

At three o'clock his body was moved, friends of his carrying it to the hearse, a number of people in the company were in tears. Theodore Van ghohg who was devoted to his brother, who had always supported him in his struggle to support himself from his art was sobbing pitifully the whole time ...

The sun was terribly hot outside. We climbed the hill outside Auvers talking about him, about the daring impulse he had given to art, of the great projects he was always thinking

11. This sentence about Ravoux and the gendarmes must have formed the basis for Adeline Ravoux's later account of the same episode.

12. Theo also described the flowers, but alluded to Gachet's special contribution. See Prologue 4, note 5.

13. Compare Theo's account of the number of mourners (Prologue 4, note 4). Lucien Pissarro (1863-1944) travelled from nearby Eragny (see French 1). A.M. Lauzet (1863-1898), Provençal-born, had recently published a folio of twenty lithographs after original paintings by Monticelli, with the help and encouragement of Theo van Gogh. The publisher, in fact, was Boussod Valadon et Cie of 19 Boulevard Montmartre, the address of Theo's gallery.

14. Bernard's account of the lying-in, with pictures hung around the walls, is supplemented by Theo's letter of 1 August (Prologue 4) and was recalled by Theo when writing to Bernard on 18 September

qu'il a donné à l'art, des grand projects qu'il avait toujours en tête, du bien qu'il a fait a chacun de nous.

Nous arrivons au cimetière, un petit cimetière neuf emaillé de pierres neuves. C'est sur la butte dominant les moissons sous le grand ciel bleu qu'il aurait encore aimé.. peut-être.

Puis on le descend dans la fosse...

Qui n'aurait pu pleurer en ce moment.. cette journée etait trop faite pour lui pour qu'on ne songeât qu'il y aurait vecu heureux encore..

Le docteur Gachet (lequel est grand amateur d'art et possède une des belles collections impressionnistes d'aujourd'hui, artiste lui-même) veut dire quelques paroles qui consacreront la vie Vincent mais il pleure lui aussi tellement qu'il ne peut que lui faire une adieu fort embrouillé.. (le plus beau n'est ce pas)

Il retrace brievement les efforts de Vincent, en indique le but sublime et [?] la sympathie immense qu'il avait pour lui (qu'il connaissait depuis peu). Ce fut, dit il, un honnête homme et un grand artiste, il n'avait que deux buts l'humanité et l'art. c'est l'art qu'il cherissait au dessus de tout qui le fera vivre encor..

Puis nous rentrons. Theodore Van ghog est brisé de chagrin, chacun des assistants très emu se retire dans la campagne, d'autres regagnent la gare.

Laval et moi revenons chez Ravoux et l'on cause de lui...

mais en voilà bien assez mon cher Aurier, bien assez n'est ce pas de cette triste journée. Vous savez combien je l'aimais et vous vous doutez de ce que j'ai pu le pleurer. ne l'oubliez donc pas et tachez, vous son critique, d'en dire encore quelques mots pour qeu tous sachent que son enterrement fut une apothéose vraiment digne de son grand coeur et de son grand talent.

Tout a vous de coeur

Bernard

about, and of the good he had done to all of us.

We reached the cemetery, a small new cemetery strewn with new tombstones. It is on the little hill[15] above the fields that were ripe for harvest under the wide blue sky that he would still have loved.. perhaps.

Then he was lowered into the grave...

Anyone would have started crying at that moment.. the day was too much made for him for one not to imagine that he was still alive and enjoying it..

Doctor Gachet (who is a great art lover and possesses one of the best collections of impressionist painting at the present day) wanted to say a few words of homage about Vincent and his life, but he too was weeping so much that he could only stammer a very confused farewell... (perhaps it was the most beautiful way of doing it)

He gave a short description of Vincent's struggles and achievements, stating how sublime his goal was and how great an admiration he felt for him (though he had only known him a short while). He was, Gachet said, an honest man and a great artist, he had only two aims, humanity and art. It was art that he prized above everything and which will make his name live.[16]

Then we returned. Theodore Van ghog was broken with grief; everyone who attended was very moved, some going off into the open country while others went back to the station.

Laval and I returned to Ravoux's house, and we talked about him...[17]

But that is quite enough, my dear Aurier, quite enough, don't you think, about this sad day. You know how much I loved him and you can imagine how much I wept. You are his critic, so don't forget him but try and write a few words to tell everyone that his funeral was a crowning finale that was truly worthy of his great spirit and his great talent.[18]

With my heartfelt wishes

Bernard

1890. In writing to Aurier, Bernard said nothing of his own role in the hanging of the pictures. Nor does he make any mention of the paintings of Auvers, selecting instead, for symbolic emphasis, the *Pietà* after Delacroix (F 630) and the *Ronde des Prisonniers* after Doré (F 669).

15. Bernard referred to 'la butte dominant les moissons' as if, on the plateau above the valley of the Oise, he was reminded of the Butte Montmartre.

16. Gachet's words, as here reported by Bernard, are elaborated by Gachet himself in his letter to Theo of mid-August (French 21).

17. Bernard makes no mention of a division of Vincent's canvases among his friends and admirers.

18. Aurier answered Bernard on 29 August 1890. See Stein 1986, pp. 234-235.

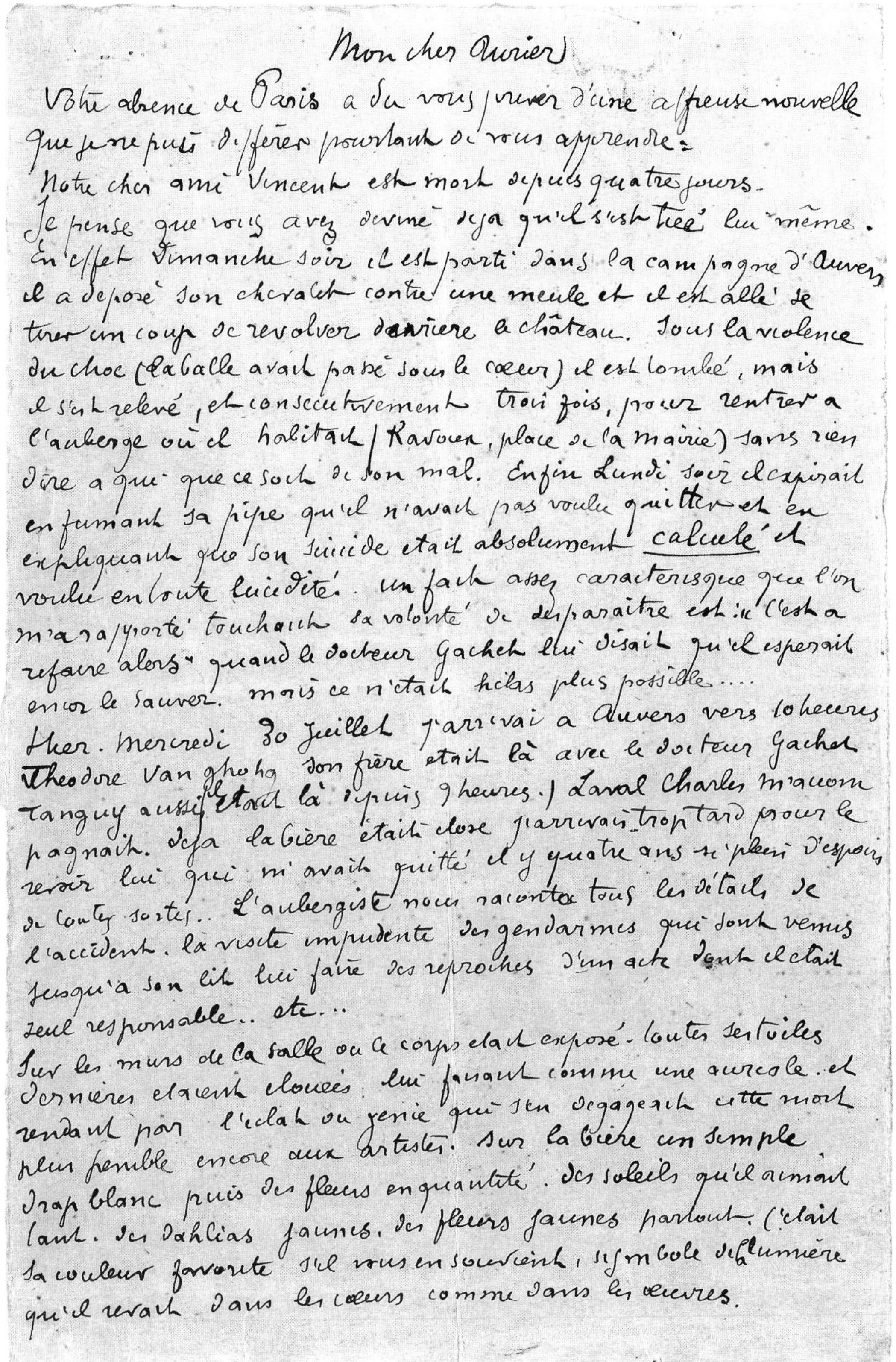

Mon cher Aurier

Votre abence de Paris a du vous priver d'une affreuse nouvelle que je ne puis différer pourtant de vous apprendre:

Notre cher ami Vincent est mort depuis quatre jours.

Je pense que vous avez deviné déja qu'il s'est tué lui même. En effet Dimanche soir il est parti dans la campagne d'Auvers il a deposé son chevalet contre une meule et il est allé se tirer un coup de revolver derriere le château. Sous la violence du choc (la balle avait passé sous le cœur) il est tombé, mais il s'est relevé, et consecutivement trois fois, pour rentrer a l'auberge où il habitait (Ravoux, place de la Mairie) sans rien dire a qui que ce soit de son mal. Enfin Lundi soir il expirait en fumant sa pipe qu'il n'avait pas voulu quitter et en expliquant que son suicide etait absolument calculé et voulu en toute lucidité. un fait assez caracteristique que l'on m'a rapporté touchant sa volonté de disparaitre est: "C'est a refaire alors" quand le docteur Gachet lui disait qu'il esperait encor le sauver. mais ce n'était hélas plus possible....

Hier. Mercredi 30 Juillet j'arrivai a Auvers vers 10 heures Theodore Van ghohg son frère était là avec le docteur Gachet Tanguy aussi (il était là depuis 9 heures.) Laval Charles m'accompagnait. Déja la bière était close j'arrivais trop tard pour revoir lui qui m'avait quitté il y quatre ans si plein d'espoirs de toutes sortes.. L'aubergiste nous raconta tous les détails de l'accident. la visite impudente des gendarmes qui sont venus jusqu'à son lit lui faire des reproches d'un acte dont il était seul responsable.. etc...

Sur les murs de la salle ou le corps etait exposé toutes ses toiles dernières etaient clouées lui faisant comme une auréole et rendant par l'eclat du genie qui s'en degageait cette mort plus penible encore aux artistes. Sur la bière un simple drap blanc puis des fleurs en quantité. des soleils qu'il aimait tant. des Dahlias jaunes. des fleurs jaunes partout. C'était sa couleur favorite s'il vous en souvient, symbole de la lumière qu'il revait dans les cœurs comme dans les œuvres.

PROLOGUE 3

près de là aussi – son chevalet son pliant, et ses pinceaux avaient été posés devant le cercueil à terre.

Beaucoup de personnes arrivaient des artistes surtout parmi lesquels je reconnais. Lucien Pissarro et Lauzet les autres me sont inconnus, viennent aussi des personnes du pays qui l'avaient un peu connu. vu une ou deux fois et qui l'aimaient. car il était si bon, si humain..

Nous voilà réunis autour de cette bière qui cache un ami dans le plus grand silence. Je regarde les études: une très belle page souffrante interprétée d'après Delacroix La vierge et Jesus. Des galériens qui tournent dans une haute prison. toile d'après Doré d'une férocité terrible et symbole pour sa fin. Pour lui la vie n'était elle pas cette prison haute de murs si hauts. si hauts.. et ces gens tournant sans cesse dans cette cave n'étaient ~~sont~~ ils pas les pauvres artistes. les pauvres maudits marchant sous le fouet du Destin...

a trois heures on lève le corps. ce sont des amis qui le portent jusqu'au corbillard. quelques personnes pleurent dans l'assemblée Theodore Van gogh qui adorait son frère, qui l'avait toujours soutenu dans sa lutte pour l'art et l'indépendance ne cessait de sanglotter douloureusement..

Dehors il faisait un soleil atroce nous montons les cotes d'auvers en parlant de lui, de la poussée hardie qu'il a donné à l'art, des grands projets qu'il avait toujours en tête, du bien qu'il a fait à chacun de nous.

Nous arrivons au cimetière. un petit cimetière neuf émaillé de pierres neuves. C'est sur la ~~côte~~ butte dominant les moissons Sous le grand ciel bleu qu'il aurait encore aimé.. peut être.

Puis on le descend dans la fosse...

Qui n'aurait pu pleurer en ce moment.. cette journée était trop faite pour lui pour qu'on ne songeât qu'il y aurait vécu heureux encore..

Le docteur Gachet (lequel est grand amateur d'art et possède une des belles collections impressionnistes d'aujourd'hui. artiste lui même) veut dire quelques paroles qui consacreront la vie de Vincent mais il pleure lui aussi tellement qu'il ne peut que lui faire une adieu fort embrouillé.. (le plus beau n'est ce pas)

PROLOGUE 3

Il retrace brièvement les efforts de vincent en
indiquant le but sublime et la sympathie
immense qu'il avait pour lui (qu'il connaissait
depuis peu) Ce fut, dit il, un honnête homme
et un grand artiste. il n'avait que deux buts
l'humanité et l'art. [redacted] c'est l'art qu'il
cherissait au dessus de tout qui le fera vivre
encor..
Puis nous rentrons. Theodore Vanghog est brisé
de chagrin; chacun des assistants très ému se
retire dans la campagne. d'autres regagnent
la gare.
Laval et moi revenons chez Ravoux et l'on cause
de lui...
mais en voila bien assez mon cher Aurier. bien
assez n'est ce pas de cette triste journée. vous
savez combien je l'aimais et vous vous doutez de
ce que j'ai pu le pleurer. ne l'oubliez donc pas
et tachez, vous son critique, d'en dire encore quelques
mots pour dire à tous que son enterrement
fut une apotheose vraiment digne de son grand
coeur et de son grand talent.

Tout à vous de coeur

Bernard

Parijs 1 Aug. 1890

Mijn liefste vrouwtje,

Uit mijn zwijgen heb je zeker wel opgemaakt dat ik in de weer was & o lieveling het was zulk moeielijk werk. Toen ik in Auvers aankwam vond ik hem gelukkig nog in leven & verliet ik hem niet weer tot het gedaan was. Je alles schrijven kan ik niet maar ik zal je alles spoedig komen vertellen. Een van zijn laatste woorden was ik wilde dat ik zóó heen kon gaan & zoo was het ook eenige oogenblikken & het was gedaan hij vond die rust die hij op aarde niet vinden kon. De twee dokters waren o zoo goed Dr. Gachet had de dorpsdokter er bij genomen omdat hij zichzelf niet vertrouwde, maar hij was het toch eigenlijk die alles deed. Later liet hij mij bijna geen oogenblik alleen en was o zoo hartelijk. De menschen waren uitsteekend, verbeeld je de volgende morgen kwamen er van Parijs & elders 8 vrienden die de kamer waar de kist stond behingen met zijn schilderijen die o zoo mooi deden. Er waren massa's bouquetten en kranzen. Dr. Gachet was de eerste die een prachtige bouquet zonnebloemen bracht omdat hij daar zooveel van hield. In Auvers wonen heel veel artisten en er waren er velen gekomen. Dries was ook gekomen. Er was van allerlij te doen om de begrafenis op tijd te kunnen doen plaatshebben, maar alles kwam in orde & het laatste uur wachten was moeielijk. Hij ligt op een zonnig plekje

Paris 1 Aug. 1890

My dearest wife,

You will have realized from my silence[1] that I have been rushing about & oh my dearest, it's been such a difficult task. When I arrived in Auvers I found him still alive fortunately & did not leave him until it was over. I cannot write to you about it all but I shall come soon and tell you everything. One of his last words was I wanted it to end like this & so it was for a few moments & it was over & he found the peace he could not find on earth.[2] The two doctors were so very good.[3] Dr Gachet had summoned the village doctor as he did not trust himself, but it was nevertheless he in fact who did everything. Later, he did not leave me alone for a second, almost, and was so very kind. The people were wonderful; imagine, the following morning 8 friends came from Paris & elsewhere and hung his paintings that looked so beautiful on the walls of the room that the coffin was in.[4] There were masses of bouquets and wreaths. Dr Gachet was the first to bring a magnificent bouquet of sunflowers because he loved them so dearly.[5] There are very many artists living in Auvers and many of them came. Dries came too.[6] There was much to be done in order to have the funeral take place on time, but everything worked out all right & waiting the last hour was difficult. He is buried

Theo to Jo, Friday 1 August 1890.
Inv. no. b 2067 VF/1982
Three passages from this letter were quoted by Johanna van Gogh-Bonger in her 1914 Introduction. These passages have often been quoted by later authors.

1. Theo had not written to his wife since Monday 28 July (Prologue 2). Jo did not receive this letter in Amsterdam until Wednesday 30 July. Theo's three-day silence was caused not only by the many tasks he had to perform after his brother's death, nor by his own distraught state, but more so by his disinclination to upset Jo, as a nursing mother, thus heeding Dr Gachet's warning (see Prologue 1). During these days, in fact, the only member of the family that Theo wrote to was his brother-in-law, Joan Marinus van Houten (see Family 1). In quoting from Theo's letter of 1 August in the 1914 Introduction, Jo does not give the date, which has led later commentators to misdate the letter to 29 July.

2. Theo arrived at Ravoux's inn on Monday 28 July, probably just after midday. Vincent died at 1.30 a.m. the following day. Theo therefore spent the last twelve hours with his brother, his only interruption being to write to Jo.

3. The village doctor was Joseph Mazery (1859-1920).

4. It is difficult to identify all 'eight friends'; seven can be named: Bernard (see Prologue 3), Charles Laval (1862-1894), A.M. Lauzet (1863-1898), Julien Tanguy, Lucien Pissarro (see French 1), Hirschig and Dr Gachet. Theo also cites 'many' other artists in a sentence not quoted in the 1914 Introduction. Hence, it has often been wrongly supposed that only eight people attended the funeral. Compare Bernard's account (Prologue 3, note 13).

5. Bernard, too, referred to the flowers, without specifying Gachet's role (see Prologue 3).

6. Dries is Theo's brother-in-law, Andries Bonger (1861-1936).

midden in de korenvelden & en het kerkhof heeft niet dat onaangename van de Parijsche kerkhoven. Dr. Gachet sprak heel mooi; ik bedankte in een paar woorden & toen was het gedaan. 's Avonds ben ik nog weg kunnen gaan maar o wat is het overal leeg, ik mis hem zoo het is of alles mij aan hem doet doet denken. Ik ben niet graag t'huis, daarom heb ik Annies aanbod om bij hun te komen slapen aangenomen. Mijn plan blijft om zondagmorgen weg te gaan & als je het goed vind hoe grooten lust ik ook heb om naar je toe te gaan in Amsterdam vind ik dat ik eerst naar Leiden moet om Moe van alles te vertellen, zij weet het al & schreef dadelijk, zij is o zoo bedroefd. Als je kan, kom dan in Leiden zoo gauw je kan (Zondag zoo mogelijk) dan gaan wij daarna weer naar Amsterdam terug. O wat zal ik blij zijn weer dicht heel dicht bij je te zijn. Heerlijk dat de jongen goed groeit en dat jij je toch wat beter gaat gevoelen. Dag mijn schat, zoen de kleine Vincent van mij & weest hartelijk omhelst door je altijd liefhebbende man

Theo

Ik schreef aan Moe of we Zondag mochten komen, maar schrijf haar ook een woordje. Groeten aan allen bij je thuis en bedank Pa voor zijn brief.

in a sunny spot in the middle of the cornfields & the churchyard doesn't have the unpleasant air of Parisian churchyards. Dr Gachet spoke beautifully; I gave a few words of thanks & then it was over.[7] I was able to get away in the evening but oh how empty it is everywhere, I miss him, everything seems to remind me of him. I don't like being at home, so I accepted Annie's invitation to sleep at their place.[8] I still intend to leave on Sunday morning & if you are agreeable, much as I long to come to you in Amsterdam I think I should first go to Leiden to tell Mother about it all, she already knows & wrote immediately, she is so very sad.[9] If you can, then come to Leiden as soon as you can (Sunday if possible) then we can return to Amsterdam together afterwards. Oh how happy I shall be to be close, very close, to you once again. Wonderful that the boy is growing well and that you are starting to feel better.[10] Goodbye my love, a kiss for little Vincent from me & a warm embrace from your ever loving husband

Theo

I have written to Mother asking if we might come on Sunday, but send her a few words too.[11] Regards to everyone at home with you and thank Father for his letter.[12]

7. Compare Bernard's account (Prologue 3), as well as Gachet's letter to Theo of mid-August (French 21).

8. Annie was the wife of Dries Bonger (see Prologue 2, note 4). They were then living at 127 rue du Ranelagh, Passy.

9. His mother's letter was written on Thursday, 31 July. See Family 2.

10. Theo wrote much the same to Joan van Houten on Tuesday, 29 July (Family 1).

11. Theo wrote to his mother earlier this same day (see Family 6).

12. Jo's father, Hendrik Christiaan Bonger (1828-1904), must have written to Theo on Thursday, 31 July; this letter is now apparently lost. But his letter of Monday, 4 August survives (see Family 12).

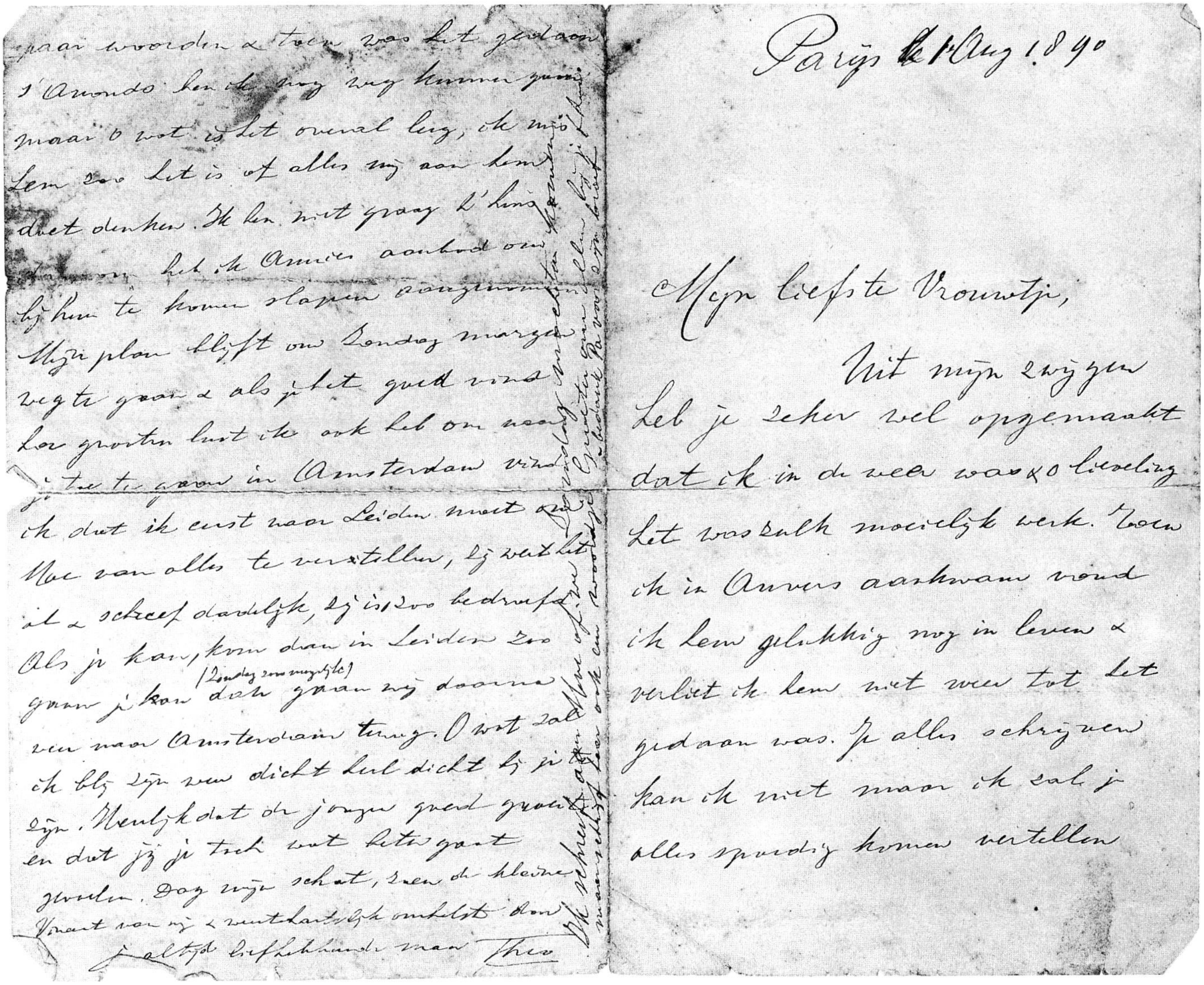
paar woorden & toen was het gedaan
's Avonds ben ik nog weg kunnen gaan
maar o wat is het overal leeg, ik mis
hem zoo het is of alles mij aan hem
doet denken. Ik ben niet graag t'huis
[illegible] heb ik Anniès aanbod om
bij hem te komen slapen aangenomen
Mijn plan blijft om Zondag morgen
weg te gaan & als je het goed vond
hoe groot en lust ik ook heb om naar
je toe te gaan in Amsterdam vind
ik dat ik eerst naar Leiden moet om
Moe van alles te vertellen, zij weet het
al & schreef dadelijk, zij is zoo bedroefd
Als je kan, kom dan in Leiden zoo
gaan je kan (Zondag zoo mogelijk) dan gaan wij daarna
een naar Amsterdam terug. O wat zal
ik blij zijn een dicht heel dicht bij je
zijn. Heerlijk dat de jongen goed groeit
en dat jij je toch wat beter gaat
voelen. Dag mijn schat, zoen de kleine
Vincent van mij & weest hartelijk omhelsd door
je altijd liefhebbende man Theo

[illegible]

Parijs 1 Aug. 1890

Mijn liefste Vrouwtje,

Uit mijn zwijgen heb je zeker wel opgemaakt dat ik in de weer was & o lieveling het was zulk moeielijk werk. Toen ik in Auvers aankwam vond ik hem gelukkig nog in leven & verliet ik hem niet weer tot het gedaan was. Je alles schrijven kan ik niet maar ik zal je alles spoedig komen vertellen.

4 I

PROLOGUE 4

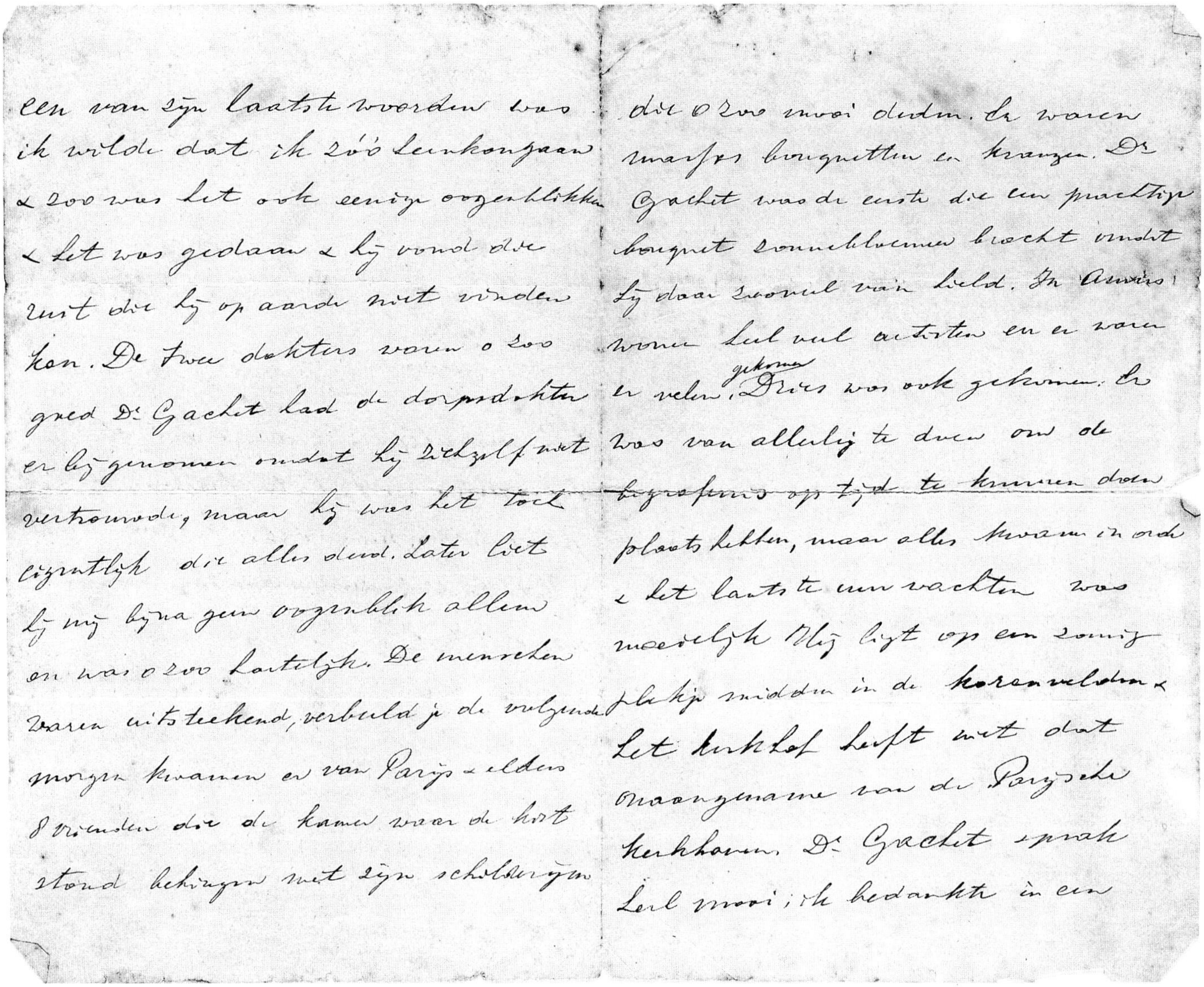
een van zijn laatste woorden was
ik wilde dat ik zóó heen kon gaan
& zoo was het ook eenige oogenblikken
& het was gedaan & hij vond die
rust die hij op aarde niet vinden
kon. De twee dokters waren o zoo
goed Dr Gachet had de dorpsdokter
er bij genomen omdat hij zichzelf niet
vertrouwde, maar hij was het toch
eigenlijk die alles deed. Later liet
hij mij bijna geen oogenblik alleen
en was o zoo hartelijk. De menschen
waren uitsteekend, verbeeld je de volgende
morgen kwamen er van Parijs & elders
8 vrienden die de kamer waar de kist
stond behingen met zijn schilderijen

die o zoo mooi deden. Er waren
massas bouquetten en kranzen. Dr
Gachet was de eerste die een prachtige
bouquet zonnebloemen bracht omdat
hij daar zooveel van hield. In Auvers
wonen heel veel artisten en er waren
er velen gekomen. Dries was ook gekomen. Er
was van allerlij te doen om de
~~begrafenis op tijd te kunnen doen~~
plaats hebben, maar alles kwam in orde
& het laatste uur wachten was
moeielijk. Hij ligt op een zonnig
plekje midden in de korenvelden &
het kerkhof heeft niet dat
onaangename van de Parijsche
kerkhoven. Dr Gachet sprak
heel mooi; ik bedankte in een

2 3

PROLOGUE 4

Family

Vincent's relationship with his family was seldom easy and often dotted with periods of estrangement and animosity. One of the longest of these was from 1885 to 1888. After his father's death in March 1885, at least one of his sisters, Anna, hitherto always close to him, broke with him. And once in Paris, Vincent became increasingly hostile to his family, bemoaning their narrowness of spirit, their lack of interest in his work, and the failure of two art-dealing uncles to help Theo launch himself as an independent dealer.

Gradually, however, perceptible changes took place in his outlook, especially once he had moved to Provence. He often wrote to his sister Wil, he began writing to his mother again, and he frequently recalled the Dutch experience – 'Northern' life and landscape, seventeenth-century Dutch artists and even contemporary Dutch painters. When he returned from Saint-Rémy to 'the North' in May 1890, he was not just conciliatory towards all members of the family, but considerably warmer towards his seventy-year old mother and his sister Wil: he even talked of wishing to see them again after a five-year separation. He wrote to them frequently from Auvers-sur-Oise. It was as if he were part of the family circle again. He discussed optimistically his health and the care and friendship of Dr Gachet; he described the congenial surroundings in the village and the landscape that inspired his painting. Moreover, Theo and Jo were now only an hour away by train: they visited him in Auvers, he visited them in Paris. He felt a renewed calm, a greater serenity, a sense of well-being. All this encouraging news was relayed by his mother and Wil to other members of the family in Holland, particularly to her sisters, as well as his own sisters, Anna and Lies. They were relieved and consoled: a happy working solution had been found. In turn, Mother and Wil sent Vincent family news – of life in their new abode in Leiden, of Anna's daughters, of Lies. And Lies herself, clearly apprised of Vincent's newly gained serenity, sent him a letter via Theo on 29 June. A month later, Vincent was dead.

For his mother and Wil in particular, the news of Vincent's death, coming so utterly unexpectedly, would be shattering. Theo was faced with a terrible dilemma in Auvers. A telegram would be too abrupt and brutal. Even a letter would be too drastic under the circumstances, not only to his mother, but also to Jo, who was then staying with her parents in Amsterdam, remembering how Dr Gachet had warned him not to alarm his wife. So Theo evolved the very simple strategy of writing to his brother-in-law, Joan van Houten who lived at Leiderdorp, just outside Leiden. At Theo's request, Van Houten would visit Mother and Wil on Wednesday afternoon and tell them that Vincent was again unwell, rather seriously unwell, but that his strong constitution had won him through in the past and could well do so again. This was how Van Houten reported it to Mother and Wil on Wednesday – the actual day of the funeral. He left them that evening and returned the following morning, breaking the news of Vincent's death to Wil, who then told her mother. They were stupefied: given all the recent assurances and encouraging signs of serenity and rehabilitation, with his painting going so well, it was all the more incredible. The rest of the day was spent sending letters: by Friday 1 August the whole family in Holland knew.

There are fourteen such family letters, including two from Theo himself to his mother and sister Elisabeth Huberta – Lies – both of which have previously been published. Jo concluded her account of Auvers with parts of Theo's letter of 1 August to his mother; and it has subsequently been printed in full. Now we have his mother's and Wil's letters to him that prompted his letter: the patchwork begins to take shape. As it does also with Theo's letter to Lies of 5 August 1890, known only from the generous excerpts printed by Lies in her book of recollections, published in 1910. Unfortunately, the original letter has still not come to light. But what has come to light is Lies' letter to Theo of 2 August that prompted Theo's response. These are certainly the most revealing of the family letters: on Theo's part, adding a further gloss on the circumstances of Vincent's death and burial; on Lies' part, combining her stunned expressions of grief with reminiscences, and comments on two of Vincent's paintings that were already in her collection.

Leiden 31/7 '90

Waarde Theo,

Je brief met het treurig bericht van Vincent's overlijden ontving ik gisteren middag. Ik kan me best voorstellen hoe ge er door geschokt zult zijn.

Ge hebt altijd zoo met hem mee geleefd en kendet hem daardoor beter dan een der anderen. 't Moet eene groote satisfactie voor je wezen te weten, dat hij op 't laatst niet geleden heeft, en dat ge nog tijdig gekomen zijt, doet me recht veel genoegen voor je. Ge zijt, ik weet dit, meer dan een broer voor hem geweest, maar juist daardoor zult ge hem nu dubbel missen.

Wees dan ook overtuigd dat ik hartelijk in je verlies deel en moge 't je een troost wezen te weten, dat hij nu rust gekregen heeft na het moeitevolle leven, dat hij achter de rug heeft.

Gisteren avond heb ik Moe & Mien meêgedeeld, dat ge weêr slechte berichten uit Auvers gekregen hadt, en van morgen deelde ik haar de tijding in haar geheel meê. Dat zij innig bedroefd zijn spreekt vanzelf; 't kwam toch nog onverwacht, te onverwacht om zich aan 't denkbeeld te kunnen wennen, want hoe dikwijls kwam Vincent na zulk een vlaag er weer boven op, dankzij zijn sterk gestel.

Ik verliet Moe kalm en berust, getroost door 't denkbeeld, dat hij eindelijk rust gevonden heeft.

Ongetwijfeld zal 't je eene groote leegte in je leven geven; gelukkig dat vrouw en kind die zullen trachten aan te vullen. Ik hoorde met zooveel genoegen uit Amst:[erdam], dat de jongen zo goed groeit, en Jo zooveel aansterkt.

Ik schrijf deze in vliegende haast; wees dus met dit korte woordje tevreê.

Adieu, geloof me

tt Joan

Leiden 31/7 '90

Dear Theo,

Yesterday afternoon I received your letter with the sad news of Vincent's death.[1] I can well imagine how shocked you must be.

You had such a strong affinity with him and consequently knew him better than anyone else. It must be a great comfort to you to know that he did not suffer at the end, and I am indeed glad for you that you arrived in time. You have, I know, been more than a brother to him, but this is precisely why you will feel the loss twice as deeply.

Be assured of my sincere sympathy on your loss and may it comfort you to know that he will now be at peace after a life full of care.

Yesterday evening I told Mother & Mien that you had again received bad news from Auvers, and this morning I told her the whole story.[2] That they are deeply upset goes without saying; it was nevertheless unexpected, too unexpected for them to have accustomed themselves to the idea since, after all, Vincent frequently recovered from such bouts, thanks to his strong constitution.[3]

I left Mother calm and composed, reassured by the thought that he has finally found peace.

It will undoubtedly leave a tremendous void in your life, which your wife and child, fortunately, will endeavour to fill. I was greatly pleased to hear from Amst:[erdam] that the boy is growing well and that Jo is gaining strength.[4]

I am writing in all haste; forgive me for keeping it short.

Adieu, believe me

yrs. ever Joan

Joan Marinus van Houten to Theo, Thursday 31 July 1890.
Inv. no. b 1007 V/1962

1. Joan Marinus van Houten (1850-1945) was Theo's brother-in-law, having married Theo's eldest sister Anna (1855-1930) in Etten in August 1878. He was of the firm of Van Houten en Ledeboer, limeburners at Leiderdorp, just outside Leiden. Partly because Van Houten lived so close to Mother and Wil, and partly because Theo trusted his discretion, it was he alone of all that family that Theo chose to inform of the death of Vincent. Obviously, this was to protect the womenfolk from the unbearable shock of receiving the news by letter or telegram. Theo's letter was sent from Auvers-sur-Oise on Tuesday 29 July. Van Houten received it the following afternoon at the very time that Vincent's funeral was taking place. Unfortunately, the letter is lost, but some of its contents can be gauged from the letters written by Mother and Wil to Theo and Jo (Family 2-3). Van Houten's reply was delayed until Thursday 31 July, giving him time to break the distressing news more gently to Theo's mother and sister.

2. See Family 2, note 1, and Family 3, note 2.

3. Theo had written in similar vein to his wife on 28 July: 'things have been as hopeless before & the doctors were surprised by his strong constitution' (Prologue 2).

4. Much the same was said by Theo to Jo on 1 August: 'Wonderful that the boy is growing well and that you are starting to feel better' (Prologue 4).

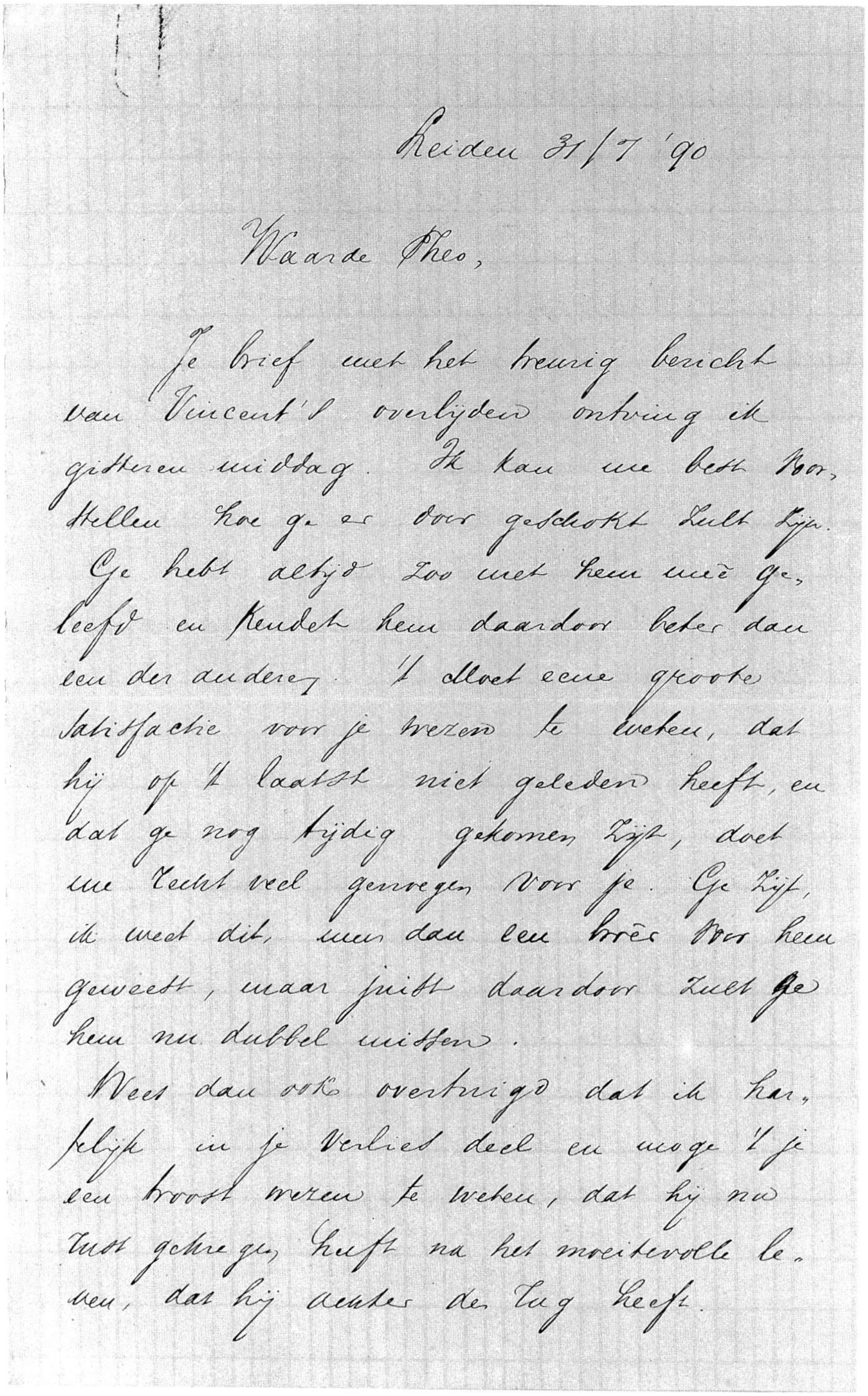

Leiden 31/7 '90

Waarde Theo,

Je brief met het treurig bericht van Vincent's overlijden ontving ik gisteren middag. Ik kan me best voorstellen hoe ge er door geschokt zult zijn. Ge hebt altijd zoo met hem mee geleefd en kendet hem daardoor beter dan een der anderen. 't Moet eene groote satisfactie voor je wezen te weten, dat hij op 't laatst niet geleden heeft, en dat ge nog tijdig gekomen zijt, doet me recht veel genoegen voor je. Ge zijt, ik weet dit, meer dan een broer voor hem geweest, maar juist daardoor zult ge hem nu dubbel missen.

Wees dan ook overtuigd dat ik hartelijk in je verlies deel en moge 't je een troost wezen te weten, dat hij nu rust gekregen heeft na het moeitevolle leven, dat hij achter den rug heeft.

Gisteren avond heb ik Moe & Mien mee ge-
deeld, dat ge weer slechte berichten uit
Auvers gekregen hadt, en van morgen deelde
ik haar de tijding in haar geheel mee.
Dat zij innig bedroefd zijn spreekt van
zelf; 't kwam toch nog onverwacht, te
onverwacht om zich aan 't denkbeeld te
kunnen wennen, want hoe dikwijls kwam
Vincent na zulk eene vlaag er weer boven
op, dank zij zijn sterk gestel.

Ik verliet Moe kalm en berust, getroost
door 't denkbeeld, dat hij eindelijk rust
gevonden heeft.

Ongetwijfeld zal 't je eene groote leegte
in je leven geven; gelukkig, dat vrouw
en kind die zullen trachten aan te vullen. Ik hoorde met zooveel genoegen uit
Amst., dat de jongen zoo goed gedijt, en
Jo zooveel aansterkt.

Ik schrijf deze in vliegende haast; wees
dus met dit korte woordje tevree.

Adieu, geloof me

t.t. Joa.

Leiden 31 Juli

Beste innig geliefde Theo.

Bedroeft zijn we door het treffend bericht! Jo bereidde ons en toen ik Wil met tranen in de oogen vanmorgen zag, zei ik is hij dood? Dank beste Theo voor al wat ge voor hem deed. Gij hebt hem het leven tot leven gemaakt door Uwe liefde en zorg. De goede God heeft dat gezien en alles zoo beschikt dat gij tot belooning hem zijn oogen hebt zien sluiten en hem ter ruste gelegd hebt. Dat is een belooning die de hoogste liefde vond je toekwam. Bij al het ontzettend onverwachte ben ik dankbaar voor de kalme goede omgeving die hij had dat hij nog met je sprak en hij na je schrijven zonder bijzonder lijden heen ging naar dat land waar geen strijd en lijden meer zijn zal. 'k Zal je laten lezen zijn brief van voor 14 dagen hoe hij uitdrukt zich te voelen. Hij schreef ook hij dikwijls verlangde ons weer te zien. Hoe goed Uwe trouwe liefde hem tot 't laatst toe nabij was. Zegen Theo van ons allen en de goede God zegene je met Jo en de lieve kleine Vincent die de vreugd van je leven mag worden. Een hartelijke kus bij de dank van:

je zoo liefh. Moe

Leiden 31 July

Dear beloved Theo.

We are upset by the distressing news! Jo prepared us[1] and when I saw Wil this morning with tears in her eyes, I said is he dead? Thank you, my dear Theo, for all you did for him. Your love and solicitude made his life worthwhile. The good Lord witnessed it and ordained that you be rewarded by seeing him close his eyes and laying him to rest. This is the reward of which the greatest love found you worthy. In all these terrible unexpected events, I am thankful that he was in calm, good surroundings, that he could still talk to you and that, according to your letter,[2] he departed without undue suffering to that land where turmoil and pain are no more. I shall let you read his letter from a fortnight ago, saying how he felt. He also wrote that he often longed to see us again.[3] How good that your abiding love was near him right to the end. Blessings, Theo, from all of us, and may the good Lord bless you and Jo and dear little Vincent. May he be the joy of your life. A grateful kiss and many thanks from:

your loving Mother

Mother and Wil to Theo, Thursday 31 July 1890.
Inv. no. b 1009 v/1962

1. Anna Cornelia Carbentus (1819-1907) married Pastor Theodorus van Gogh (1822-1885) on 21 May 1851. They had seven children, Vincent Willem (still born 30 March 1852), Vincent Willem (born 30 March 1853), Anna Cornelia (born 17 February 1855), Theodorus (born 1 May 1857), Elisabeth Huberta (born 16 May 1859), Willemina (born 16 March 1862) and Cornelis Vincent (born 17 May 1867). After the death of her husband in Nuenen on 26 March 1885, Anna Cornelia moved first to Breda and then, in late October 1889, to 100 Herengracht, Leiden. Only Willemina, known as Wil (1862-1941), lived with her at this time. And it was Wil, of the three sisters, who was closest to Vincent, receiving some twenty-three letters from him between 1887 and July 1890.

Jo is Joan van Houten, who, having received Theo's letter on Wednesday afternoon, 30 July, announcing Vincent's death, visited Mother and Wil at 100 Herengracht that same evening (see Family 1-2). At Theo's request, he refrained from telling them immediately the devastating news. Instead, he returned the following morning and broke the news to Wil, who then told

Beste Theo,

Ik kan 't haast niet gelooven en er me nog niet indenken, dat hij er niet meer is. We mogen hem de rust niet misgunnen, maar wat zal 't jou ook hard vallen. Heerlijk dat je bij hem was, trouwe, dat had je verdiend. En dat hij kalm is heengegaan is de grootste zegen die mogelijk was. Wat wonderlijke samenloop dat alles zóó ging, dat hij zijn wensch had van meer als gewoon mensch te doen en te wonen, en nu zoo dicht in je buurt was. Zoo was hij toch zeker gelukkiger voor zichzelf wat hij trouwens in zijn laatste schrijven zelf uitdrukte. Wat zal je blij zijn dat Jo hem nog zag, wie dacht toen dat 't voor 't laatst zou zijn en hij 't kleine Vincentje ook gezien heeft. Arme jongen dat je vrouwtje nu niet bij je is, kom maar gauw naar Holland, we verlangen zoo naar je, zou 't de volgende week zijn? Houd je goed en pas op je zelf, een zoen van

je Wil.

Bedankt Dr Gachet ook uit onze naam.

Dear Theo,

I can hardly believe and cannot yet imagine that he is no more. We should not begrudge him his peace, but how hard it will be for you. Wonderful that you were with him, loyal, you deserved it. And that he passed away peacefully is the greatest blessing possible. What a strange coincidence, the course that events took, that he had his wish to be and to live more like ordinary people, and was now so near to you. He was certainly happier like this as he himself said, incidentally, in his last letter.[4] How glad you must be that Jo managed to see him, who would have supposed then that it would be for the last time, and that he also saw little Vincent.[5] Poor fellow, not having your wife with you now; come to Holland soon, we long so much for you, could you manage next week? Keep well and take care of yourself, a kiss from

your Wil.

Thank Dr Gachet on our behalf too.[6]

her mother. Their letter of condolence to Theo was written later that day. Theo received it in Paris on Friday 1 August (see Family 6).

2. Mother is referring to Theo's letter to Joan van Houten (see Family 1).

3. Vincent wrote two letters to his mother from Auvers (LT 639 and LT 641a), and two to his sister Wil (W 22 and W 23; W 21 is a draft for W 22). Only in his last letter did he write to them jointly (LT 650).

4. Wil is referring to LT 650. See note 3.

5. Wil knew that Vincent had been in Paris from 17 to 20 May. And she also knew of the visit to Auvers on Sunday 8 June: Vincent wrote of it to her (W 23) as well as to his mother (LT 641a).

6. Dr Gachet must have been spoken of highly in Theo's (lost) letter to Joan van Houten, just as he had been in Theo's letters of 1 August to Jo (Prologue 4) and his mother (Family 6).

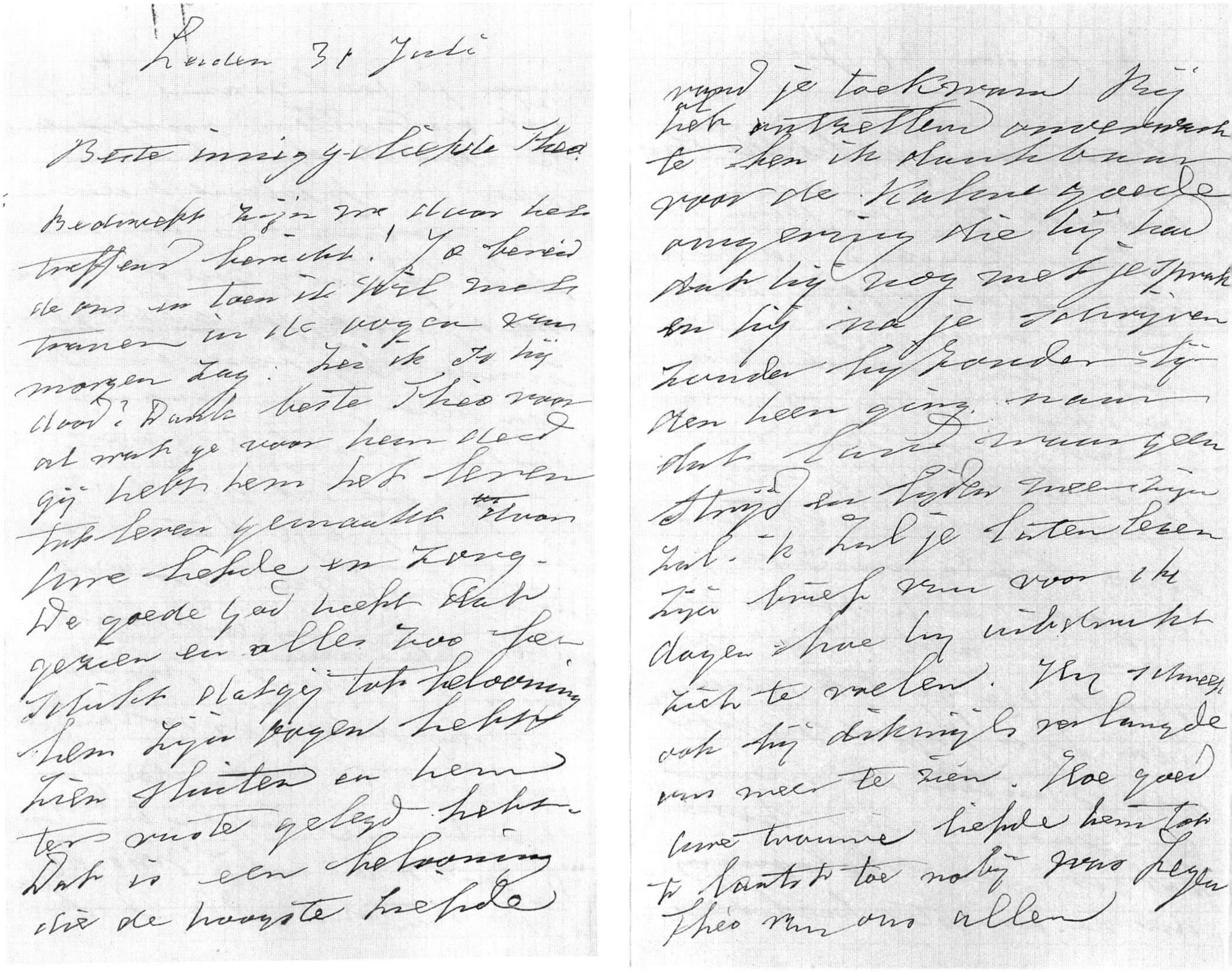

Leiden 31 Juli

Beste innig geliefde Theo

Bedroefd zijn we, door het treffend bericht! Jo bereidde ons er toen ik Wil met tranen in de oogen dien morgen zag. Zei ik is hij dood? Dank beste Theo voor al wat ge voor hem deed gij hebt hem het leven tot leven gemaakt door uwe liefde en zorg. De goede God heeft dat gezien en alles zoo geschikt dat gij tot belooning hem zijn oogen hebt zien sluiten en hem ter ruste gelegd hebt. Dat is een belooning die de hoogste liefde

vond je toekwam. Bij het afzetten onderweg te zien ik dankbaar voor de kalme goede omgeving die hij had dat hij nog met je sprak en hij na je schrijven zonder strijd aan der zijde heen ging, naar dat laatste vreeselijke strijd en lijden meer zijn zal. 'k had je laten lezen zijn brief van voor 14 dagen hoe hij uitdrukt hoe te voelen. Hij schreef ook hij dikwijls verlangde ons meer te zien. Hoe goed uwe trouwe liefde hem tot het laatst toe nabij was zegen Theo van ons allen

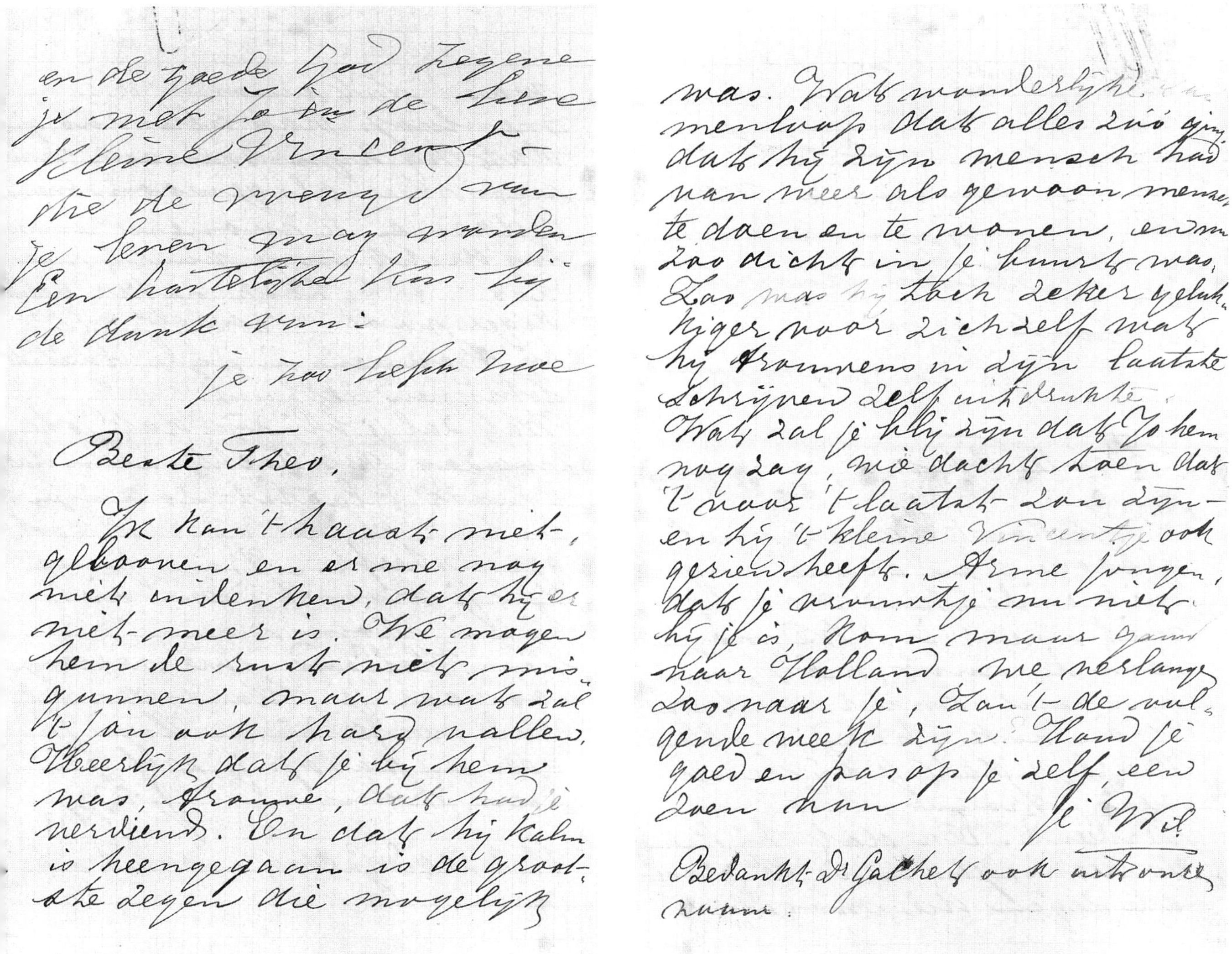

en de goede God zegene
je met Jo en de lieve
kleine Vincent &
dat de vreugd van
je leven mag worden
Een hartelijke kus bij
de dank van:
je zoo liefh. Moe

Beste Theo,

Ik kan 't haast niet
gelooven en er me nog
niet indenken, dat hij er
niet meer is. We mogen
hem de rust niet mis-
gunnen, maar wat zal
't jou ook hard vallen.
Heerlijk dat je bij hem
was, trouwe, dat had je
verdiend. En dat hij kalm
is heengegaan is de grootste zegen die mogelijk
was. Wat wonderlijke sa-
menloop dat alles zoo ging
dat hij zijn mensch had
van meer als gewoon mensch
te doen en te wonen, en in
zoo dicht in je buurt was.
Zoo was hij toch zeker gelukkiger voor zichzelf wat
hij trouwens in zijn laatste
schrijven zelf uitdrukte.
Wat zal je blij zijn dat Jo hem
nog zag, wie dacht toen dat
't voor 't laatst zou zijn-
en hij 't kleine Vincentje ook
gezien heeft. Arme jongen,
dat je vrouwtje nu niet
bij je is. Kom maar gauw
naar Holland we verlangen
zoo naar je, zal 't de volgende week zijn? Houd je
goed en pas op je zelf, een
zoen van
je Wil

Bedankt Dr Gachet ook uit onze
naam.

FAMILY 2

Leiden donderdag avond

Beste Jo,! Een enkel woordje maar, ik kan niet goed schrijven, ge kunt denken hoe bedroefd we zijn. 'k Had al gewacht of er ook een woordje van U kwam maar nu begin ik maar wat, misschien morgenochtend. Gisterenavond kwam Jo van Houten die een brief van Theo had, hij moest 't voorzichtig zeggen en zei ons 't weer niet goed met Vincent was. Morgen hoorden wij meer. Hij wilde de nacht laten voorbijgaan en toen Wil vanmorgen met betraande oogen in mijn kamer kwam zei ik dadelijk O is Jo er, Is Vincent dood, helaas 't was zoo. –

O lieve Jo we zijn zielsbedroefd, maar wat zegen die beste broer onze lieve Theo bij hem was en hij hem tot 't einde mocht bijstaan. Theo schreef hoe alles ging, hoe zacht ontsliep hij en nu rust hij van dat onvermoeid streven en strijden en lijden. Weet ge wel hij ons schreef hij ongekend kalm was en zijn hoofd zoo rustig door de gedachte meer in de nabijheid te zijn. Och beste Jo wat goed Ul.[ieden] lief kindje nu Vincent Willem heet, hij heeft het toch nog gezien. Wat zal Theo bedroefd zijn, hoe verlangen we naar hem. Zou hij nu toch Zondag komen, ge moet ons toch schrijven als ge wat weet. Hoe verlangend zijn we naar al de bijzonderheden. Wat een zegen Theo in Parijs was, de goede God Die Hem onder

Leiden Thursday evening

Dear Jo,! Just a few words, as I can't really write, you can imagine how miserable we are. I was expecting to hear from you, but I shall make a start now, perhaps tomorrow morning.[1] Jo van Houten came last night with a letter from Theo.[2] He had to break the news to us gently and said that all was not well with Vincent again. The next morning we would hear more. He wanted to wait the night and when Wil came into my room weeping this morning I immediately said Oh, is Jo here, is Vincent dead, alas, he was. –

Oh dear Jo we are heartbroken, but what a blessing that fine brother, our dear Theo, was with him to attend him to the end. Theo wrote what happened, how gently he passed on and now he is at rest from that tireless striving and struggling and suffering. Do you know that he wrote that he was more at peace than ever before and that his mind was at rest, knowing that he was nearer.[3] Ah my dear Jo how fine that your lovely child is called Vincent Willem, and that he was able to see it. How sad Theo must be, how we miss him. Will he be coming on Sunday, please write to us when you know. We are so anxious to hear the details. What a blessing that Theo was in Paris.[4] The good Lord who was near him throughout, has called

Mother and Wil to Jo, Thursday 31 July 1890.
Inv. no. b 1003 V/1962

1. This letter to Johanna was clearly begun in the late evening of Thursday 31 July, after Mother and Wil had already sent their letter to Theo (Family 2). It is conceivable that Mother actually finished it that evening – the holograph shows no change in the writing, nor a hiatus in the flow of thought. Wil may well have added her short message on the last page, exhausted at the end of a long and deeply distressing day in which she and her mother had written many letters to members of the family and friends.

2. See Family 1.

alles nabij was, heeft hem tot zich genomen. Wie zal hem de rust misgunnen, maar o wat smartelijk! Wat lief van Uw vader mij zoo vriendelijk te schrijven. En nu lieve Jo, ik kan niet meer, maar verlangde zoo naar je. Och 'k ben Theo zoo dankbaar die altijd zóó lief voor hem was, 't Zal in zegen op Ul.[ieden] kindje neerkomen bid en vertrouw ik. Wil is bitter bedroefd. Ge weet ze hield zooveel van hem, wat zal Cor schrikken en Lies en Anna.

Groet Theo toch hartelijk. Wij schreven hem dadelijk. Wat was die doctor lief! En nu goeden nacht, groet de Uwen en een kus voor U en de kleine Vincent van

je bedroefde Moe

him. Who would deny him his rest, but oh what anguish! How kind of your father to write to me so cordially.[5] And now, dear Jo, I can't go on, but missed you very much. Oh how grateful I am to Theo who was always so very kind to him. I trust and pray that it will be a blessing upon your child. Wil is bitterly upset. You know how much she loved him. It will certainly come as a shock to Cor and Lies and Anna.

Give Theo my fondest regards. We shall write to him soon. How very kind that doctor was![6] And now, goodnight, greetings to your dear ones and a kiss to you and little Vincent from

your sorrowful Mother

Lieve Jo, Wat zal je verlangen bij Theo te zijn in zijn droefheid. Maar wat een zegen dat hij in Parijs was en bij Vincent blijven kon. Zou Theo nu Zondag komen. 'k Heb zoo veel geschreven dat 'k eigenlijk niet meer schrijven kan. Een zoen van

je Wil.

Dear Jo, How much you must long to be with Theo in his sadness. But what a blessing that he was in Paris and could stay with Vincent. Is Theo coming on Sunday? I have written so much that I can't actually write any more.[7] A kiss from

your Wil.

3. A reference to Vincent's last letter to Mother and Wil of circa 16 July (LT 650).

4. Theo had returned to Paris on Saturday 19 July.

5. Johanna's father had probably written on 30 July (the letter is lost), doubtless sharing his worries over Vincent's health.

6. The reference is to Dr Gachet (see Family 2).

7. Wil, probably more than her mother, must have written letters to family relatives throughout the day, after hearing of Vincent's death that morning.

Dennenoord 1 Aug.

Lieve Jo!

Wat trof mij het bericht van het onverwachte sterven van Vincent, hoe zult gij en Theo, die hem nog zoo kort geleden wèl zagen, er van ontsteld zijn. Hoe gelukkig voor beide broers, zij tot het einde toe bij elkaar waren, dat zal Moe ook zoo tot troost zijn, dat Theo bij hem was, en hem kon bijstaan. Hem zal de rust zeker welkom geweest zijn, want wat heeft hij het toch altijd moeilijk gehad, gelukkig hij de laatste tijd toch nog zooveel satisfactie van zijn werk gehad heeft, en hij zijn naamgenootje ook nog gezien heeft. Gij zult nu zeker dubbel naar Theo verlangen. Wat zal hij het eenzaam gehad hebben in deze treurige dagen. Komt hij nu toch morgen? Van morgen hoorde ik van Moe, het jongetje het toch zoo goed maakt, en het met die flesschen goed gaat. Ik zag dezer dagen een kindje dat er mee groot was gebracht, maar dat geeft wel vidutie. Hij geniet zeker veel van buiten zijn ook, met dit mooie weer. En voel je je zelf wat sterker, dat hoop ik zoo voor je, eer ge weer naar Parijs gaat. Gij verlangt zeker geducht naar Theo, want al is men ook in 't ouderlijke huis, zoo gescheiden is toch niet meer het ware. Dat ondervind ik ook en verlang er naar Jo [van Houten] weer eens te zien. Voor het oogenblik doet het buitenzijn nog niet zooveel goed als we wel zouden wenschen, maar de koorts is gelukkig geheel weg. We zouden zoo graag onze meisjes wat sterker zien, vooral over Ann zijn we steeds in zorg. En nu moet ik het hierbij laten, groet je familie s.v.p. voor me en geef het jongetje eens een hartelijke kus voor mij en de meisjes. Geloof mij steeds

je liefhebbende
Anna.

Dennenoord 1 Aug.

Dear Jo!

How upset I was to hear the news of Vincent's unexpected death; how distressing for you and Theo, who saw him fit such a short time ago.[1] How fortunate for the two brothers that they were together to the end; it will also be a great comfort to Mother that Theo was with him and able to help him. The peace will certainly be welcome, as things were always difficult for him. It is fortunate that he was gaining such satisfaction from his work recently, and that he managed to see his little namesake. You will surely be longing for Theo all the more now. How lonely he must have been in these unhappy days. Will he be coming tomorrow? Mother told me this morning that your little boy is doing very well and that the bottles are no problem. I recently saw a child that had been brought up on the bottle, and found it most reassuring. He must enjoy being out in the open, especially in this fine weather. And are you feeling stronger now, I do hope so for you, before you return to Paris. You must be longing for Theo most awfully, because even if one is staying with one's parents, such a separation is simply not right. I feel the same and am longing to see Jo [van Houten] again. For the moment, being out is not as beneficial as we might wish, but the fever has fortunately subsided completely. We should so like to see our girls a little stronger; Ann in particular is a constant worry.[2] And now I must end; please give my good wishes to your family and an affectionate kiss to your little boy from me and the girls. Believe me always,

your loving
Anna.

Anna van Houten-Van Gogh to Jo, Friday 1 August 1890.
Inv. no. b 1004 V/1962

1. Anna Cornelia was the eldest of the three Van Gogh sisters, having been born at Zundert on 17 February 1855. She died at Dieren on 20 September 1930.

Only two years younger than Vincent, Anna was close to him as a child and they continued the best of friends until their father's death in March 1885. Anna felt that Vincent's behaviour partly caused his father's death (LT 398). Anna is referring to Vincent's visit to Paris on Sunday 6 July, the last time he saw Jo, Theo and the baby together.

2. Anna and Joan Marinus van Houten (1850-1945) were married by her father at Etten church on 22 August 1878. Their two daughters were Sara Maria, born 22 July 1880, and Anna Theodora, born 8 February 1883. There is a reference to Anna's children in Vincent's last letter to Mother and Wil of circa 16 July (LT 650). This sentence, 'Wat zullen Anna's kinderen al groot worden' ('How big Anna's children must be getting') was omitted from all editions of Van Gogh's correspondence until it was printed in the 1990 Letters (no. 904).

Leiden Vrijdag avond

Beste Théo!

Hoe gaat het je. We zijn ontsteld dat uw Jo na 't bericht uit Auvers dat Vincent ziek was maar geen oogenblikkelijk gevaar dat ze niets meer hoorde. Wij konden ons niet begrijpen we niets van Jo hoorden en dachten ze zou komen toen we vrijdag morgen nog niets hoorden schreef ik haar waarom en nu zegt ze ze nog niets wist en hebben wij onschuldig haar verschrikt. 'k hoop zoo ge niet ziek zijt en spoedig 't zich opheldert. Hoe we verlangen van alles te hooren kunt ge denken vooral van je zelf. Lies kwam vanmorgen al vroeg, zoo welkom Anna is ook erg bedroeft. Dag beste Theo van ons allen ook van Jo van Houten.

Een kus van

je bedroefde
Moe

Leiden Friday evening

Dear Théo!

How are you. We are worried that, after the news from Auvers that Vincent was ill but in no immediate danger, your Jo heard nothing more.[1] We could not understand why we heard nothing from Jo and thought she would call on us; when we still didn't hear anything on Friday morning, I wrote to ask her why and now she says she did not yet know anything and that we had inadvertently given her a fright.[2] I hope you are not ill and that things will be cleared up soon. We look forward to hearing everything as you can imagine, especially about you. Lies arrived early this morning,[3] so very welcome. Anna is also deeply upset.[4] Greetings dear Theo from us all and from Jo van Houten too.

A kiss from

your sorrowful
Mother

Mother to Theo, Friday 1 August 1890.
Inv. no. b 1008 v/1962

1. Theo had last written to Johanna on Monday 28 July (Prologue 2). He had not written a word to his mother. To protect the womenfolk against the shock, Theo decided to inform Joan van Houten first (see Family 1-3). He broke his silence only on Friday 1 August, writing to both his mother and his wife on that day. His letter therefore crossed with this one from his mother.

2. See Family 2. Johanna's letter appears to be lost.

3. On Theo's sister, Elisabeth Huberta (1859-1936), see Family 11.

4. See Family 4.

Parijs 1 Aug 1890

Lieve beste Moedertje,

Men kan niet schrijven hoe bedroefd men is nog troost vinden in uitstorting op het papier. Mag ik gauw bij U komen? Ik moet hier nog allerlei regelen maar als het kon zou ik graag Zondag morgen van hier gaan om s' avonds bij U te zijn. Het is een smart die mij lang zal wegen en die mij mijn heele leven zeker niet uit de gedachte zal gaan, maar als men iets ervoor zou willen zeggen is het dat hijzelf rust heeft waar hij naar verlangde. Als hij had kunnen zien hoe de menschen voor mij waren nadat hij weg was gegaan en de attenties van zoovelen voor hem had kunnen zien zou hij voor het oogenblik er niet toe gekomen zijn om te willen sterven. Ik ontving van daag Uw brief en die van Wil en dank er U beiden wel voor. Alles kan ik U beter

Paris 1 Aug 1890

Dear beloved Mother,

One cannot write how sad one is nor find solace in pouring out one's heart on paper. May I come to you soon? I still have to make all sorts of arrangements here but if it is possible I would like to leave here on Sunday morning to be with you in the evening.[1] It is a sadness which will weigh upon me for a long time and will certainly not leave my thoughts as long as I live, but if one should want to say anything it is that he himself has found the rest he so much longed for.[2] If he could have seen how people behaved to me when he had left us and could have seen the kindness which so many showed for him, he would for the moment not have decided that he wanted to die. Today I received your letter and the one from Wil and I thank you both.[3] It would be better to tell you

Theo to Mother, Friday 1 August 1890.
Inv. no. b 934 V/1962
Partly published by Johanna van Gogh-Bonger in her 1914 Introduction, where it was used to conclude the Auvers period. The excerpt, in part or wholly, has often been used in later books and articles on Van Gogh. The letter was first published in its entirety, with its four holograph pages illustrated, and with an English translation, by J. Hulsker, 'What Theo really thought of Vincent', *Vincent: Bulletin of the Rijksmuseum Vincent van Gogh* 3 (1974), no. 2, pp. 2-28. Hulsker also published it in full in *Lotgenoten. Het leven van Vincent en Theo van Gogh*, Weesp 1985, p. 634, and idem, *Vincent and Theo: a dual biography*, Ann Arbor 1990, p. 449.

1. Theo's letter is in response to his Mother's and his sister Wil's letter of Thursday 31 July (Family 2). He had not written a word to them since his arrival in Auvers the previous Monday. Now, on Friday, he conveys something of his intense anguish and profound grief, and promises to tell more when he arrives in Leiden on Sunday 3 August.

vertellen dan schrijven Dr Gachet en ook de andere dokter waren voorbeeldig en hebben goed voor hem gezorgd maar van het eerste oogenblik af wisten zij wel er niets aan te doen was. Vincent zei: Ik zou zoo weg willen gaan en een half uur later had hij zijn zin. Het leven woog hem zoo zwaar maar zooals het meer gaat is nu ieder vol lof ook over zijn talent. Misschien is het gelukkig dat Jo niet hier was, het zou haar hebben doen schrikken. Mag zij ook komen zoodra ik er ben. Wij gaan dan later nog een dag of wat naar Amsterdam. O, Moeder ik verlang zoo om bij U te zijn. U heb het zeker wel aan Lies geschreven. Ik kan het niet goed doen op dit oogenblik. Morgen zal ik het eerst zeker weten of ik weg kan en kom ik niet dan krijgt U nog een brief. O Moeder hij was zoo mijn eigen broer. In gedachten een kus voor U en voor Wil van Uwe liefhebbende

Theo

everything instead of writing. Dr Gachet and the other doctor were excellent and looked after him well, but they realized from the very first moment that there was nothing one could do.[4] Vincent said: This is how I would like to go and half an hour later he had his way. Life weighed so heavily upon him, but as happens more often everyone is now full of praise for his talent too.[5] Maybe it was fortunate that Jo was not here for it might have given her a shock. May she also come once I am there. Later we will go to Amsterdam for a couple of days. Oh Mother, I so much long to be with you. I suppose you have written to Lies.[6] I can't do it at the moment. Only tomorrow will I know for certain whether I can leave and if I cannot come I will send you another letter. Oh Mother, he was so very much my own brother.[7] In my thoughts a kiss for you and Wil from your loving

Theo

2. This passage was published by Johanna van Gogh-Bonger in 1914.

3. That is, Mother's and Wil's letter of 31 July (Family 2).

4. The 'other doctor' was Dr Joseph Mazery (1859-1920), who, in 1890, actually lived in part of Daubigny's house, the garden of which Vincent painted on three occasions (F 765, F 776, F 777).

5. This sentence was published by Johanna van Gogh-Bonger in 1914.

6. Mother and Wil had written to Theo's sister, Elisabeth Huberta (Lies), on Thursday 31 July. Lies then wrote to Theo – from Leiden – on Saturday 2 August (Family 11). Theo eventually replied to Lies on Tuesday 5 August, also from Leiden, where he had been since Sunday 3 August.

7. This sentence was published by Johanna van Gogh-Bonger in 1914.

Parijs 1 Aug 1890 38

Lieve beste Moedertje,

Men kan niet schrijven hoe bedroefd men is nog troost vinden in uitstorting op het papier. Mag ik gauw bij U komen? Ik moet hier nog allerlei regelen maar als het kon zou ik graag Zondag morgen van hier gaan om 's avonds bij U te zijn. Het is een smart die mij lang zal wegen & die mij mijn heele leven zeker niet uit de gedachte zal gaan, maar als men iets ervoor zou willen zeggen is het dat hijzelf rust heeft waar hij naar verlangde. Als hij had kunnen zien hoe de menschen voor mij waren nadat hij weg was gegaan & de attenties van zoovelen voor hem had kunnen zien zou hij voor het oogenblik er niet toe gekomen zijn om te willen sterven.

Ik ontving van daag Uw

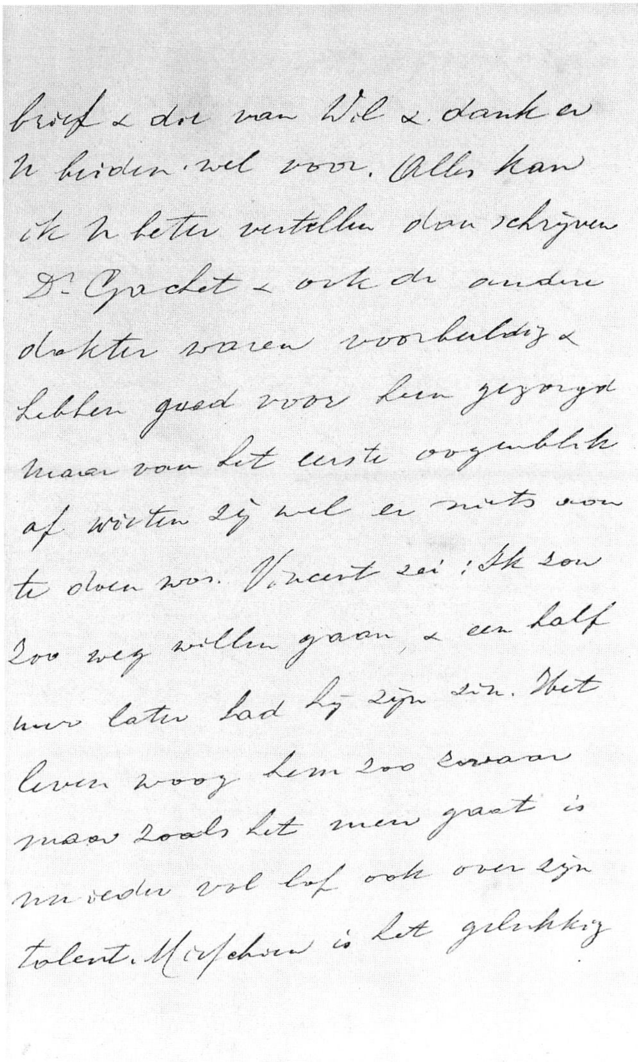

brief & die van Wil & dank er
u beiden wel voor. Alles kan
ik u beter vertellen dan schrijven
Dr Gachet & ook de andere
dokter waren voorbeeldig &
hebben goed voor hem gezorgd
maar van het eerste oogenblik
af wisten zij wel er niets aan
te doen was. Vincent zei: Ik zou
zoo weg willen gaan, & een half
uur later had hij zijn zin. Het
leven woog hem zoo zwaar
maar zoals het meer gaat is
nu iedereen vol lof ook over zijn
talent. Misschien is het gelukkig

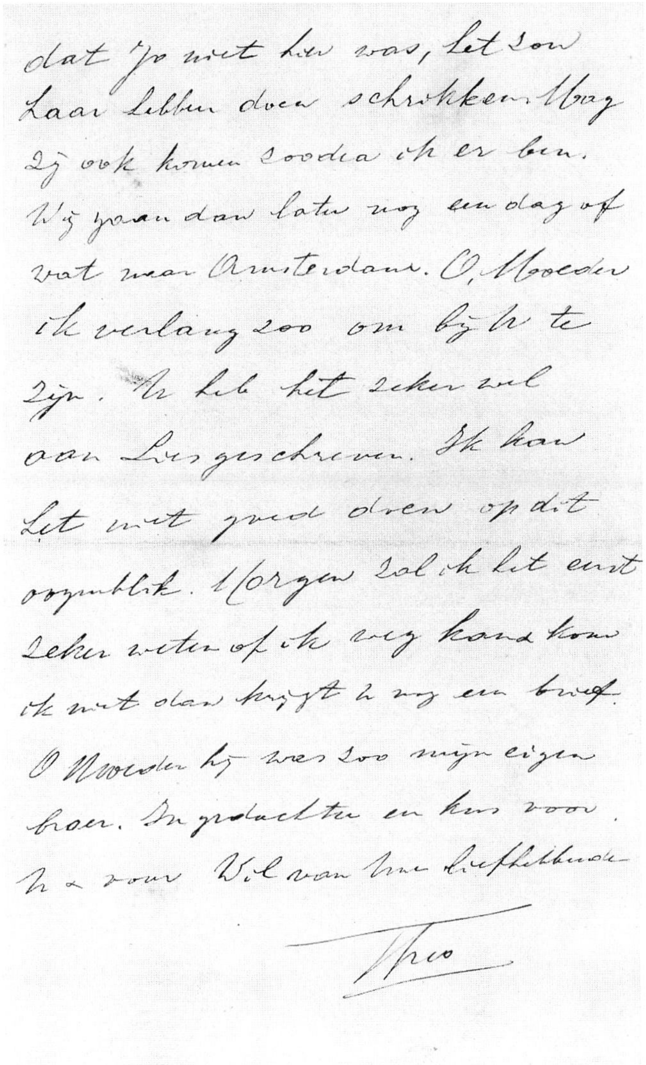

dat Jo niet hier was, het zou
haar hebben doen schrikken. Mag
zij ook komen zoodra ik er ben.
Wij gaan dan later nog een dag of
wat naar Amsterdam. O, Moeder
ik verlang zoo om bij u te
zijn. Ik heb het zeker wel
aan Lies geschreven. Ik kan
het niet goed doen op dit
oogenblik. Morgen zal ik het eerst
zeker weten of ik weg kan & kom
ik niet dan krijgt u nog een brief.
O Moeder hij was zoo mijn eigen
broer. In gedachten een kus voor
u & voor Wil van uw liefhebbende

Theo

FAMILY 6

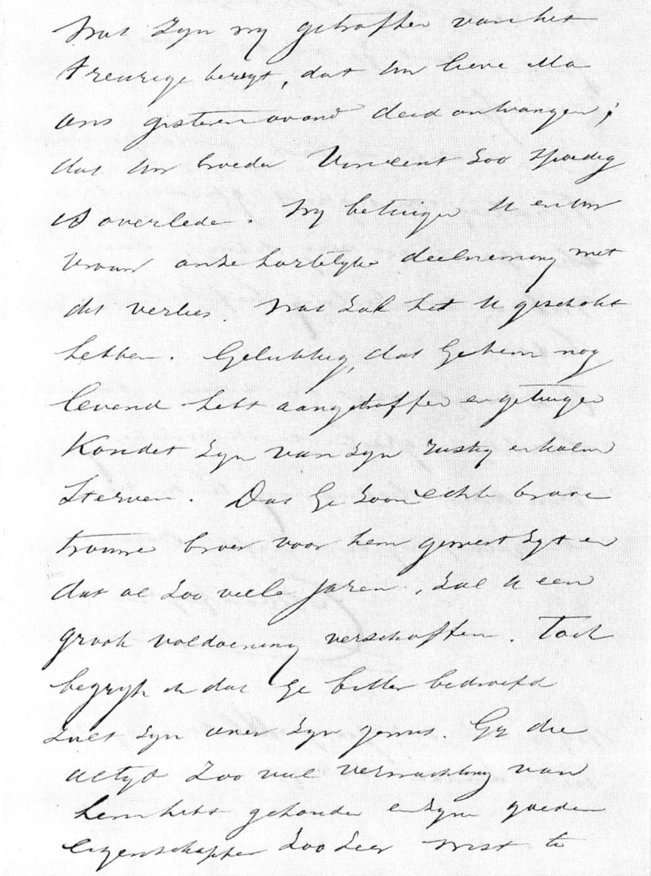

Amsterdam 2 Augs 1890

Waarde Théo!

Wat zyn wy getroffen van het treurige bericht, dat Uw lieve Ma ons gisteravond deed ontvangen; dat Uw broeder Vincent zoo spoedig is overleden. Wy betuigen U en Uw vrouw onze hartelyke deelneming met dit verlies. Wat zal het U geschokt hebben. Gelukkig dat Ge hem nog levend hebt aangetroffen en getuige konden zyn van zyn rustig en kalm sterven. Dat Ge zoo'n echte brave trouwe broer voor hem geweest zyt en dat al zoo vele jaren, zal U een groote voldoening verschaffen. Toch begryp ik dat Ge bitter bedroefd zult zyn over zyn gemis. Gy die altyd zoo veel verwachting van hem hebt gehouden en zyn goede eigenschappen zoo zeer wist te

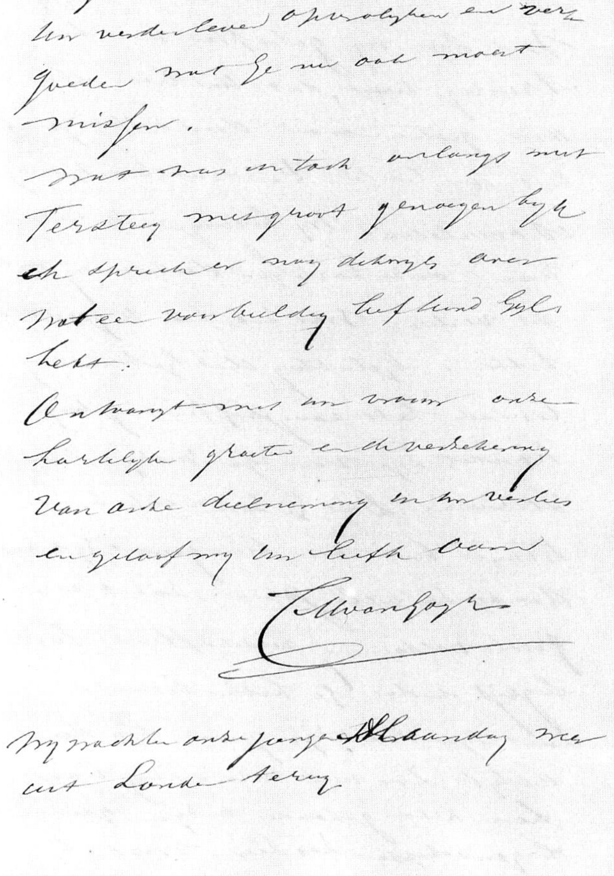

waardeeren! Maar die voldoening zal nu ook Uw troost zyn en moge het geluk van Uw vrouw en kind Uw verdere leven opvrolyken en veel goeden wat Ge nu ook moest missen.

Wat was ik toch onlangs met Tersteeg met groot genoegen by U; ik spreek er nog dikwyls over wat een voorbeeldig lief kind Gyl. hebt.

Ontvangt met Uw vrouw onze hartelyke groeten en de verzekering van onze deelneming in Uw verlies en geloof my Uw liefh. Oom

C.M. van Gogh

Wy wachten onze jongen Maandag weer uit Londen terug

Amsterdam 1 Aug. 1890

Waarde Théo!

Wat zijn wij getroffen van het treurige berigt, dat Uw lieve Ma ons gisterenavond deed ontvangen; dat Uw broeder Vincent zoo spoedig is overleden. Wij betuigen U en Uw vrouw onze hartelijke deelneming met dit verlies. Wat zal het U geschokt hebben. Gelukkig, dat ge hem nog levend hebt aangetroffen en getuigen kondet zijn van zijn rustig en kalm sterven. Dat ge zoo'n echte brave trouwe broer voor hem geweest zijt en dat al zoo veele jaren, zal U een groote voldoening verschaffen. Toch begrijp ik dat ge bitter bedroefd zult zijn over zijn gemis. Gij die altijd zoo veel verwachting van hem hebt gehouden en zijne goede eigenschappen zoo zeer wist te waardeeren! Maar de voldoening zal nu ook Uw troost zijn en moge het geluk van Uw Vrouw en kind Uw verder leven opvrolijken en vergoeden wat ge nu ook moest missen.

Wat was ik toch onlangs met Tersteeg met groot genoegen bij U. Ik spreek er nog dikwijls over wat een voorbeeldig lief kind Gijl.[ieden] hebt.

Ontvangt met Uw vrouw onze hartelijke groeten en de verzekering van onze deelneming in Uw verlies en geloof mij Uw liefh. oom

C.M. van Gogh.

Wij wachten onze jongen Maandag weer uit London terug.

Amsterdam 1 Aug. 1890

My dear Théo!

We were most upset by the sad news your mother conveyed to us last night; that your brother Vincent had died so soon.[1] We express our deepest sympathy to you and your wife in this bereavement. What a shock it must have been. It is fortunate that you found him still alive and could witness his quiet and peaceful death. Having been such a truly good, devoted brother to him and for so many years, must give you great satisfaction. Nevertheless, I know how bitterly sad you must be at this loss. You who always had such faith in him and were so well able to appreciate his good qualities! But the satisfaction will now give you comfort and may the happiness of your wife and child cheer the rest of your life and make up for what you have lost.

How agreeable it was to visit you with Tersteeg recently.[2] I still frequently remark upon your most delightful child.

Accept our best wishes to you and your wife, and be assured of our sympathy with you in your loss and believe me, your affect. uncle,

C.M. van Gogh.

We are expecting our son back from London on Monday.[3]

Cornelis Marinus van Gogh to Theo, Friday 1 August 1890.
Inv. no. b 1006 V/1962

1. Cornelis Marinus van Gogh (1824-1908) was a bookseller and art dealer in Amsterdam from 1849 onwards. He had three children to his second wife, Johanna Franken (1836-1919), whom he married on 30 May 1862. Known as Uncle Cor or C.M. to both his nephews, he played an important part in Vincent's life in the 1870s, and even commissioned two sets of drawings in The Hague in 1882. Thereafter, however, the two drifted apart, having little in common, and showing little sympathy or understanding for one another.

2. There is no printed evidence of this visit with H.G. Tersteeg (1845-1917): it must have taken place at Leiden on Wednesday 16 July.

3. The reference is probably to his elder son, Vincent (1866-1911), who succeeded to his father's business, rather than to the younger son Daniel (1867-1909).

Helv:[oirt] 1 Aug. 90

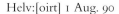

Lieve Theo, Vroeg of laat vraag ik Moe om dit woordje aan U in te sluiten want gij begrijpt dat ik zeer voor U gevoel bij het verlies van Vincent. Hoe zal die U in het bijzonder treffen die altijd zoo een goeden broeder voor hem waart en nu ook weer meer omgang met hem hadt nu hij meer in de buurt woonde.

Welk een genoegen zal het U zijn te denken dat hij Uw vrouw en kind nog heeft leeren kennen en Uwe Jo dus met U over hem spreken kan. Wat zult gij haar nu dubbel missen of komt ge ook d.d. reeds naar het land. Uw taak jegens Uw oudsten broeder is dus afgeloopen, ik voel voor U welk ene leegte U dit zal geven en betuig U wel zeer mijne deelneeming in die smart.

Gij zult Uwe vrouw die ook met mijne groeten overbrengen. Moge Uw jongen gezond en goed opgroeien en Ul.[lieden] tot vreugde blijven. Welk een rust voor Moe ook dat gij bij Vincent waart, dus trouw tot het einde kondt zijn.

Moge gij allen nog voor elkander gespaard blijven en die goede Moe de schok niet te veel zijn.

Het is goed dat gij spoedig naar Amst.[erdam] en Leiden komt en de zusters weer ziet. Gij allen zult wel veel aan Cor schrijven die zoo ver in den vreemde dit verneemt. Ja, het ga hem daar goed, maar nog liever gunde ik U allen dat hij dichterbij kon komen. De hemelsche Vader zij met U allen! De fam.[ilie] 's Gr.[aeuwen] voegt zeker deelnemende groeten aan U, ontvang die van

Uwe U liefheb.

tante Mietje

Helv:[oirt] 1 Aug. 90

Dear Theo, Sooner or later I shall ask [your] Mother to enclose these few words for you as you know I deeply sympathize with you at the loss of Vincent.[1] You in particular will be upset, as you have always been such a good brother to him and have had more contact with him since he moved closer to you.

How gratifying it must be for you to think that he was able to meet your wife and child so that your Jo can talk about him with you. You must be missing her all the more now or will you also be coming to the country in the next few days? Your duty towards your eldest brother is now over. I can imagine how empty you must feel and sympathize most sincerely.

Please convey this to your wife with my regards. May your son grow up in good health and remain a joy to you. How comforting for Mother too that you were at Vincent's side and could be steadfast to the end.

May you all be spared for one another and the shock not prove too much for your good Mother.

It is a good thing that you will be coming to Amst.[erdam] and Leiden shortly and seeing your sisters again. I am sure that you all keep in touch with Cor, who will learn of this so far away.[2] Yes, may he fare well there, although I should rather for all your sakes that he could be nearer. May the Heavenly Father be with you all! The 's Gr.[aeuwen] fam.[ily] include their condolences and regards,[3] accept those of

Your affect.

aunt Mietje

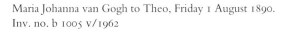

Maria Johanna van Gogh to Theo, Friday 1 August 1890.
Inv. no. b 1005 v/1962

1. Maria Johanna van Gogh (1831-1911) was the youngest of the eleven children born to Parson Vincent van Gogh (1789-1874). Known as Aunt Mietje to Vincent and Theo, she lived at Helvoirt (her address is given as Molenstraat A25 in Theo's address book; see Pabst no. 106).

2. Vincent's younger brother Cornelis Vincent (1867-1900) was in South Africa (see Family 14).

3. Aunt Mietje's eldest sister, Geertruida Johanna (1826-1891), married a naval commander, Abraham Antonie 's Graeuwen (1824-1903) in 1858. He was a friend of Vincent's uncle, Johannes van Gogh (1817-1885), who, on his retirement, went to live with his sister and her husband at Helvoirt. Hence, the reference to the 's Graeuwen family.

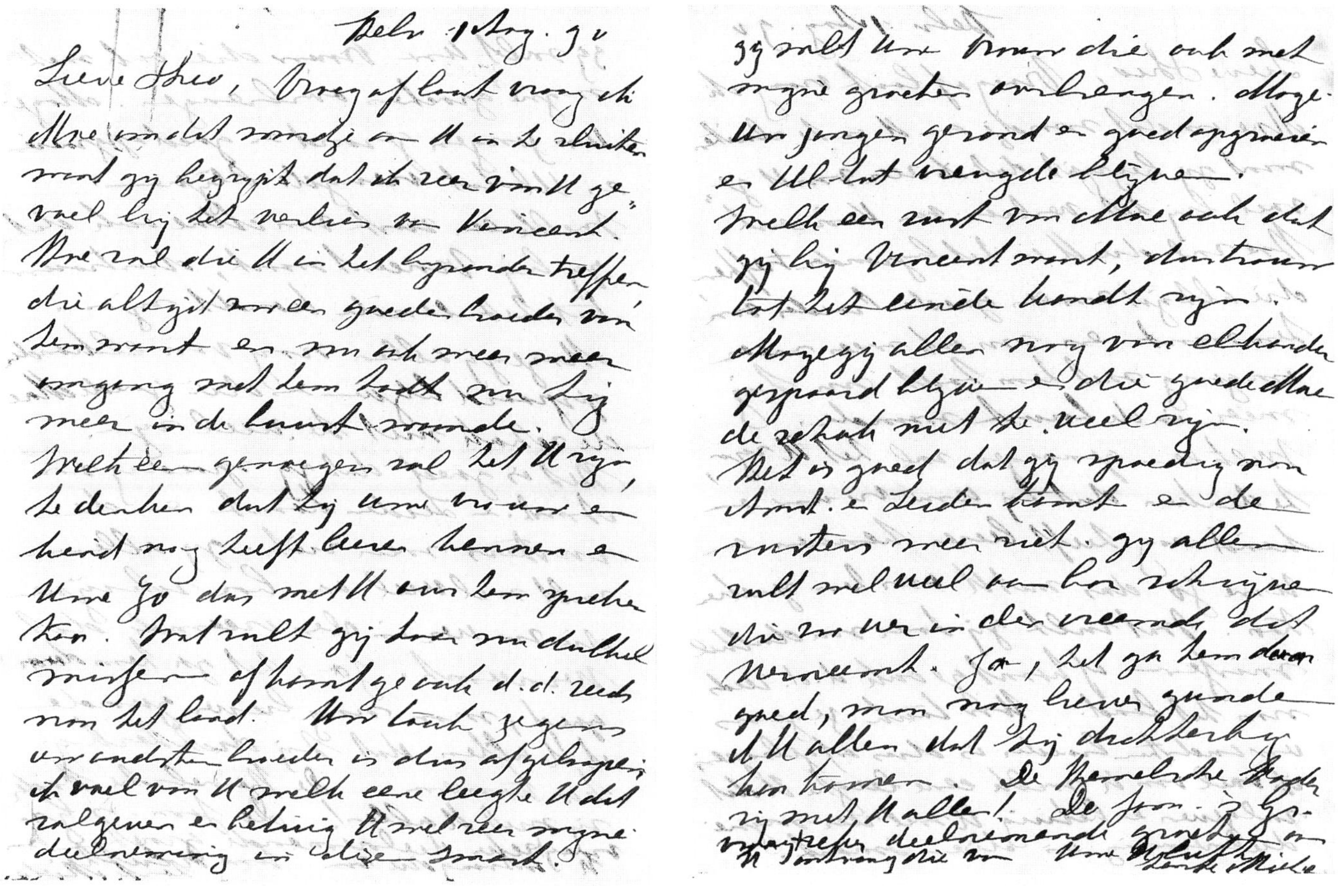
Helv. 1 Aug. 90

Lieve Theo, Vroeg af laat nog ik
Moe van dit woordje om U in te sluiten
want gij begrijpt dat ik zeer innig gevoel bij het verlies van Vincent.
Hoe zal dit U in het bijzonder treffen
die altijd voor een goede broeder van
hem waart en van ook meer meer
omgang met hem hadt dan hij
meer in de kunst woonde.
Welk een genoegen zal het U zijn,
te denken dat hij Uwe vrouw en
kind nog heeft leeren kennen en
Uwe Jo dus met U over hem spreken
kan. Wat zult gij hem van dichtbij
missen of hoort ge ook d.d. reeds
van het land. Uw toch zegen
[illegible] broeder is dus afgeloopen
ik voel van U welk eene leegte U dit
zal geven en betuig U wel zeer mijne
deelneming in Uwe smart.

gij zult Uwe vrouw die ook met
mijne groeten overbrengen. Moge
Uw jongen gezond en goed opgroeien
en U tot vreugde blijven.
Welk een zucht van Moe ook dat
gij bij Vincent waart, daar trouw
tot het einde bevonden zijn.
Moge gij allen nog van elkander
gespaard blijven en die goede Moe
de zorgen niet te veel zijn.
Het is goed dat gij spoedig naar
Amst. en Leiden komt en de
zusters weer ziet. gij allen
zult wel veel aan hun schrijven
die zoo ver in den vreemde dit
vernamen. Ja, het ga hem daar
goed, maar nog liever gunde
ik U allen dat hij dichterbij
had kunnen. De Hemelsche Vader
zij met U allen! De [illegible]
[illegible] deelnemende groeten aan
U [illegible]
Uwe liefh. tante Mieke

Waarde Theo!

Zeer trof ons het berigt van den dood van Uw broeder. Wij weten hoe lief gij hem had en begrijpen gij hem betreurt. Maar gij weet nog beter dan wij, hoe 'n moeijelijk leven hij had. Om Zijnent wil zult gij hem zijn rust niet misgunnen. Gij hebt Uw best voor hem gedaan zoo lang hij leefde en zult het zeer waardeeren dat gij hem hebt zien heengaan. Hoe gelukkig dat gij onder zijn bereik was. Het was voor Uw beiden bevredigend. Wij gaan dinsdag naar Leiden en hopen dan nog wat van Vincent te hooren. Zorg gij toch goed voor je zelf nu Uw vrouwtje het niet doen kan, al hebt gij er geen lust in. In droefheid moet men dubbel oppassen. Dat zal je ter wille van je vrouwtje en je jongen wel doen niet waar? Dochter Kee neemt er ook veel deel in. Het is goed dat het treft wij naar Leiden gaan. Uwe moeder en Wil zullen er gaarne over willen spreken en dat kan ze zoo goed met ons die in U allen zoo veel belang stellen. Spoedig hopen wij je ook te zien. Ontvang intusschen onze hartelijke groeten,

Uwe liefh.
tante Mina

Dear Theo!

We were most sorry to hear the news of your brother's death.[1] We know how you loved him and can imagine how you will miss him. But you know even better than us how difficult his life was. For his sake you would not wish to deny him his peace. You did your best for him as long as he was alive and will cherish the knowledge that you saw him pass away. How fortunate that you were within reach. It was gratifying to both of you. We are going to Leiden on Tuesday and hope to hear more about Vincent then.[2] Take good care of yourself now that your wife is unable to do so, even if your heart is not in it. One must be twice as careful in sorrow.[3] You will, of course, for the sake of your wife and little boy, won't you? Daughter Kee also conveys her deepest sympathy.[4] Our going to Leiden works out well. Your Mother and Wil will be wanting to talk about it, which she can do so well with us, who are so concerned with all of you. We hope to see you soon too. For the time being, accept our kind regards,

Your affect.
aunt Mina

Willemina Catharina Gerardina Stricker-Carbentus to Theo, circa Friday 1 August 1890.
Inv. no. b 1001 V/1962

1. Aunt Mina was the sister of Vincent's mother and of his aunt Cornelia (see Family 10). She was Willemina Catharina Gerardina Carbentus (1816-1904) who married Pastor Johannes Paulus Stricker (1816-1886). It was their daughter Cornelia Adriana, known as Kee (1846-1918), who was the object of Vincent's unrequited love in 1881. Hence, the 'we' refers to Kee and herself and possibly to Kee's son, Johannes Paulus (born 13 April 1873). Aunt Mina is listed in Theo's address book (Pabst no. 215) at Anna Vondelstraat 13, Amsterdam.

2. That is, Tuesday 5 August. Theo was due to arrive in Leiden on Sunday 3 August.

3. Pastor Stricker had died on 27 August 1886, so Aunt Mina was four years a widow, like her sister Cornelia who had lost her husband two years previously (see Family 10).

4. The reference is to her daughter, Cornelia Adriana (1846-1918), widow of Christoffel Martinus Vos (1841-1878). See note 1.

's Prinsenhage.

Beste Théo, Wat waren wij gister av.[ond] getroffen bij dat onverwacht berigt van het overlijden van Vincent. Wat zult gij bedroefd zijn want wat zijt gij veel voor hem geweest, wat zijt gij een zegen voor hem geweest en met wat een gevoel van voldoening kunt gij achteruitdenken. Toch zult gij hem willen laten rusten en hem om zijn eigen wil niet terug wenschen want zijn beste deel was toch maar moeite en verdriet daar zijn gezondheid toch zoo geschokt was en wat had hij daardoor toch eene onzekere toekomst en wie weet hoe zwaar je die zorgen toch door de tijd zouden zijn gaan vallen en nu is het zoo goed want wat hebt ge hem nog gelukkig gemaakt door hem daar te brengen door hem nog je eigen interieur te hebben laten kennen en je kindje zijn naam te hebben gegeven, en daar zamen bij hem te zijn geweest en dan met zij werk ook hoe heerlijk dat hij die voldoening nog gehad heeft dat hij nog een schilderij verkocht heeft en immers nog wel eens; en je

's Prinsenhage.

Dear Théo, We were so upset yesterday evening at the unexpected news of Vincent's death.[1] How sad you must be as you meant so much to him, what a blessing you were to him and with what satisfaction you can now look back. Nevertheless you will want him to be at peace and for his own sake not wish him back as his lot was only trouble and sorrow anyway since his health was so upset; and how uncertain his future was because of it and who knows how heavy a burden this might have become for you over the years and now all is well because you made him happy by showing him your own home and naming your child after him, and having been there with him and then his work how wonderful that he had the satisfaction of selling a painting and in fact more than once;[2] and your Mother also recently received such a nice letter from him so

Cornelia van Gogh-Carbentus to Theo, circa Saturday 2 August 1890.
Inv. no. b 1000 V/1962

1. Aunt Cornelia Van Gogh-Carbentus (1829-1913), younger sister of Vincent's mother, married the art dealer Vincent van Gogh (1820-1888) in 1850. 'Uncle Cent' was a highly successful art dealer, who later sold his business to Goupil et Cie of Paris. Childless himself, he appears to have placed great faith in his nephew Vincent, whom he clearly wanted to groom as an important member of the firm of Goupil. Extremely upset by Vincent's failure as an art dealer, Uncle Cent became strongly opposed to his nephew's subsequent attempt to become a preacher. In the 1880s, very little contact was maintained between them.

The letter is undated. Mother's letter, one of the many written on Thursday 31 July, was probably received in the evening of Friday 1 August ('yesterday evening'); hence, a date of Saturday 2 August is suggested. Aunt Cornelia lived in a large country house at 's-Prinsenhage near Breda, which contained a specially built picture gallery to house Uncle Vincent's considerable collection. Vincent and Theo knew it well.

2. This is an extremely revealing statement: not only that Vincent sold more than one painting, but that his aunt Cornelia should have known about it. Presumably, she learned of these sales from Mother and Wil. It is yet another instance of the 'spreading' of news about Vincent within the family.

Moe had ook pas nog zoo'n goede brief van hem gehad dus alles is zoo af. *Och beste Théo laat je daar toch allemaal mee troosten en denk dat* hij *al niet terug zou willen keeren op deze onvolmaakte wereld. Nu zal hij pas tot zijn regt komen. Ik hoop maar dat de onvermijdelijke schok die het je gegeven moet hebben je geen nadeel zal doen. Arme wat treurige vacantie maar hoe goed ge er juist weer waart om zijne oogen toe te drukken het had ligt kunnen zijn dat ge ver weg waart geweest.*

Wat zal je je vrouwtje missen maar voor haar goed zij in die warmte niet daar is. Kom maar liever gaauw bij haar. Hoe heerlijk gij nu niet meer alleen zijt. de vroegere tijd zal je nu zoo goed voor de geest kunnen stellen en aangenaam wakker komen het nu zoo anders is.

Ik herdacht dd ook weer mijn lievelings heengaan al of pas 2 jaar! O ik mis hem zoo en 't went niets.

Adieu beste Théo ik hoop Ul.[ieden] toch ook nog eens te zien. Pas op je zelf nu je alleen ben en in deze droeve omstandigheden en geloof aan de deelneeming van je liefh. tante Cornelie.

everything is *finished.*[3] Ah dear Théo be comforted by all this and remember that *he* would not wish to return to this imperfect world. Only now will he find his place. I hope that the inevitable shock this must have given you will not prove detrimental to you. Poor fellow what a sad holiday but how fortunate that you were there right then to close his eyes, you might have been far away.

How you must be missing your wife but it is better for her not to be in that heat. Come to her soon instead. How wonderful that you are no longer alone. You will remember those former times and wake up comfortably as things are so different now.

I recently commemorated my darling's passing away, already or only 2 years ago! Oh I miss him so and haven't got used to it at all.[4]

Adieu dear Théo I hope I shall still see you again. Take care of yourself now that you are alone and in these sorrowful circumstances and accept the sympathy of your affect. aunt Cornelie.

3. A reference to Vincent's last letter to Mother and Wil (LT 650) of circa 16 July (see Family 2, note 3), which his mother must have mentioned in her letter to her sister Cornelia.

4. Aunt Cornelia's husband died on 28 July 1888, when Vincent was in Arles. It was Theo's legacy from his uncle Cent that enabled him to send 300 francs to Vincent in September 1888, with which Vincent then furnished his Yellow House. Because of their long estrangement, Vincent was excluded from his uncle's will.

Leiden 2 Augustus 1890.

Beste Theo, en Jo,

Welk een treffend bericht ontving ik Vrijdag! Het was mij een ondenkbaar iets dat het leven van Vincent zóó plotseling was afgebroken, juist nu het in den laatsten tijd zulk een veel vriendelijker aanzijn had gekregen; maar toen ik de brieven herlas van Moeder en Wil, waarin zij mij alles schreven wat zij tot hier toe van zijn heengaan wisten, en ik mij zijn leven in het geheel voorstelde, – toen kwam het mij voor, als had God hem zelf zacht te slapen gelegd, na hem eerst getroost en gesust te hebben. Welk een overgang liefelijk en opwekkend tevens, de omgeving van zieken, voor het leven in het midden der heerlijke natuur, die zich overal en geheel aan hem gaf in al de nieuwheid van een andere landstreek, dan die waaraan hij meer gewoon was geraakt. En dan daarbij de nabijheid van Parijs, de bereikbaarheid van je beiden, en het zien van zijn petekind, waarvoor hij zijn illusies zal hebben gemaakt, in wie hij misschien ook een kleinen toekomstigen schilder zag. Al die vriendelijke zonnestraaltjes heeft hij gehad, tot nu toe had zijn ongesteldheid nog geen invloed op zijn werkkracht, maar zou dit op den duur zoo gebleven zijn...? Hij heeft deze niet zien verminderen, niet als een verminkte, maar in 't vuur van den strijd is hij gevallen.

Met Theo bij hem, niet alleen in den vreemde, is hij heengegaan. Ik herinner mij, toen hij eens van uit Etten naar

Leiden 2 August 1890.

Dear Theo, and Jo,

What upsetting news I received on Friday![1] Never could I have imagined that Vincent's life would come to such an abrupt end, especially since it had taken a far more agreeable course of late; but when I re-read the letters from Mother and Wil, telling me all they knew so far about his passing away, and I thought about his life as a whole, – it seemed to me that God himself had gently laid him to sleep, having first comforted and soothed him. What a pleasant and inspiring change, from being surrounded by illness to a life in the midst of glorious nature, which was all around and all there for him, with all the novelty of a different part of the country from the one he had grown more accustomed to.[2] And then Paris being so near, the two of you within reach, and seeing his godchild, of whom he will certainly have had high expectations and in whom he may also have seen a future little painter. Indeed, he had all these cheerful little rays of sunshine; up to now his indisposition had not affected his stamina to work, but would this have been the case in the long run...? He did not see this stamina diminish; he fell, not as one wounded, but in the fire of battle.

He was not alone in a foreign country when he departed, but had Theo at his side. I remember once when

Lies van Gogh to Theo, Saturday 2 August 1890.
Inv. no. b 2002 VF/1982

1. Mother and Wil wrote to Elisabeth Huberta (1859-1936), known as Lies, soon after receiving the news of Vincent's death from Joan van Houten on Thursday 31 July. Lies was then living at Soesterberg, where, since February 1880, she had been housekeeper to the family of the lawyer Jean Philippe Theodore du Quesne van Bruchem (1840-1921), and in particular nursed his gravely ill wife. When the latter died in 1891, Lies married du Quesne van Bruchem. Lies received the letter on Friday 1 August, and went directly to join Mother and Wil at Leiden (confirmed in Family 5). Her reply to Theo was sent from Leiden on Saturday 2 August; and Theo must have received it before leaving Paris for Leiden on Sunday 3 August.

2. Lies is referring to Vincent's move from the asylum of Saint-Rémy ('surrounded by illness') to Auvers-sur-Oise ('life in the midst of glorious nature') in mid-May 1890.

Zundert wandelde, en ook Aarsen bezocht. Hij kwam daar net, om hem te zien sterven en bij zijn terugkomst zei hij: 'als ik sterf, hoop ik precies zoo te liggen als hij', en bleef nog lang onder dien indruk. Toen Pa dood was en vrouw Poots Pa nog eens zien wôu, stond Vincent bij haar, en zei: 'ja, vrouw Poots, sterven is moeilijk, maar leven is nog moeilijker.'

Ik behoef je niet te zeggen, Theo hoeveel wij over je spreken en hoe verlangend wij zijn nog meer te weten. Wij zijn ook bezorgd over je; want je droefheid zal zoo ontzettend groot zijn en het is niet gemakkelijk nu er je lichamelijk en geestelijk boven op te houden, onder zooveel wee. Het spijt mij, o! zoo erg, dat ik je nu niet dadelijk zie. maar ik kon niet anders doen, dan dadelijk hierheen komen, en mocht niet wachten tot dat jullie hier zoudt zijn. Nu zal ik niet zoo dadelijk wêer kunnen komen; maar je weet er de reden van.

Moeder en Wil houden zich flink het is ons een genot bij elkander te zijn, en over alles te spreken, en wij verlangen er naar, dat Jo en jij weder bij elkander zijt. Geen ander dan je

he went tramping from Etten to Zundert and also called on Aarsen.[3] He arrived just as he was dying and upon his return he said: 'when I die, I hope I shall be lying just like him', and the impression remained with him long afterwards. When Father died and Mrs Poots wanted to see Father once again, Vincent stood beside her and said: 'yes, Mrs Poots, dying is hard, but living is harder still'.[4]

I need not tell you, Theo, how much we talk about you, and how anxious we are to know more. We are also worried about you, as you must be overcome with grief and it is no easy matter for body and spirit to cope with such great sorrow. I deeply regret that I shall not be seeing you soon, but I had no alternative other than to come directly here, and could not wait until you were here. Now I shall not be able to return for some time; but you know why.[5]

Mother and Wil are coping bravely and it is agreeable to be together and to talk about everything, and we hope that Jo and you will soon be reunited. No-one can comfort you better than your wife and the little one,

3. Vincent's 'long walk' took place on Saturday 7 March and Sunday 8 March 1877. On Saturday night, he 'took the last train from Dordrecht to Oudenbosch and walked from there to Zundert' where he arrived on Sunday morning (LT 91, 8 April 1877). This letter has always been given the date of 3 April in printed editions, because the '8' was carelessly read as '3'. Only in the 1990 Letters, no. 111, has it been correctly dated to (Sunday) 8 April.

Johannes Aertsen (1805-1877) was a day labourer who also acted as gardener at the parsonage in Zundert during the Van Gogh family's stay there until 1871. He was much admired by Vincent's father, as well as by Vincent himself. He actually died on the Saturday evening, a few hours before Vincent arrived. 'I shall never forget that noble head lying on the pillow: the face showed signs of suffering, but wore an expression of peace and a certain holiness' (LT 91). Vincent then walked back from Zundert to Etten.

4. Lies recalled Vincent's remark – without citing Mrs Poots – in her personal recollections (E.H. du Quesne-Van Gogh, *Vincent van Gogh. Persoonlijke herinneringen aangaande een kunstenaar*, Baarn 1910, pp. 74-75). While Vincent had already expressed similar sentiments in a letter to Theo, a year before his father's death: 'dying is perhaps not so difficult as living' (LT 358, circa 1-2 March 1884, and 1990 Letters, no. 434: 'het sterven [is] misschien niet zo moeilijk [...] als het leven zelf').

5. Lies left Leiden before Theo's arrival there on Sunday 3 August, returning to Soesterberg. That is why Theo, unable to talk with her, sent a letter on Tuesday 5 August (see Family 11a).

vrouwtje zal je nu zoo goed kunnen troosten, en het kleine ventje ook al heeft hij nog niets te vertellen.

Ik heb hier de schilderijtjes gevonden, die mij nu nog veel meer waard zijn. Van het landschapje vooral zal ik heel veel gaan houden; ik verlang er naar het in mijn kamer te zien hangen. Ik heb ook nog den Nuenenschen toren van hem, met sneeuw, die zoo prachtig mooi is! En nu adieu lieve Theo en Jo; moge het rustig thuis zijn je goed doen. Met een hartelijke kus ook voor Vincentje, dat nu nog meer een soort van nalatenschap van Hem aan ons allen is geworden.

Je zoo innig liefhebbende
Lies.

Heb je hem toen nog mijn brief gestuurd, en mijn boodschap over gebracht? Ik zou daar zoo blij om zijn.

Wel bedankt voor het boekje. Niet meer doen, het is te duur en te mooi!

young though he still may be.

I have found the paintings and they are now even dearer to me. I shall become immensely fond of the little landscape in particular; I look forward to seeing it hanging in my room. I also have the Nuenen tower he did, with snow, which is wonderfully beautiful![6] And now adieu dear Theo and Jo; I hope that being quietly at home will do you good. With a fond kiss for little Vincent, who has now become even more a sort of legacy from *Him* to us all.[7]

Your dearly loving
Lies.

Did you send him my letter and convey my message?[8] I should be very glad if you did.

Thank you for the book. Don't do that again, it is too costly and too beautiful![9]

6. Vincent – and Theo – had often talked of some of Vincent's pictures going to Lies, just as he had designated certain paintings for his Mother and Wil (see LT 602, 629, W 20). Of the two paintings mentioned by Lies in her letter, the Nuenen tower with snow is clearly F 87, while the 'little landscape' could well be the Paris painting of early summer 1887, now in the De Boer Collection, Amsterdam (F 291).

7. On 4 August 1890, the Van Gogh family renounced all claims to Vincent's painted legacy in favour of Theo. The document is quoted by Johan van Gogh, 'The history of the collection', cat. Amsterdam 1987, pp. 1-8, on p. 3.

8. That Lies had written to Vincent is confirmed in a brief postscript to her letter of 29 June 1890 to Theo (Rijksmuseum Vincent van Gogh, inv. no. b 2413 V/1982). But there is no proof that Vincent in fact received the letter. Lies is never mentioned in Vincent's letters from Auvers, and nor does Theo refer to her in his letters to Vincent. The reason for her writing is unclear; but it must have been prompted, in part, by the news of Vincent's letters to Mother and Wil from Auvers (LT 639 and LT 641; W 22 and W 23), which displayed a renewed warmth toward his family. Lies must have been told of this by her mother and decided to write herself to Vincent to enhance further the feelings of family closeness.

9. Theo had clearly sent Lies an expensive book (no longer identifiable). It acted as a symbolic token of the warm relationship that existed between Theo and Lies so beautifully expressed in her letter of condolence.

te zijn, en nu alles te spreken, en nog verlangen er naar dat Jo en jij weder bij elkander zijt. [illegible] anders dan je [illegible] zal je nu zoo goed kunnen troosten en het kleine ventje ook al heeft hij nog niets te vertellen.

Ik heb hier de schilderijtjes gevonden, die mij nu nog [illegible] zijn. Van het landschapje vooral zal ik veel [illegible] gaan in Leiden, ik verlang er naar het in mijn kamer te zien hangen. Ik heb ook nog den Nuenenschen toren van hem [illegible], die zoo prachtig [illegible] is! En nu adieu lieve Theo en Jo, mogen het jullie thuis zijn [illegible] dagen. Met een hartelijken kus ook voor Vincentje, dat er nog meer een spoor van [illegible] van hem aan ons allen is gegeven.

Je zoo innig liefhebbende
Lies

Heeft je Leen(?) toen nog mijn brief gegeven(?) en mijn boodschap over gebracht? Ik zou daar zoo [illegible] om zijn

Leiden 2 Augustus 1890.
63

Beste Theo, en Jo,

Welk een treffend bericht ontving ik Vrijdag! Het was voor mij een ondenkbaar iets dat het leven van Vincent zóó plotseling was afgebroken, juist nu het in den laatsten tijd zulk een veel vriendelijker aanzien had gekregen, maar toen ik de brieven las van Moeder en Wil, waarin zij mij alles schreven wat zij [illegible] van zijn heengaan [illegible] en ik mij zijn leven in het geheel voorstelde – toen kwam het mij voor als had God hem zelf [illegible] te slapen gelegd, na hem eerst getroost en gesust te hebben. Welk een [illegible] lieflijke en opwekkende [illegible], de omgeving [illegible], voor het leven in het midd[illegible]

4

I

dan der heerlijke natuur die
zich meest en geheel aan hem
gaf in al de rijkdom van
een andere landstreek, dan die
waaraan hij meer gewoon was
geraakt! En dan daarbij de
vrijheden van Parijs, de heerlijk-
heden van je theaters en
wat zou niet zijn opgetogenheid, maar
voor hij zijn illusies zal hebben
[illegible]
ook geen kleinen toekomstigen
schilder zag. Al die vreselijke
zonnestraaltjes heeft hij gehad
tot nu toe [illegible] zijn ooge-
[illegible] nog geen [illegible] op
zijn werkkracht, maar zou dit
op den duur zoo gebleven zijn...?
Hij heeft ~~niets~~ niet zien verminderen, niet als een verminkte,
maar in 't vuur van den
strijd is hij gevallen.
[illegible] niet alleen
in den vreemde, als hij heengegaan.
Ik herinner mij, hoe hij eens van
uit ~~Etten~~ naar Zundert wandelde, en ook [illegible] bezocht. Hij
kwam daar net, om hem te zien

2

sterven en bij zijn terugkomst zei
hij: als ik dood ben, hoop ik precies
zoo" te liggen als hij, in slaap
nog lang [illegible] die indruk.
Toen Pa dood was en vrouw
Poots Pa nog eens zien won, stond
Vincent bij haar, en zei: "ja
vrouw Poots, sterven is moeilijk
maar leven is nog moeilijker."
Ik behoef je niet te zeggen
hoe hevig wij over je spreken en
hoe verlangend wij zijn nog meer
te weten. Wij zijn ook bezorgd
over je; [illegible]
zoo ontzettend groot zijn en het
is niet gemakkelijk om je te
[illegible] en geestelijk boven op te
houden, onder zooveel zorg.
Het spijt mij o zoo erg, dat ik
je nu niet dadelijk help, maar
ik kon niet anders doen dan
dadelijk hierheen komen en mocht
niet wachten tot dat jullie hier
zoudt zijn. Nu zal ik niet zoo dadelijk weer kunnen komen, maar je
weet er de reden van.
Moeder en Wil houden zich flink
het is ons een genot bij elkander

3

Zeggen dat het goed is, dat hij rust, – ik aarzel nog het te doen. Misschien vind ik het een van de groote wreedheden van het leven op deze aarde en is hij zelf onder de martelaren te rekenen die met een glimlach op het gelaat stierven.

Hij verlangde niet te blijven leven, en was zoo kalm van geest, omdat hij altijd gestreden had voor zijn overtuiging, die hij getoetst had aan die der Besten en Edelsten die hem voorgingen: Zijn liefde tot zijn vader, voor het Evangelie, voor de armen en ongelukkigen, voor de groote mannen in literatuur en in schilderkunst, bewijst dit wel. In den laatsten brief dien ik van hem heb, en die dateert een dag of vier vóór zijn dood, staat: 'Je cherche à faire aussi bien que de certains peintres que j'ai beaucoup aimés et admirés.'

Men moet het wél weten, dat hij een groot Artiste was, wat dikwijls samengaat met een groot Mensch te zijn. Door den tijd zal dat wel erkend worden en zal menigeen betreuren, dat hij zo vroeg is weggegaan.

Hij zelf verlangde te sterven; toen ik bij hem zat en hem zeide, dat wij zouden trachten hem te genezen en dat wij dan weêr hoopten dat hij verder bewaard zou blijven van die

Saying it is good that he is at rest – I would hesitate to do. I think perhaps that it is one of the cruellest things of life on this earth, and he may be counted among the martyrs who died with a smile on their lips.[1]

He had no desire to go on living,[2] and was at peace with himself because he had always fought for what he believed in, which he had measured against the Best and the Noblest of those who had gone before him: his love for his father, for the gospel, for the poor and downhearted, for the great men of literature and art, all attest to this. In the last letter I received from him, dating from four days before his death, he says: 'I'm trying to do as well as other painters whom I have loved and admired'.[3]

People should know that he was a great Artist, which often goes hand in hand with being a great Human Being. Time will bring recognition, and many will regret his having passed away so soon.

He himself wanted to die; when I was sitting with him and told him we would try to cure him and that

Theo to Lies van Gogh, Tuesday 5 August 1890.
Theo's letter of 5 August 1890 to his sister is known only from the printed excerpts first published by Lies in her book on Vincent (E.H. du Quesne van Gogh, *Vincent van Gogh. Persoonlijke herinneringen aangaande een kunstenaar*, Baarn 1910, pp. 95-97). These passages were subsequently translated into English by Katherine S. Dreier in: Elizabeth du Quesne van Gogh, *Personal Recollections of Vincent van Gogh*, Boston & New York 1913, pp. 52-53. The same passages have been used by Hulsker in his *Lotgenoten. Het leven van Vincent en Theo van Gogh*, Weesp 1985, pp. 634-635, and idem, *Vincent and Theo: a dual biography*, Ann Arbor 1990, p. 450 (with a different translation from Katherine Dreier's). The excerpts printed here have been retranslated for the present publication.

1. Theo's reference to martyr may not have met with Vincent's approval; he denied that he was a martyr.

soort wanhoop, zeide hij: 'La tristesse durera toujours.' Ik voelde wat hij daarmeê zeggen wilde.

Kort daarop kreeg hij een benauwdheid en in één minuut sloot hij de oogen. Hij kwam toen tot groote rust en kwam niet meer bij.

De menschen hielden veel van hem in dat mooie dorp, en van alle kanten hoorde men, dat hij bemind was, zoodat er velen hem naar het graf hebben gedragen, waar een steen zijn naam aan den voorbijganger zal vertellen.

Ik ben van plan om over eenige maanden te trachten een tentoonstelling van zijn werken in Parijs te organiseren. Ik wilde wel u alles eens bijeen kunnen laten zien; men moet er veel van bij elkander zien, dan begrijpt men het beter.

Er zal ook nog wel over hem geschreven worden. Als ik een lokaal kan krijgen dan zal de tentoonstelling plaats hebben in de maand October of begin November; dan zijn de Parijzenaars in de stad [...]. Hij zal zeker niet vergeten worden.

(5 Augustus 1890)

we kept hoping he would be spared this sort of despair, he said: 'Sadness will last forever'.[4] I understood what he meant.

Shortly afterwards, he gasped for breath, and a moment later closed his eyes. He found tremendous peace, and did not regain consciousness.

The people in that beautiful village loved him dearly, and everyone was saying how cherished he was, and many of them carried him to his grave,[5] where passers-by will see his name on a stone.[6]

I intend to try and arrange an exhibition of his work in Paris in a few months' time.[7] I wanted to show you everything together; one should see lots of pieces side by side, the better to understand them.

He will also be written about. The exhibition will take place in the month of October or at the beginning of November if I can get a venue; that's when Parisians are in town [...]. He will certainly not be forgotten.

(5 August 1890)

2. Vincent's lack of the will to live was also reported by Bernard (who gathered it from Dr Gachet) in his letter of 31 July to Aurier (Prologue 3).

3. This quotation is from Vincent's last letter to Theo of 23 July (LT 651). There, Vincent wrote: 'je cherche à faire aussi bien que de certains peintres que j'ai beacoup aimé et admiré' (I'm trying to do as well as other painters whom I have loved and admired). The accuracy of the quotation confirms that Theo took Vincent's last letter with him to Leiden on 3 August especially to show to Mother, Wil and Jo: it would seem in any case perfectly natural for him to have done so. Just as, for her part, Mother would show Theo Vincent's last letter to her (LT 650), which he had not yet seen, and which she promised to do in her letter of 31 July.

4. This sentence has been much quoted by later writers.

5. That many people attended Vincent's funeral is corroborated by Bernard's letter to Aurier of 31 July (Prologue 3) and by Theo's to Jo of 1 August (Prologue 4).

6. The gravestone was in place by early September 1890 when Bernard returned to Auvers and saw it *in situ* with Dr Gachet. See Theo's letter to Dr Gachet of 2 September. Though Theo spoke of returning to Auvers to see the grave, he never did so.

7. This is the first intimation of Theo's determination to organize an exhibition of Vincent's work in Paris. Already the notion of arranging such a show in October was firmly planted in his mind by early August. See also his letter to Dr Gachet of 12 August (French 21a). Together with the writing of a biography, eventually to be entrusted to Aurier, it fully preoccupied Theo until his own breakdown on 9 October 1890.

Amsterdam 4 Aug^{s} 90

Waarde Theo!

Toen Lien gisterenavond van Leiden terug kwam en ons het bericht bracht ge goed en wel aldaar van Parijs waart aangekomen, gaf dat mij werkelijk eenige verademing. Want inderdaad: wat dan ook zal blijken de reden te zijn geweest Jo in de laatste dagen niets van je hoorde, en hoe betrekkelijk kalm zij daaronder ook was; Zaterdag begon ook ik eenigsints ongerust te worden en te vreezen dat ook gij door overspanning wellicht ziek geworden waart. Die vrees is nu geheel geweken en kunt ge thans rustig van elkanders bijzijn genieten.

Ja Theo, ik besef volkomen welke treurige dagen gij hebt doorgebracht. Het verlies van je geliefde broer zal je onbegrijpelijk zwaar hebben getroffen. Juist nu zijn gezondheid blijkbaar zoo vooruitging, zijn naam als artist meer en meer bekend en als zoodanig gevestigd begon te worden; hem nu te moeten missen is een harde slag. Alleen het besef steeds alles voor hem te hebben gedaan wat in je vermogen was en hem tot in zijn laatste oogenblikken te hebben bijgestaan, zal steeds de liefelijkste herinneringen bij je opwekken.

Je zult Jo wel al wat beter hebben gevonden; maar toch is ook zij nog alles behalve op haar verhaal. Rust en kalmte zijn voor haar ook medicijn. De kleine Vincent is allerliefst. In gedachten heb ik hem altijd lief en aardig gevonden, maar in de werkelijkheid vond ik hem nog liever. Hij is zoo zoet en gezellig, je kunt het niet begrijpen. Hij kan zoo'n heel uur als het ware liggen keuvelen en het zal heel kort duren of hij kan al kunstjes leeren. Het is voor ons een leegte dat hij er niet meer is. Uw moe zal hem ook wel lief vinden. Geniet nu maar in rust van het mooije wêer; ga vooral in de lucht en tracht zoodoende nieuwe kracht te verzamelen.

Vele groeten aan Jo, je moe en Wil en in de hoop je spoedig ook hier te zijn, als steeds

Je liefh.
Pa.

Amsterdam 4 Aug 90

My dear Theo!

I was really quite relieved when Lien returned from Leiden yesterday evening and told us that you had arrived there from Paris safe and sound.[1] For indeed: whatever turns out to be the reason for Jo not having heard from you these past few days, and although she was relatively unperturbed about it, I started to get rather worried on Saturday fearing that you too had probably taken ill from the stress.[2] That fear has now been dispelled, and you can enjoy each other's company again.

Yes Theo, well do I realize how sad the past few days have been for you. The loss of your beloved brother must have affected you more deeply than one can imagine. Especially now that his health appeared to be improving, his reputation as an artist was becoming better known, and he starting to become established; losing him now is a painful blow. Only the knowledge that you always did everything in your power for him and stood by him until his last hour, will always arouse in you the sweetest memories.

I trust that you will have found Jo somewhat improved, although she too is anything but recovered. Peace and quiet are medicine for her as well. Little Vincent is most charming. I had always imagined him a dear and amiable child, but in reality I found him dearer still. He is so sweet and agreeable, you cannot imagine. He can spend a whole hour as it were lying chattering, and it won't be long before he starts learning to do things. His absence leaves a void. Your mother must also be fond of him. Relax and enjoy the fine weather now; take the air whenever you can and try to regain your strength.

Kindest regards to Jo, your mother and Wil and hoping you will be here soon, as ever

Your affect.
Father.

Hendrik Christiaan Bonger to Theo, Monday 4 August 1890.
Inv. no. b 1002 V/1962

1. Hendrik Christiaan Bonger (1824-1904) was Jo's father. Theo arrived in Leiden on Sunday 3 August. Lien was Bonger's eldest daughter Carolina (1856-1919) who had probably accompanied Jo and her baby from Amsterdam to Leiden that same day, and then returned to Amsterdam.

2. Bonger is referring to Theo's four-day silence between Monday 28 July (Prologue 2) and Friday 1 August (Prologue 3), which also caused concern to his mother (see Family 5).

Vader en moeder Bergsma, vrouwtje en ik, wij betuigen u onze hartelijke deelneming in het verlies van Uwen broeder Vincent.

Met onze vriendelijke groeten ook aan uwe vrouw

t.a.v.
A. le Comte
Schiedam, 4 Aug. 90.

Father and mother Bergsma, my wife and I, wish to express our heartfelt sympathy at the loss of your brother Vincent.

With our kind regards to you and your wife[1]

yrs truly
A. le Comte
Schiedam, 4 Aug. 90.

Adolf le Comte to Theo, Monday 4 August 1890.
Inv. no. b 1886 v/1962
This card was initially sent to Theo in Paris: 'Monsieur Th. van Gogh / à / 8 Cité Pigalle / Paris'. It was then redirected to his mother, as the last lines were deleted and replaced by: 'chez Mad. Vve Van Gogh / Carbentus / 100 Heerengracht / Leyde / Hollande'.

1. Adolf le Comte (1850-1921) was an artist of no marked originality who exhibited a mixture of landscapes and portraits in Amsterdam and The Hague from 1881 to 1905. He was, however, a cousin by marriage of Vincent's and Theo's. Their maternal uncle, Arie Carbentus (1816-1875), married Sophia Cornelia Elisabeth Carbentus-van Bemmel (1828-1897), known to her nephews as Aunt Fie. They lived in The Hague and had three daughters, two of whom married artists – Ariette Sophia Jeanette, known as 'Jet' (1856-1894), to Anton Mauve (1838-1888), who acted as mentor to Vincent in The Hague in 1881-82, and Anna Cornelia (1852-1925) to Adolf le Comte. Vincent referred to their marriage in a letter of December 1881 (the sentence was first published in 1990 Letters, no. 191). Otherwise, he cited his cousin (but not her artist husband) in letters of 1889 to Theo (LT 582) and Wil (W 15), asking Theo to give his kindest regards to the cousins Mauve and Le Comte (March 1889), and suggesting to Wil (October 1889) that, should she 'meet our cousins Mesdames Mauve and Lecomte in Leiden, please tell them, in case they like my work, I shall be pleased, to do things for them'. Nothing ever came of this suggestion that he might do painted versions of some of his Saint-Rémy compositions for his cousins. And it seems unlikely that Vincent ever met Adolf le Comte.

Cornelis Bergsma (1831-1913), junior notary, was the second husband of Sophia Carbentus. They married 14 February 1877.

Johannesburg. 8 October 90.

Beste Jo en Theo,

Het is waarlijk schande, ik jullie zoo lang heb laten wachten met schrijven, maar denk daarom niet ik je vergeet hoor, maar ik geloof niet een slechten briefschrijver voor veel verbetering vatbaar is, en in mijn geval is het wel een 'hopeless case'.

Je weet niet hoe versteld ik stond, toen ik de treurige tijding van Vincent hoorde, volkomen begrijp ik het een enorm gemis en leegte voor je wezen zal, hoewel ik geloof het voor hemzelf beter is, zooals nu. Dikwijls nog denk ik aan de pleizierige dagen een grootjaar geleden terug; mijn kamer herinnert zo mij dagelijks, daar alle platen, die ik meebracht aan de muur hangen. Van Moe zul je misschien nu en dan wel eens wat van hier hooren. Bepaald nieuws is er niet, om je te vertellen, daar er niet veel variatie in ons leven hier is. Natuurschoon bestaat hier in of rondom Johannesburg volstrekt niet, wij zijn rondom voor in een woestijn opgesloten, zonder eenige boomen, niets dan kort, hard gras, dat zelfs niet eens groen is, zooiets als het helm op de duinen.

Wat mijn werk aangaat, dat bevalt mij vrij goed tegenwoordig. Je weet natuurlijk ik hier aan de spoor ben. Voor veertien dagen heb ik met twee anderen eene nieuwe locomotief afgeleverd, die wij gemonteerd hebben.

Johannesburg. 8 October 90.

Dear Jo and Theo,

It is truly shameful that I have kept you waiting so long for a letter, but don't think that I have forgotten you,[1] however, I don't believe a poor correspondent can be much improved, and I am indeed a 'hopeless case'.

I can't tell you how upset I was to hear the sad news about Vincent, I know it will be a terrible loss and emptiness for you, although I believe that it is better for him as things are. I often recall the happy days a little more than a year ago; my room reminds me of it daily, as all the prints I brought with me are hanging on the walls.[2] I suppose Mother gives you news from here from time to time. There is nothing special to tell you, as there is not much variety in our lives. The area in and around Johannesburg has no natural beauty, we are surrounded by desert on all sides, with no trees, nothing but short, coarse grass that is not even green; it is a little like the marram grass on the dunes.

As far as my work is concerned, I am quite content at present. You know, of course, that I am on the railways. A fortnight ago, two other people and I completed a new train engine that we had been assembling.

Cor van Gogh to Jo and Theo, Wednesday 8 October 1890.
Inv. no. b 837 V/1962
First published in D. Bax, 'Nog 'n keer Cor van Gogh', *Standpunte* 8 (1953), pp. 76-80, on p. 79.

1. Cornelis Vincent, known as Cor (1867-1900), was the youngest of the six Van Gogh children. He was fourteen years younger than Vincent, ten years younger than Theo. This disparity in age – and Vincent's long periods of absence from home between 1869 and 1881 – meant that the relationship between Cor and Vincent was never close. In the 1880s, they saw little of each other and had little in common. The gulf that separated them is made clear in Vincent's letter to Theo of circa 6 August 1888: 'I am glad that our brother Cor has grown bigger and stronger than the rest of us. And he must be stupid if he does not get married, for he has nothing but that and his hands. With that and his hands, or his hands and that, and what he knows of machinery, I for one would like to be in his shoes, if I had any desire at all to be anyone else' (LT 518). Cor is then forgotten for almost a year: until July 1889, when he decided to

Wij hadden hem aangenomen om voor £ 50 op te stellen en hebben er slechts £ 30 aan verwerkt, dus dat is altijd nog eens een buitenkansje.

En nu, hoe gaat het met mijn neefje, gaat hij goed vooruit en wat denkt hij wel van zijn oom in Transvaal. Ik ben er niet weinig trotsch op; zoogauw hij lezen kan, krijgt hij ook eens een brief van mij.

Het stormt vanavond geweldig; en het is na de donderbui van vanmiddag geweldig koud geworden, maar nu jullie de kou tegen gaan, krijgen wij de hitte en braaien kan het hier, you bet; dit vooruitzicht is anders niet zoo heel pleizierig, want menig zweetdruppeltje laten wij dan in de shop achter. Wij hebben een nieuwen superintendent gekregen, de vorige hebben wij door een strike, die wij tegen hem hielden er tusschen uit gejaagd. Je kunt wel nagaan hij nu knorrig op ons is. De toestanden hier zijn anders treurig, zeer weinig werk in de stad en aan de reef; twee banken zijn reeds gesprongen met een enorm tekort, wat velen groote verliezen heeft doen lijden.

Maar nu ga ik voor vanavond uitscheiden daar ik slaap heb, geloof veel aan je denkt, met een kus en een poot,

je liefhebbende broer
Cor.

We had taken it on for £ 50 and spent only £ 30 on it, which was quite a windfall.

And how is my little nephew; is he coming along well, and what does he think of his uncle in the Transvaal. I am more than a little proud; as soon as he can read, I shall write to him too.

It's terribly windy this evening and bitterly cold after the thunderstorm we had this afternoon; but now that you have the cold weather ahead, we shall be getting the heat, and it can certainly bake here, you bet. The prospect is rather disagreeable, because the sweat just pours off us in the shop. We have a new foreman, having driven the last one out by staging a strike against him. You can imagine how vexed he is with us now. Otherwise, the situation here is bleak; there's very little work in the city or on the Reef. Two banks have already collapsed, with enormous deficits, and many people have suffered substantial losses.

But now I shall end off for this evening, as I am sleepy. Know that I often think of you, with a kiss and a handshake,

your loving brother
Cor.

emigrate to the Transvaal. A flurry of references ensued, mostly in Vincent's letters to his mother. But Jo's letter to Vincent of 16 August 1889 (T 15) reveals that just before Cor's departure for South Africa, when he spent some days with Jo and Theo in Paris, Vincent actually wrote him a letter. Unfortunately, it is now lost.

So the two brothers were separated by continents, just as they had long been separated in physique, outlook, interests, and profession. Given that, it comes less as a surprise that Cor should have been so long in sending his letter of condolence, and so insensitively brief in speaking of his dead brother. Cor's letter is dated 8 October, the day before Theo's breakdown, so it is unlikely that Theo ever knew of it.

2. Though it initially seemed possible that this referred to works by Van Gogh, just before the manuscript went to press it transpired from a comparison with another letter from Cor, likewise published in D. Bax, op. cit., p. 78, that the prints were in fact from an 'exhibition', presumably the World Exhibition held in Paris in 1889.

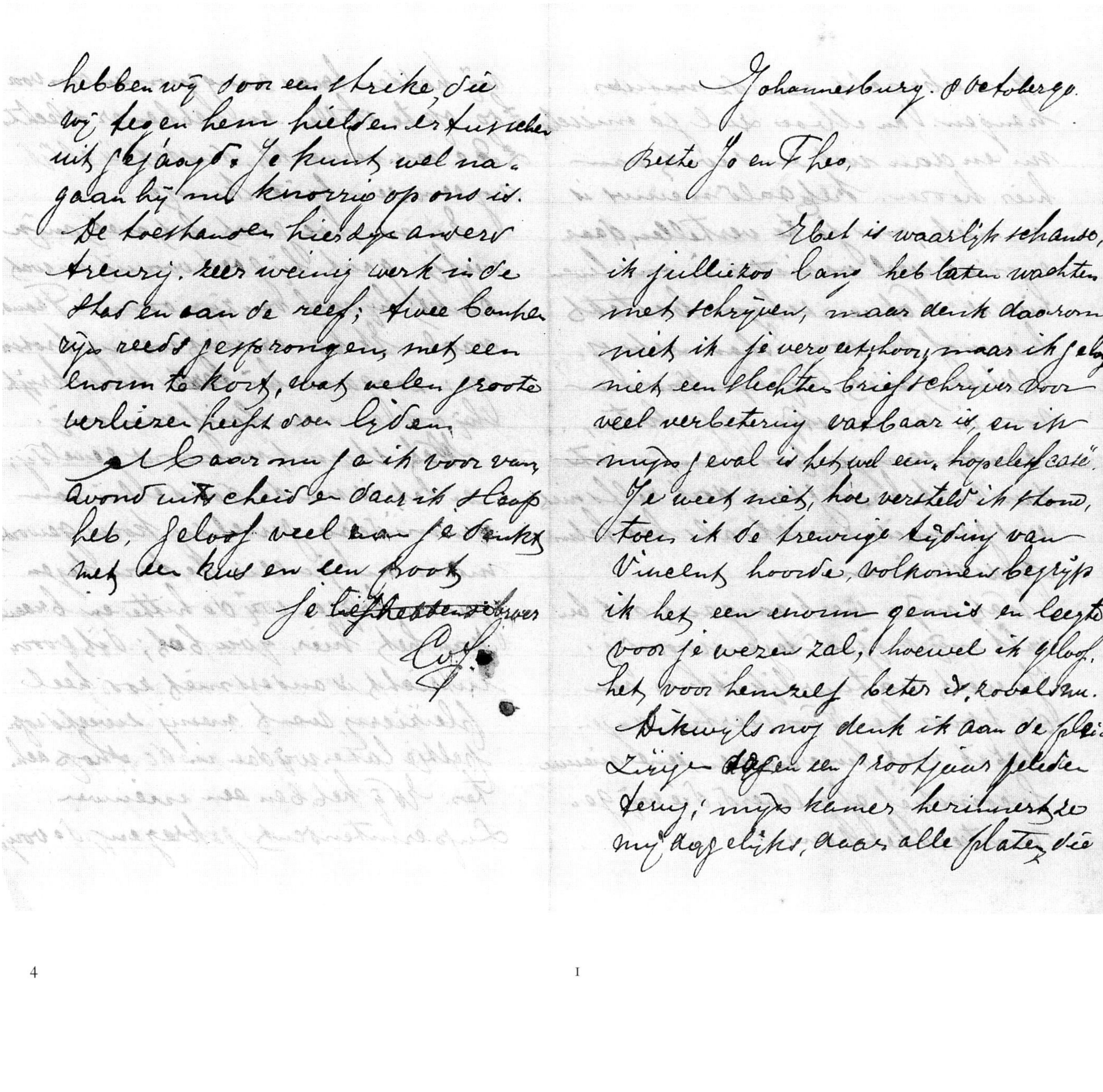
hebben wij door een strike, die
wij tegen hem hielden er tusschen
uit gejaagd. Je kunt wel nagaan hij mij knorrig op ons is.
De toestanden hier zijn anders
treurig. zeer weinig werk in de
stad en aan de reef; twee banken
zijn reeds gesprongen, met een
enorm tekort, wat velen groote
verliezen heeft doen lijden.
Maar nu ga ik voor van-
avond uitscheiden daar ik slaap
heb. Geloof veel aan je denkt
met een kus en een groot
Je liefhebbende broer
Cor.

4

Johannesburg. 8 October 90.

Beste Jo en Theo,

Het is waarlijk schande,
ik jullie zoo lang heb laten wachten
met schrijven, maar denk daarom
niet ik je vergeten heb, maar ik geloof
niet een slechter briefschrijver voor
veel verbetering vatbaar is, en in
mijn geval is het wel een hopeless case.
Je weet niet, hoe versteld ik stond,
toen ik de treurige tijding van
Vincent hoorde, volkomen begrijp
ik het een enorm gemis en leegte
voor je wezen zal, hoewel ik geloof
het voor hemzelf beter is, zoo als het nu.
Dikwijls nog denk ik aan de pleizierige dagen een groot jaar geleden
terug; mijn kamer herinnert ze
mij dagelijks, daar alle platen die

I

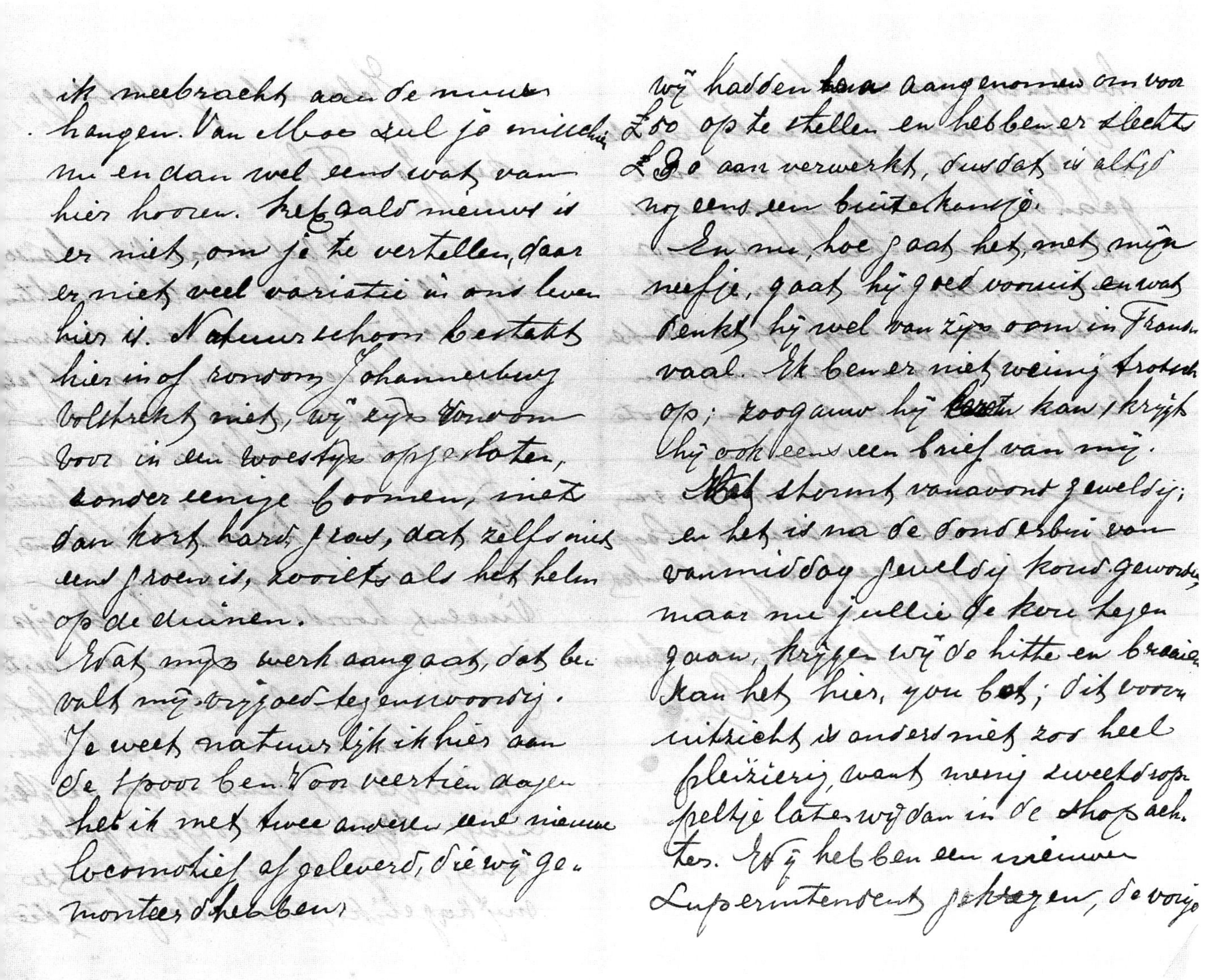

ik meebracht aan de muur
hangen. Van Elboo zul jij misschien
nu en dan wel eens wat van
hier hooren. Het zaldmeuws is
er niet, om je te vertellen, daar
er niet veel variatie in ons leven
hier is. Natuurschoon bestaat
hier in of rondom Johannesburg
volstrekt niet, wij zijn rondom
door in een woestijn opgesloten,
zonder eenige boomen, niets
dan kort hard gras, dat zelfs niet
eens groen is, zooiets als het helm
op de duinen.
Wat mijn werk aangaat, dat bevalt mij wijgoed tegenswoordig.
Je weet natuurlijk ik hier aan
de spoor ben. Voor veertien dagen
heb ik met twee anderen eene nieuwe
locomotief afgeleverd, die wij gemonteerd hebben.

2

wij hadden ~~kan~~ aangenomen om voor
£50 op te stellen en hebben er slechts
£30 aan verwerkt, dus dat is altijd
nog eens een buitekansje.
En nu, hoe gaat het met mijn
neefje, gaat hij goed vooruit en wat
denkt hij wel van zijn oom in Transvaal. Ik ben er niet weinig trotsch
op; zoodra hij ~~lezen~~ kan, krijgt
hij ook eens een brief van mij.
~~Het~~ stormt vanavond geweldig;
en het is na de donderbui van
vanmiddag geweldig koud geworden,
maar nu jullie de kou tegen
gaan, krijgen wij de hitte en braaien
kan het hier, you bet; dit vooruitzicht
is anders niet zoo heel
pleizierig want menig zweetdrop-
peltje laten wij dan in de shop achter. Wij hebben een nieuwen
Superintendent gekregen, de vorige

3

FAMILY 14

Dutch

The Dutch letters of condolence are dominated by artists. Eight of the eleven surviving letters come from six painters, a sculptor and (possibly) a book-illustrator. The remaining three letters show a mixture of professions – a minor civil servant in The Hague, a journalist-publisher also from The Hague, and a Dordrecht bookseller. Yet these three belong together in that they alone 'represent' the 1870s, and each knew Vincent in other guises than that of artist.

The most important of this trio to Vincent – and to Theo – was the Roos family in The Hague. Employed in the Ministry of Finance, W.M. Roos (1816-1893) also ran a small boarding house with his wife at 32 Lange Beestenmarkt. It was there that Vincent stayed during his time as apprentice art dealer at Goupil in The Hague, from the age of 16 to 20. Soon after he left for London in May 1873, his brother Theo followed him to Goupil and the Roos', where he stayed from November 1873 to spring 1879. It is hardly surprising that Vincent wrote to Theo in December 1875: 'Give my very best love to the Roos family. Both of us have enjoyed many good things in their house, and they have proved faithful friends' (LT 48). Jo wrote in 1914 of the Roos household: 'It was a comfortable home where his [Vincent's] material needs were perfectly provided for, but there was no intellectual intercourse'. Their essential goodness and simplicity of outlook glows through their letter of condolence. Yet one small remark is worth noting. Willem Valkis (1853-1935), a fellow-boarder, was evidently taught French by Vincent, thus underlining the fact that Vincent was already proficient in that language before his first visit to Paris in May 1873. And it may suggest that he was reading French literature before he was twenty, for which there is no evidence in his letters to Theo.

It was also in The Hague, most probably in January 1873, that Vincent met P.A.M. Boele van Hensbroek (1853-1912). Like Valkis, he too was Vincent's age. He was journalist and publisher with Martinus Nijhoff in The Hague. Nothing was said of this meeting at the time; nor was Boele van Hensbroek ever mentioned in Vincent's letters. It was a brief, passing acquaintanceship. 'I have not seen him for years', Boele van Hensbroek wrote in his letter of condolence.

The third member of the 1870s trio was the Dordrecht book and printseller, Dirk Braat (1851-1926), son of the owner of Blussé and Van Braam, where Vincent was employed as a not very efficient clerk in the early months of 1877. Dirk Braat later said more openly what he hinted at tactfully in his letter of condolence. 'He was not an attractive boy, with those small, narrowed peering eyes of his and, in fact, he was always a bit unsociable. And then I remember well that he always preferred to wear a top hat, a bit of respectability he had brought back from England'.[1]

It is quite extraordinary how the eight Dutch artists who wrote their letters of condolence to Theo, or Theo and Jo, or to Theo's mother, 'cover' successively the whole decade of the 1880s. Van Rappard takes care of 1880-1885, with Breitner providing additional material in February-March 1882. Koning covers Paris from September 1887 to February 1888. De Haan, while not meeting Vincent, knew his work, his letters to Theo and to Gauguin, and eagerly wished to meet him from October 1888 onwards. Isaac Israëls also saw the work at Theo's in October 1889. Sara de Swart met Vincent on Sunday 6 July 1890, and certainly knew his work. The little-known Thijsen and the mysterious Van Teijn likewise must have known the work well, without having met the artist.

In brief, we have an even split: four artists who knew him (or at least met him) and four who did not.

Clearly, Van Rappard is the most important. His letter of condolence to Vincent's mother was available to Johanna van Gogh who used excerpts at three points in her Memoir. Since 1914, however, the letter has been lost. This is a great pity, since Van Rappard was Vincent's closest and longest surviving friend. Its appeal is nostalgic, yet not sentimental; appreciative and utterly sincere; appraising, but not sycophantic. It must have consoled Vincent's mother, aware of the quarrel that had ended the five-year friendship so finally in the late summer of 1885. And consoling not only because it recalled the stays at Etten and Nuenen, but also of its assessment of Vincent's work as an artist: 'He was of the breed from which great artists are born'.

No such assessments and comparable recalling of their times spent working in Vincent's company were expressed by Breitner or Koning. Their brevity is disappointing. But Koning at least made up for his laconic salute in later recollections of the five months he and Vincent spent together in Paris in 1887-1888.[2]

The most outstanding and astonishing letter of the Dutch group is Van Teijn's, if such be the identity of the writer. One can only hope that his true identity may be confirmed as a result of this publication. He is not to be found in Theo's address book, yet he was a fairly close friend of Theo's, visiting both the gallery and the appartment in Paris. No other letter from him to Theo or Jo appears to exist; and he is never cited in Theo's letters. Whoever he may have been, he deserves his small niche among the earliest and warmest appreciators of Vincent's achievement.

Other Dutch friends and acquaintances, whom one would have expected to write either did not do so, or their letters have been lost. Most prominently, perhaps, H.G. Tersteeg (1845-1917), Vincent's former boss at Goupil in the Hague. And, from Theo's circle of friends, the critics Jan Veth, Johannes de Meester and A.L.H. Obreen, as well the painter Willy Martens.

But enough survives to provide an interesting first stage assessment by Dutch artists before the art critics (such as de Meester and Jan Veth) began their interpretive analyses. Vincent was neither forgotten nor unknown because he left Holland in 1885. And these Dutch artists who saw his work in Paris – De Haan, Isaac Israëls, Van Teijn – were not only struck by it, but were surely influenced as well in ways that were not always immediate nor blatantly obvious.

1. *The Complete Letters of Vincent van Gogh*, 3 vols., Greenwich (Conn.) 1958, vol. 1, p. 109.
2. See Dutch 6, note 2; and Han van Crimpen, 'Friends remember Vincent in 1912', in *Vincent van Gogh. International Symposium*, Tokyo 1988, pp. 83-85.

Beste van Gogh.

De treurige mededeeling – het overlijden van je geachte Broeder Vincent doet me erg leed: ik gevoel in dit oogenblik hoe veel smart je zulks veroorzaakt, jij die zoo veel van hem hield. In dergelijke omstandigheden is niemand in staat, troost aan te brengen – echter beste vriend – het bewust zijn dat de overledene een braaf mensch was – en nog veel meer – een Artist van groote beteekenis – Zulks moet je kalmeeren: hij is niet dood hij leeft voor jou voor ons – en voor allen in zijne werken die hij ons achterliet.

Ik heb altijd gehoopt hem nog eens te spreken. Zelfs met hem en Gauguin gelukkig te werken volgens het projet Gauguin in een ver en vreemd land – Zelfs Vincent gaf zulks in zijn laatst schrijven aan Gauguin te kennen – echter er is niets aan te veranderen. Geloof me steeds je vriend

Meyer de Haan

Dear van Gogh.

I am most sorry to hear the sad news – the death of your dear brother Vincent: I know what pain this must cause you, who loved him so dearly.[1] No one can give solace in such circumstances – nevertheless, dear friend – the knowledge that the deceased was a good person – and far more – an extremely important Artist – must be a comfort to you: he is not dead he lives for you for us – and for everyone, in the work that he has left behind.

I always hoped to speak to him one day.[2] Even to work happily with him and Gauguin on Gauguin's project in a far and foreign land – Vincent also mentioned this in his recent letter to Gauguin – but none of it can be changed.[3] Believe me ever your friend

Meyer de Haan

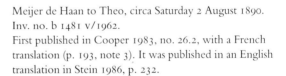

Meijer de Haan to Theo, circa Saturday 2 August 1890.
Inv. no. b 1481 V/1962.
First published in Cooper 1983, no. 26.2, with a French translation (p. 193, note 3). It was published in an English translation in Stein 1986, p. 232.

1. Meijer de Haan (1852-1895) first met Theo in September 1888 when he arrived in Paris with his friend, the painter and art critic J.J. Isaacson (1859-1942). Shortly afterwards, Theo invited De Haan to share his apartment at 54 rue Lepic. De Haan stayed until spring 1889. He met Gauguin in January or February 1889, and later that year the two were working together in Brittany, at Pont-Aven and Le Pouldu. Throughout the winter of 1889-1890, they shared an apartment and a studio in Le Pouldu. And it was there that they received Theo's announcement of Vincent's death, probably by 1 August. Gauguin replied, on one side of a page (French 15), De Haan on the other – the one in French, the other in Dutch.

2. Although Meijer de Haan knew Theo well, he never met Vincent, who, for his part, often expressed the desire to meet his fellow-Dutchman.

3. We know from a brief postscript in Gauguin's letter to Theo of 7 July (Cooper 1983, no. 25) that he had recently received two letters from Vincent – 'assez calmes qui m'ont fait plaisir'. Only a draft of part of the first of these, written about 16 June, survives (LT 643). De Haan's reference is to the second letter, written on 1 or 2 July, where Gauguin's project of going to Madagascar was discussed by Vincent.

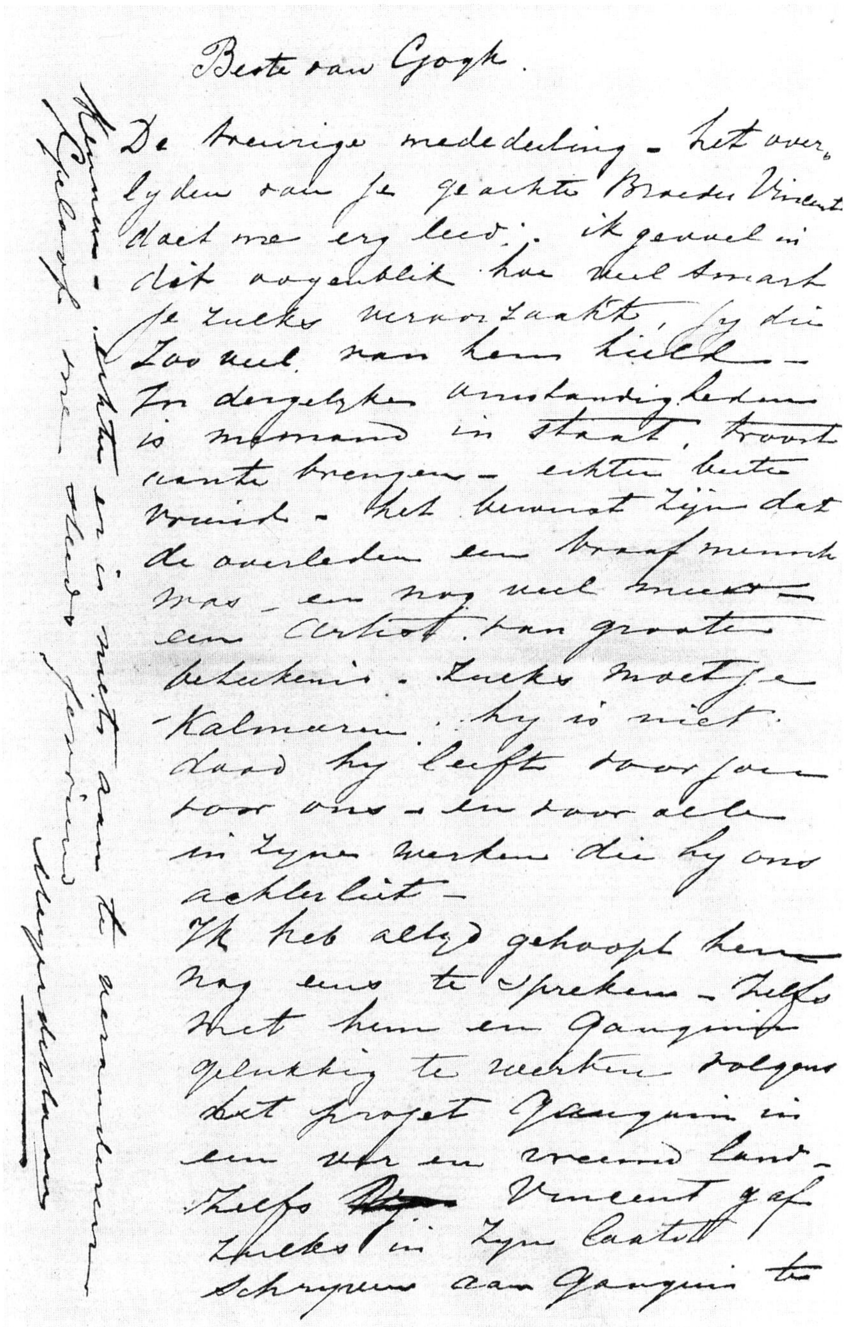

Beste van Gogh.

De treurige mededeeling - het overlyden van je geachte Broeder Vincent doet me erg leed; ik gevoel in dit oogenblik hoe veel smart je zulks veroorzaakte, gy die zoo veel van hem hield -
In dergelyke omstandigheden is niemand in staat, troost aan te brengen - echter beter vriend - het bewust zyn dat de overledene een braaf mensch was - en nog veel meer - een Artist van grooten beteekenis. Zulks moet je kalmeeren. hy is niet dood hy leeft voor jou voor ons - en voor allen in zyne werken die hy ons achterliet -
Ik heb altyd gehoopt hem nog eens te spreken - zelfs met hem en Gauguin gelukkig te werken volgens het project Gauguin in een ver en vreemd land - Zelfs ~~hy~~ Vincent gaf zulks in zyn laatst schryven aan Gauguin te

kennen - Echter er is niets aan te veranderen
Geloof me steeds Je vriend
Meyerdehaan

Paris. 2. Aug 90.

Geachte Mijnheer en Mevrouw.

Heden ochtend kwam ik in het bezit van de treurige tijding aangaande het smartelijk verlies van Mr. Vincent. Het is een ware troost, dat ZEd [Zijne Edele] als oprecht lijdend kunstenaar heeft geleefd, en gestorven is door *de kunst* voor *de kunst.*

Hij zal blijven voortleven door de meenigvuldige origineele en vooruitschreidende werken. waarvan U voor een gedeelte de gelukkige bezitter zijt. Aanvaard dus Mijnheer en Mevrouw mijn oprechte deelneming in dit voor ons allen zoo smartelijk verlies.

Uw toegenegen dienaar
W.J. Thijsen

Paris. 2. Aug 90.

Dear Sir and Madam.

This morning I learned the unfortunate news concerning the sad loss of Mr Vincent.[1] It is indeed comforting to know that he lived the life of an honest suffering artist and that he died *through* art *for* art.

He will live on through his many original and innovative works, some of which you have the good fortune to possess. Please accept my condolences on this sad loss to us all.

Your affectionate servant
W.J. Thijsen

Willebrordus Johannes Thijsen to Theo and Jo, Saturday 2 August 1890.
Inv. no. b 1011 V/1962

1. Willebrordus Johannes Thijsen was a little-known Dutch artist, born in Rotterdam on 29 October 1864; his date of death is unknown. This is his only surviving letter to Theo.

's Gravenhage, 4 augustus 1890.

Bedroefde Vrienden!

Het heeft ons veel leed gedaan te vernemen als dat uw Geliefde Broeder Vincent zoo onverwacht is heengegaan.

Wij betuigen in deze onze hartelijke deelneming, in dat treurig verlies, het was toch voor U één genoegen zoo in de verte, een Broeder te mogen bezitten, en nu Vincent zoo met lust en kennis de schilder-studie voortzette.

Het was toch altijd voor ons zulk Een Lieve en hartelijke jongen van wien men veel hield, die ons Willem Valkis, meenige les in de Fransche taal heeft gegeven, en die van Vincents dood erg stond op te zien, Wim verzoekt mij, ook zijn deelneming in dat treurig verlies mede te deelen. Ook mijn Dientje herinnerde zich ook de gezelligen tijd noch van ons tezamenzijn, doch heelaas, zoo gaat alles voorbij. Het doet ons genoegen Gij Beste Theo, *zoo erg gelukkig zijt, in U Huwelijksleven, en nu zal de treurige stemming, door U* Lieve Gade *veel worden verzoet.*

God! sterke U tezamen en geeve U zijn Zegen!

Van U Lieve Moeder! ontvingen wij Een Briefkaart, den dood van Vincent vermeldende zijde dat Goede Mensch: zij wist de overledene een oude vriend van ons geweest ware, en het

The Hague, 4 August 1890.

My sorrowful Friends!

We were so sorry to hear that your beloved brother Vincent had passed away so unexpectedly.[1]

We would hereby convey our heartfelt condolences on this sad loss, it was such a joy to you to have a brother, far away though he was, and now that Vincent was pursuing his painting studies with such enthusiasm and knowledge.

He was always such a warm, kindly fellow and so well liked, who gave our Willem Valkis many a French lesson, and who is also most upset at Vincent's death.[2] Wim has requested me to convey his feelings of sympathy on this sad loss. My Dientje too remembered the pleasant times we spent together; but alas, all things must pass. We are glad that you, dear *Theo*, are so happy in your marriage, and that your *Dear Wife* will brighten the gloom.

May God! grant you both strength and give you his blessing!

We received a card from your dear Mother! informing us of Vincent's death, said that good person: she knew

Willem Marinus Roos to Theo and Jo, Monday 4 August 1890.
Inv. no. b 2003 VF/1982

1. Willem Marinus Roos (1816-1893) was born and died in the Hague. He was a clerk at the Ministry of Finance. His second wife, three years his senior, was Dina Magrieta van Aalst. Vincent lodged with the Roos family during his stay in The Hague from 1869 to 1873. After Vincent's departure for London in May 1873, Theo also lodged with them from November 1873 to spring 1879.

2. Willem Marinus Valkis (1853-1935), born the same year as Vincent, was a fellow-lodger at the Roos', and like W.M.Roos was employed at the Ministry of Finances. Vincent often mentioned Valkis in his early letters.

3. Mother's postcard, probably written on 31 July, together with

*H[are]Edele een behoefte was dat te berichten, wij hebben gelukkig de vermelding van H[are]Edele adres: ontvangen: (*Heerengracht *100 Leiden). En een condoliantie briefje geschreven.*

Wij zijn gelukkig welvarender ofschoon wij knap ouwetjes zijn. mijn lief Dientje wordt met September 77 jaren, en Roosje 74 jr. het was 31 July Feest op de Beestemart 32, waar wij herdagten toen onze veertig *jarigen trouwdag en hoe aardig van Teunis van Iterson, die kwam met zijn vrouw en twee kinderen ons feliciteren.*

De Vriendinnen en Vrienden hebben ons dien dag heel erg in de Roozen gezet, de Tafel in de voorkamer was te klein om de Boequête! te plaatsen.

Houd mij nu ten goede dat ik het treûrige met het Dankbare te zamen voeg.

Maar zie daarin liever de wisseling van des Menschen Leven in, immers vreûgde en Droefheid volgen elkander op.

En nu Zeer Geachte! Heer! Mevrouw! –

Weest tezamen Al het goede toegewenscht en geloofd wij gaarne zijn:

UEd[ele] DW [Dienstwillige] Dienaar!
en oude vrienden

W M Roos en Echtgenote

that the deceased had been an old friend of ours, and she wanted to tell us about it. Fortunately we received notification of her address: (*Heerengracht* 100 Leiden). And we have written a few words of condolence.[3]

We are faring better, I am happy to say, though getting on a bit in years. My dear Dientje will turn 77 in September, and Roosje 74yrs.[4] There was great festivity at 32 Beestemart[5] on 31 July, as we celebrated our *fortieth* wedding anniversary, and how kind of Teunis van Iterson to come with his wife and two children to congratulate us.[6]

Friends and acquaintances indulged us and our whole day was strewn with roses; the table in the front room was too small to put the bouquets on!

Forgive me for mixing the sorrows and the blessings.

But see it more as the ups and downs of human life, because joy and sorrow always follow one another.

And now dear! Sir! Madam! –

We wish both of you all the very best and believe us:

Your servants!
and old friends

W M Roos and Wife

the Roos' 'few words of condolence' on the death of Vincent, have not survived.

4. W.M. Roos was born on 28 September 1816, and would therefore have been seventy-four years old in 1890, while his wife Dina, known as Dientje, was three years his senior.

5. The couple continued to live at 32 Lange Beestenmarkt after the Van Gogh brothers had left them, and celebrated their fortieth wedding anniversary there on 31 July 1890.

6. Teunis van Iterson (1847-1925) was an employee of Goupil in The Hague under H.G. Tersteeg (1845-1917), and therefore knew Vincent and Theo well. Vincent often referred to Van Iterson when writing to his brother – not always in the most complimentary terms. Many more references have emerged as a result of the unabridged publication of the letters in 1990.

's Grav. 4 Aug. 1890.

Amice,

Gisteren ontving ik het treurige bericht van het overlijden van je broeder, en ik wil je even zeggen hoezeer ik in je verlies deel.

Hem heb ik in jaren niet gezien; maar wij hebben zóoveel over hem gesproken en ik heb zóo dikwijls van je gehoord hoezeer gij met hem dweepte en hoe hoog gij zijn streven in de kunst stelde, dat ik volkomen begrijp hoe zijn heengaan je diep moet treffen. Voor hem, den zoeker, is het mogelijk goed, dat hij rust.

Meld mij eens bij gelegenheid hoe het jelui beiden gaat, of het vrouwtje zich nogal tehuis vindt in Parijs en of de jonge man het goed maakt? Mocht de zomer een van allen of allen tesamen in Holland brengen, dan houden wij ons aanbevolen voor een bezoek.

Mijn vrouw laat u beiden hartelijk groeten. Zij spreekt nog dikwijls over jelui vriendelijk intérieur.

Groet Joh. ook van mij en geloof mij met een handdruk

tt
P Boele v H

The Hague 4 Aug. 1890.

My dear friend,

Yesterday I received the sad news of your brother's death, and I just want to tell you how deeply I sympathize.[1]

I have not seen him for years;[2] but we have talked about him so much and you have so frequently expressed your affection for him and your admiration of his endeavours in art that I know how deeply you will feel the loss. For him, the seeker, it may be good that he is at rest.

When you have an opportunity, let me know how the two of you are, whether your wife is feeling reasonably at home in Paris and whether the young man is all right? Should the summer bring any or all of you to Holland, we would be pleased to have you call on us.

My wife sends kind regards to you both. She still talks about your charming home.[3]

Give my regards to Joh. and believe me cordially

yours truly
P Boele v H

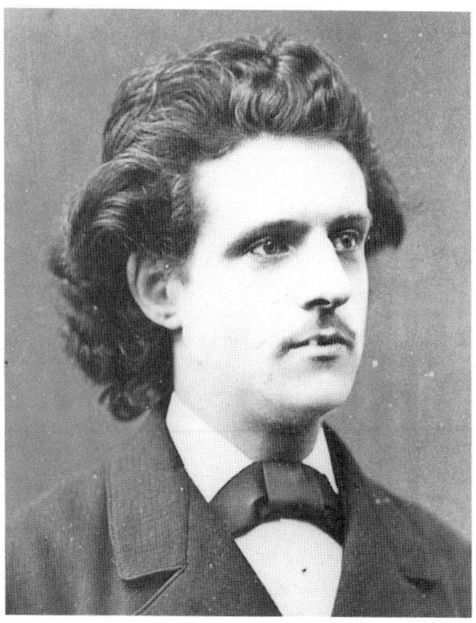

Pieter Andreas Martin Boele van Hensbroek to Theo, Monday 4 August 1890.
Inv. no. b 1012 V/1962

1. Pieter Andreas Martin Boele van Hensbroek (1853-1912) was a journalist, writer, and bookseller in The Hague at the publishers Martinus Nijhoff.

2. Boele van Hensbroek had met Vincent in The Hague, probably in January 1873, if one is to believe his reference to a New Year's day encounter, published in the *Nederlandsche Spectator*, 26 August 1893. He appears not to have seen Vincent after this.

3. Even though he did not meet Vincent in Paris in 1890, Boele van Hensbroek clearly saw Theo there. And, conversely, Theo may have visited him in The Hague – fairly frequently, judging from the earlier part of his letter. He and his wife must also have visited Theo and Jo at 8 Cité Pigalle, ('your charming home'), probably within the past few months, since the reference to the baby suggests they had seen young Vincent Willem (born 31 January 1890). It is not surprising, then, to find Van Hensbroek listed in Theo's address book twice (Pabst nos. 23 and 35).

Waarde Vriend! Met leedwezen nam ik kennis, van het overlijden van uw broeder Vincent dat zoowel voor jou als voor de andere familie leden nog een groot verlies zal zijn: misschien grooter dan menigeen oppervlakkig denkt. Want al had V. in sommige opzichten wat vreemds, van de andere zijde beschouwd had hij toch ook veel goeds – trouwens na zijn vertrek uit Dordt[recht] heb ik hem nimmer meer gezien.

Blijft het met u en uw familie overigens goed gaan? Spoedig hoop ik u eens een ander schrijven van u te ontvangen van meer opgewekter aard; waardoor ik weer wat meer op de hoogte kom van u en de uwen.

Hier loopt alles, zoowel wat gezondheidtoestand der familieleden als de zaken aangaat, naar wensch

Na vriendschappelijke groeten

tt
Dirk Braat.

My dear friend! It was with sorrow that I learned of the death of your brother Vincent, which will be a great loss both to you and to the rest of your family: greater perhaps than many might realize at first.[1] For even though V. was rather odd in some respects, on the other hand he also had many fine qualities – incidentally after his departure from Dordt[recht] I never saw him again.[2]

Are you and your family keeping well otherwise? I hope I shall soon receive another, more cheerful letter from you, with more news about yourself and your nearest and dearest.

All is satisfactory here, both as far as the family's health and the business are concerned.

With friendly greetings

yours truly
Dirk Braat.

Dirk Braat to Theo, circa Thursday 7 August 1890.
Inv. no. b 1013 V/1962
This card was redirected from Paris. Theo's address on the front – 'Monsieur Th. van Gogh / Paris, 8, Cité Pigalle' – has been deleted and replaced by that of Jo's father: 'chez M.[onsieur] H C Bonger / 121 Weteringschans / Amsterdam'.

1. Dirk Braat (1851-1926) was the son of Pieter Kornelis Braat (1823-1888), proprietor of the bookshop Blussé and Van Braam in Dordrecht, where Vincent was briefly employed in the early months of 1877. His brother Franciscus – known as Frans – (1852- ?) worked at Boussod, Valadon et Cie in Paris and was a good friend of Theo's. Dirk Braat is listed in Theo's address book at Schefferplein, Dordrecht (Pabst no. 24).

2. That is, in May 1877, when Vincent left Dordrecht for Amsterdam.

Westerbork, 7 Augustus 1890

Amice van Goch!

Tot mijn diep leedwezen las ik heden ochtend in het door mij ontvangen bericht de dood van Vincent. Je kunt wel nagaan dat mij dit na de prettige herinneringen die ik nog van hem overgehouden heb tijdens mijn verblijf te Parijs, erg frappeert. Wees zoo goed ook aan Mevrouw Uw echtgenoote en Moeder mijn deelneming in dit sterfgeval te betuigen.

Na groeten
Je vriend A.H. Koning.

Westerbork, 7 August 1890

My dear friend van Goch!

I was so sorry to read this morning the announcement I received of Vincent's death.[1] You can well imagine that I was much affected after the pleasant memories I have of him during my stay in Paris.[2] Be so kind as to express my condolences on this loss to your Wife and your Mother.

Regards
Your friend A.H. Koning.

Arnold Hendrik Koning to Theo, Thursday 7 August 1890. The orginal letter is lost. The text is printed here from a typescript copy, inv. no. b 4421 v/1962.

1. Arnold H. Koning (1860-1945) was a Dutch artist who came to Paris in September 1887, when he quickly became a friend of Vincent and Theo. He painted some views of Montmartre, as well as portraits. Soon after Vincent's departure for Arles in February 1888, Koning moved into Theo's apartment at 54 rue Lepic, staying there until late May 1888. He exchanged letters with Vincent (see LT 498a, 571a) and several of Koning's works were acquired by Theo (see cat. Amsterdam 1987, nos. 1.287-1.300; 2.726-730).

2. Koning remained close to Vincent in Paris from September 1887 to February 1888. For his memories of this time, see his letter of 8 May 1912 to Albert Plasschaert, published by Han van Crimpen, 'Friends remember Vincent in 1912', in *Vincent van Gogh. International Symposium*, Tokyo 1988, pp. 83-85.

Waarde Jo en v. Gogh.

Tot mijne groote ontzetting las ik zoo straks dat Uw broer Vincent overleden is. Het is wel ontzettend! nog zoo pas was hij gezond en vol werklust! Ik kan niet laten U even te schrijven hoe innig of ik in Uw verlies deel. Het is een vreeselijk ding – juist nu hij zulke mooie krachtige werken gemaakt had en nog maken zou. Het is voor Ul.[ieden] een droeve zomer.

Hartelijk hoop ik dat Uw jongen geheel hersteld is van zijn sukkelen te Parijs, en zich hier flink houdt.

Steeds met de meeste achting en toegenegenheid

Sara de Swart
Arnhem. 13 Aug 90

My dear Jo and v. Gogh.

I have just read to my great sorrow that your brother Vincent has passed away. It really is awful! only such a short time ago he was in good health and so eager to work![1] I simply must write a few words to tell you that I sympathize most sincerely with you. It is a terrible thing – especially since he had done and would have continued to do such beautiful powerful work.[2] It is a sad summer for you.

I do hope that your son has recovered from the poor health he was suffering in Paris and that he is keeping well here.[3]

Yours ever with the greatest respect and affection

Sara de Swart
Arnhem. 13 Aug 90

Sara de Swart to Jo and Theo, Wednesday 13 August 1890.
Inv. no. b 1334 v/1962

1. Elizabeth Sara Clasina de Swart (1861-1951), sculptor (who worked in Rodin's studio for a time), probably met Theo and Jo in Paris in 1890. Her father, Dr de Swart, is listed at 80 avenue du Maine, Paris, in Theo's address book (Pabst no. 216). But she certainly met Vincent on his visit to Theo's apartment on Sunday 6 July 1890. When he returned to Auvers, Vincent wrote of her: 'I think the Dutch lady has much talent' (LT 649).

2. Sara de Swart would have seen Vincent's paintings at Theo's apartment, and probably also at Tanguy's.

3. Vincent Willem caught a cold at the end of May, and then had a feeding problem in late June. Sara de Swart must have discussed the latter with Jo on Sunday 6 July.

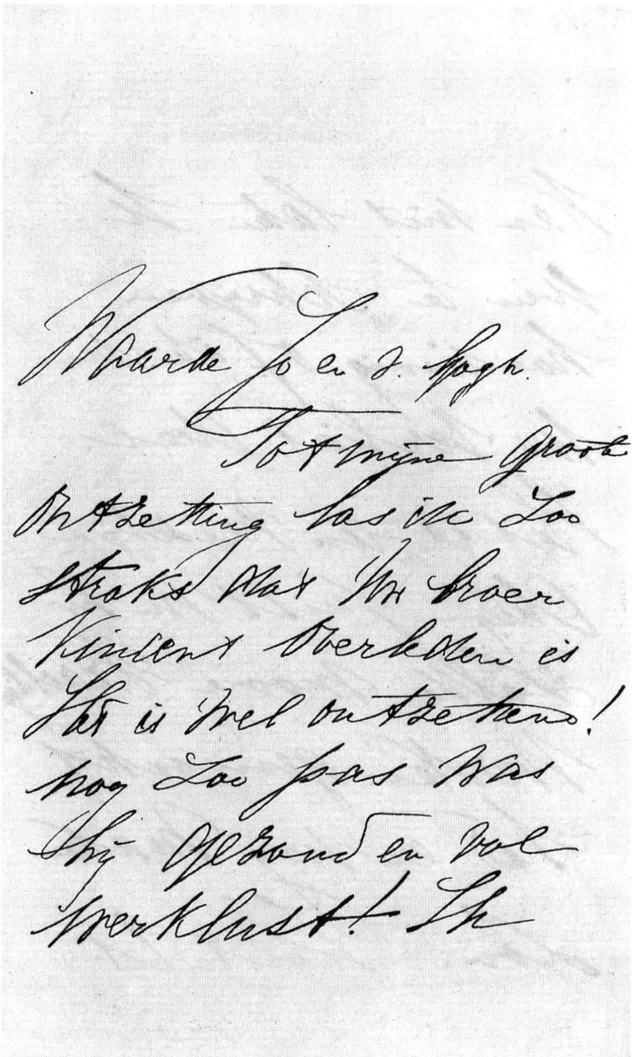
Waarde Jo v. Gogh.
Tot mijne groote
ontzetting las ik zoo
straks dat Uw broer
Vincent overleden is
Het is wel ontzettend!
nog zoo pas was
hij gezond en vol
werklust! Ik

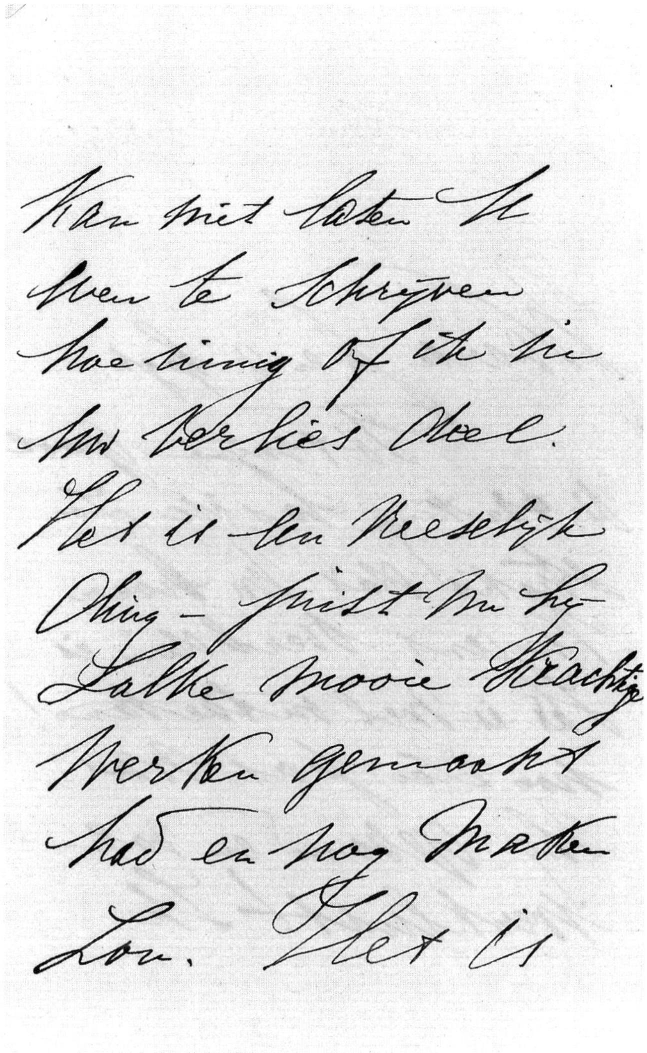
kan niet laten U
even te schrijven
hoe innig ik in
Uw verlies deel.
Het is een vreeselijk
ding - juist nu hij
zulke mooie krachtige
werken gemaakt
had en nog maken
zou. Het is

DUTCH 7

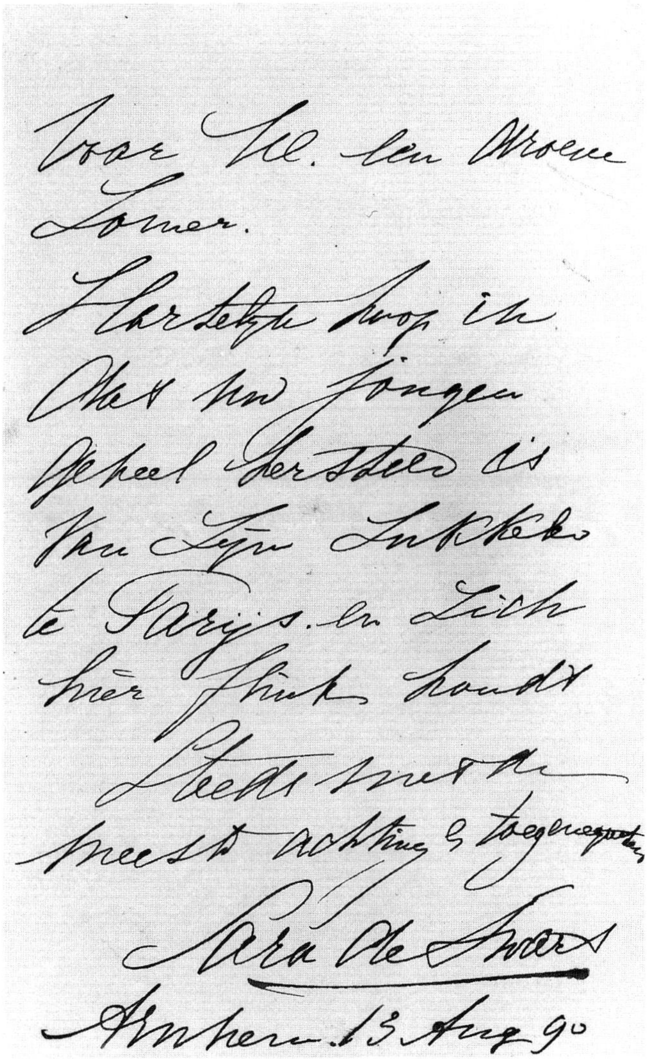

voor UE. een brave
Zoon.
Hartelijk hoop ik
dat uw jongen
geheel hersteld is
van zijn [illegible]
te Parijs en zich
hier flink houdt
Steeds met de
meeste achting & toegenegenheid
Sara de Swart
Arnhem 13 Aug 90

DUTCH 7

Amsterdam 17 Aug. 90.

Amice, ik condoleer je met het treurige geval met je broer. Het spijt mij dat ik nooit in de gelegenheid was kennis met hem te maken, maar ik dacht dat het er nog wel eens van zou komen – kom je niet eens over? Dan houd ik me zeer aanbevolen. Mijn adres is 438 1e Parkstraat. Zoodra ik kan kom ik eens wat te Parijs werken, dus hier of daar, tot ziens.

Groeten van je vriend tav.
Isaac Israels

Amsterdam 17 Aug. 90.

Dear friend, I sympathize with you in these sad circumstances with your brother. I regret never having had the opportunity to meet him, but I had expected this yet to be the case[1] – don't you ever come over? If you do I should be pleased to see you. My address is 438 1st Parkstraat.[2] I shall come to work in Paris for a while as soon as I can, so whether here or there, I look forward to seeing you.

Best wishes from your friend, yours truly.
Isaac Israels

Isaac Lazarus Israëls to Theo, Sunday 17 August 1890.
Inv. no. b 1015 V/1962
This card was sent to Theo's business address: 'Monsieur van Gogh, (Maison Boussod Valadon e. Co) / Boulevard Montmartre / à Paris'.

1. Isaac Lazarus Israëls (1865-1934), son of Josef Israëls (1824-1911), probably first met Theo in Paris in 1889. Theo reported to Vincent on 22 October 1889 (T 19) that several people had called on him 'to see your work', among them 'Israël's son, who is staying in Paris for some time'. Isaac Israëls is listed in Theo's address book at Parkstraat, Amsterdam (Pabst no. 131). Like Meijer de Haan (see Dutch 1), Israëls never met Vincent. But he greatly admired his work, and later owned a Saint-Rémy painting of olive trees (F 711).

2. This studio was situated in the same building as that of G.H. Breitner (see Dutch 9).

Amice.

Bij mijn terugkomst van Noorwegen, las ik de droevige tijding en hierbij zend ik u de verzekering van mijn oprechte deelneming.–

Ik vernam van Groesbeek dat ge u hier had opgehouden, maar vond geen bewijs dat ge bij mij geweest waart – Doe me het genoegen en schrijf me eens wat –

Na groeten ook aan uwe echtgenoote.

tt
G H Breitner
1.ste Parkstraat 438.
Amsterdam 19 Augs. 90

Dear friend.[1]

I read the sad news upon my return from Norway,[2] and hereby send you the assurance of my condolences.–

I heard from Groesbeek[3] that you had been here, but found no sign of your having visited my home – Please oblige me by writing a few words –

Kind regards to you and your wife.

yours truly
G H Breitner
1.st Parkstraat 438.
Amsterdam 19 Aug. 90

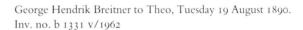

George Hendrik Breitner to Theo, Tuesday 19 August 1890.
Inv. no. b 1331 V/1962

1. George Hendrik Breitner (1857-1923), like Van Rappard (Dutch 11) and Koning (Dutch 6), actually worked with Vincent. In Breitner's case, this occured when the two artists were living in The Hague in 1882. They often drew together in waiting-room and soup-kitchen in February-March of that year (LT 174 and LT 178). And like Vincent, Breitner spent some weeks in hospital in spring 1882. Subsequently, they saw little of each other, but Vincent occasionally referred to Breitner – as late as April 1888 in Arles he even thought of dedicating a still life to him (LT 473). Unfortunately, Albert Plasschaert appears not to have written to Breitner in 1912, when he was contacting friends of Vincent's for their recollections (see Dutch 6, note 2). Breitner was greatly admired by Theo; and he is listed in Theo's address book (Pabst no. 21; and also Pabst no. 43, without address).

2. Little or nothing is known about this trip. There is no evidence either in correspondence, photographs or in Breitner's oeuvre, of its ever having taken place. Only Y.V. Pols, *George Hendrik Breitner*, dissertation Amsterdam 1960, p. 67, mentions that Breitner went to Norway with the art dealer A.P. Nielsen – in 1900, according to the author. I wish to thank Paul Hefting for this information.

3. Klaas Groesbeek (1858-1935) was closely associated with the art dealer Van Wisselingh, who had been a friend of Vincent's in London and The Hague. Groesbeek became manager of the Amsterdam branch of the firm in 1892. Earlier, he was closely connected with the bookshop of Scheltema and Holkema.

BRIEFKAART
(CARTE POSTALE)
ALGEMEENE POSTVEREENIGING (UNION POSTALE UNIVERSELLE)
Zijde voor het adres bestemd. (Côté réservé à l'adresse.)
AMSTERDAM 17 AUG 90 1-2 N.
PARIS 18 AOUT 90 ETRANGER
5 CENT

Monsieur van Gogh maison Boussod
Valadon & C°
Boulevard Montmartre
à Paris.

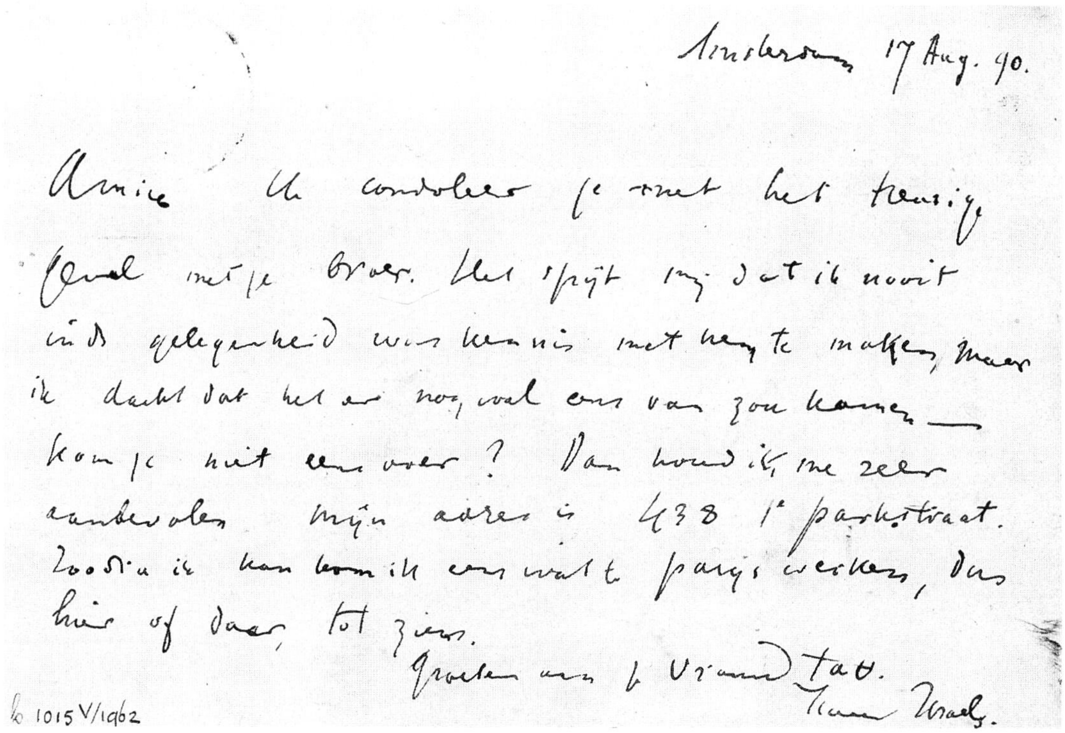
Amsterdam 17 Aug. 90.

Amice Ik condoleer je met het treurig geval met je broer. Het spijt mij dat ik nooit eens gelegenheid wis kennis met hem te maken, maar ik dacht dat het er nog wel eens van zou komen — kom je niet eens over? Dan houd ik me zeer aanbevolen. Mijn adres is 438 1e parkstraat. Zoodra ik kan kom ik eens wat te parijs werken, dus hier of daar, tot ziens.
Groeten aan je vrouw tav.
Isaac Israels.

b 1015 V/1962

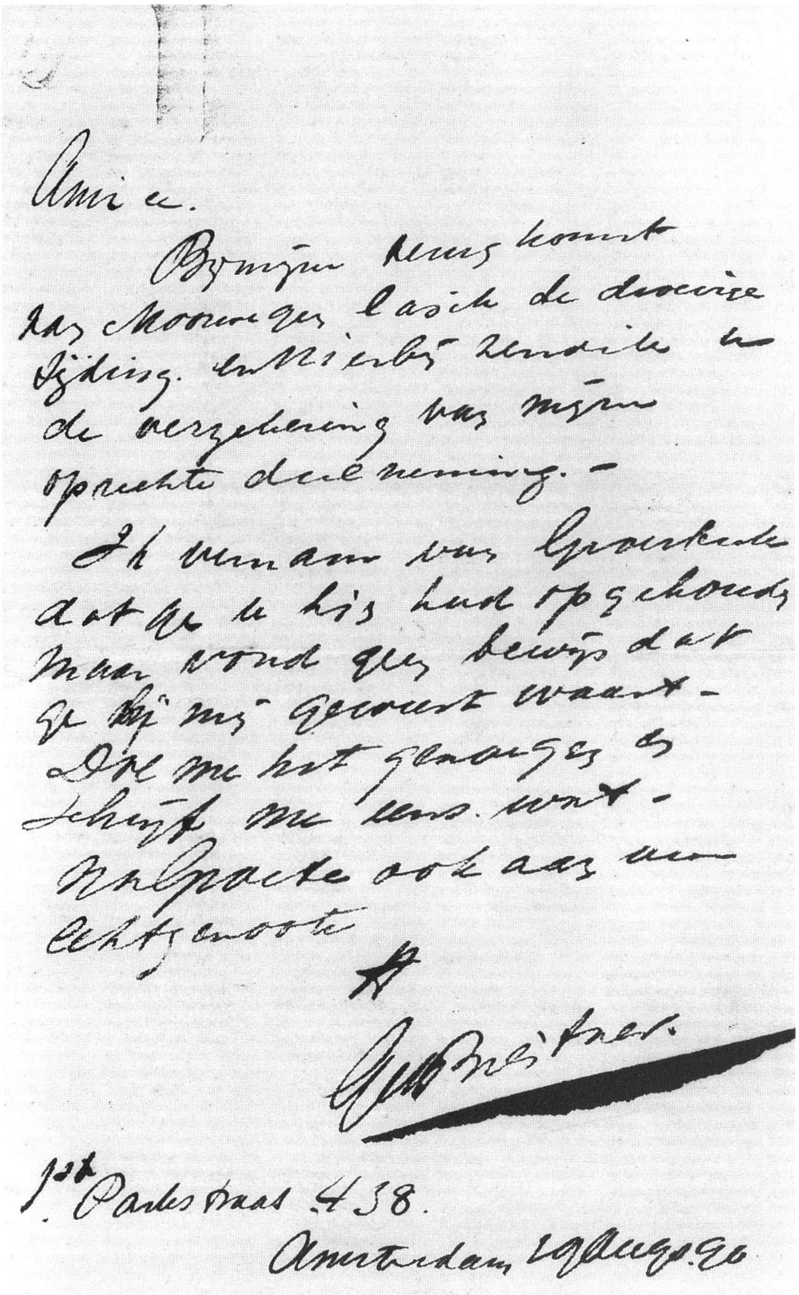

Amice.

Bij mijn terugkomst van Noorwegen las ik de droevige tijding. En hierbij zend ik u de verzekering van mijn oprechte deelneming. —

Ik vernam van Groenkade dat ge u bij hem had opgehouden maar vond geen bewijs dat ge bij mij geweest waart. —

Doe me het genoegen en schrijf me eens. wat. —

[illegible] ook aan uw echtgenoote

t.t.

GH Breitner.

1ste Parkstraat 438.

Amsterdam 29 Aug. 90

DUTCH 9

Den Haag. 30 Sept. 1890.
Monsieur Van Goch à Paris

Beste vriend Van Goch! –

Heden eerst vernam ik het treurig bericht der doodstijding van Uwen genialen broeder wiens werk ik zoo hoog heb leeren waardeeren en wiens talent ik zoo goed begreep. Reeds had ik er mij mede gevleid na mijn terugkeer te Parijs persoonlijk zijn kennis te maken en ziedaar nu al mijn hoop vervlogen. Ik had u reeds willen verzoeken hem mijn litteraire schetsen te toonen, maar mijn vertrek is plotseling opgekomen en ik was eens Bd. Montmartre en Cité Pigalle zonder u te vinden. Gij zult mij dus niet ten kwade duiden dat ik u niet goeden dag ben komen zeggen. Ik dacht ook spoediger terug te zijn. – Nu zou ik u graag persoonlijk de hand komen drukken en van mijn innigen deelneming met uw groot verlies komen betuigen, een verlies dat ieder die het werk van den overledene zoo als ik gezien heeft medegevoelt. Over 14 dagen hoop ik u zelf te komen bezoeken. Ik kan nu niet veel schrijven, waarlijk de tijding heeft mij te zeer getroffen. Ik had dat niet verwacht, en hoe graag had ik den grooten artiest wiens werk één levenden en vroolijken kleur is een verder leven nog gegund met wat meer kleur in vergoeding van al wat hij al geleden had. Arme kerel wiens gevoel te fijn

The Hague. 30 Sept. 1890.
Monsieur Van Goch à Paris

Dear friend Van Goch! –

I only heard today the unhappy news of the death of your brilliant brother, whose work I have come to admire very greatly and whose talent I understood so well.[1] I had been flattering myself that I should meet him personally upon my return to Paris, but my hopes have now been dashed. I had been intending to ask you to show him my literary sketches,[2] but I was unexpectedly obliged to depart and I went to Bd. Montmartre and Cité Pigalle but was unable to find you.[3] You will therefore forgive me for not having come to say goodbye. I had also expected to return sooner than I did.– Now I should like to clasp your hand in person and express my deepest condolences at your terrible loss, a loss that will be shared by all who, like myself, have seen your late brother's work. I hope to visit you in person in a fortnight. I am unable to write much at present, as I am indeed much affected by the news. I had not expected it, and how ardently I should have wished the great artist, whose work is all animated and cheerful colour, himself a longer life with more colour in recompense for all that he

Anton van Teijn (?) to Theo, Tuesday 30 September 1890.
Inv. no. b 2006 VF/1982
The identity of the writer of this remarkable letter has not been convincingly established. First, the deciphering of the signature: 'Anton Van' is relatively easy, but the last and crucial part of the surname proved more intransigent. Next, the writer's profession: 'literary sketches' might suggest a writer, a Dutch journalist perhaps sending back reports from Paris. But he could equally be an illustrator doing 'literary sketches' for periodicals or books. 'Dear friend' and 'my good friend', suggests that he knew Theo fairly well. And, clearly, he knew Theo's gallery, as well as his apartment at 8 Cité Pigalle. Above all, he knew Vincent's work. Yet, in Theo's address book, there is not one name that corresponds with the sender of this letter. Nor, in the archives of the Van Gogh Museum, is there another letter in this hand.

One credible candidate could be Anthonie van Teijn, born at Naaldwijk on 3 November 1863, who lived and worked for a time in Paris, and who did landscapes, etching, watercolours and book illustrations signed Vanteyn. He died at Amersfoort on 28 May 1943.

1. Whether Van Teijn left Paris in early August (during Theo's absence in Amsterdam), and then spent two months in Holland is unclear. Whether he received Theo's card announcing Vincent's death, or heard, or read about it, remains uncertain.

2. 'Literary sketches': here lies an ambiguity – is he author or artist-illustrator?

3. The addresses refer to 19 Boulevard Montmartre, the gallery of

was om met die ruwe werkelijkheid te kunnen harmonieeren. Ik denk aan de laatste woorden van Oskar uit Ibsens 'Spoken': 'Gib mir die Sonne!' Hij trachtte hem vast te houden op zijn doeken en er het leven van zoo menige armen en eenvoudigen mede te verkwikken, en ziedaar nu zullen wij niets meer van hem zien... Maar wat ik hoop van harte wensch en wat moet gebeuren, dat is dat men zijn werk in ruimen kring zal zien en zeker zullen er dan vele zijn die zullen zien welk een gevoelig mensch welk een groot artiest Vincent van Goch geweest is en zoo zal hij toch leven blijven onder ons jongeren hoe vroeg te *vroeg ook heengegaan! – Voor u echter beste vriend die ik heb leeren hoogachten en waardeeren is deze slag echter een der pijnlijkste. Wij moeten ons echter bukken voor die noodzakelijkheid waartegen alles machteloos is. Wees er verzekerd van dat de deelneming in uw rouw als vriend en ook als medewerker aan dat doel waarvan uw broeder een zoo talentvolle bevorderaar was: het ware het levensvolle in de kunst. en laat dat ons troosten waarde vriend dat de overledene niet voor niets geleefd heeft. Van hoeveel quasie grootheden kan men hetzelfde zeggen? – Groet uw waarde vrouw hartelijk voor mij, ook haar mijn condoleances en gij hartelijk gegroet met een handdruk van uw vriend*

Anton Van Teijn

suffered. Unfortunate fellow, whose sensibility was too fine to be in harmony with this harsh reality. I am reminded of Oscar's final words in Ibsen's 'Ghosts': 'Gib mir die Sonne!' [Give me the sun!].[4] He tried to capture this on his canvases and to brighten the lives of many a poor and simple souls, and now, alas, we shall see no more of it...[5] But what I hope and wish with all my heart, and what indeed must happen is that more people must get to see his work,[6] and many there will certainly be who will see what a sensitive person, what a great artist Vincent van Goch was, and so he shall live on, with us, despite his early, his *too* early demise!– But for you, my truly dear friend, whom I have come to respect and cherish, the blow comes hardest. However, we must yield to that inevitability against which all is impotent. Be assured that I mourn together with you, both as a friend and as one striving towards the same goal as that to which your brother aspired with such talent: the authentic, the vitality in art,[7] and let us find comfort, my good friend, in the knowledge that the deceased did not live in vain. Of how many quasi great men can this be said?- Please give your wife my kind regards and convey to her, too, my sincere condolences. My cordial good wishes to you from your friend

Anton Van Teijn

Boussod Valadon et Cie, where Theo worked, and 8 Cité Pigalle, Theo and Jo's apartment.

4. *Ghosts*, by the Norwegian dramatist Henrik Ibsen (1828-1906), was written in September-October 1881 and published in December of that year. It was so attacked and vilified that no Scandinavian theatre would stage it (its first performance was actually given by a touring Danish company in Chicago in May 1882). It was translated into German in 1884: the quotation comes from this German edition. Translated into French in 1889, the play was first performed in Paris (as *Les revenants*) at Antoine's Théâtre Libre on 30 May 1890, a few weeks before this letter was written. The doomed artist Osvald, dying of inherited syphilis, utters the words 'Give me the sun' to his mother, Mrs Alving, in the closing exchanges of the third and last act. Osvald's last words, in his state of collapse, are 'The sun.. the sun..'.

5. This implies that the writer was familiar with Vincent's paintings of Arles and Saint-Rémy, where the sun often plays a crucial role: e.g. F 422, F 450, F 737.

6. The notion of showing Vincent's work was taken up by Theo, who in August and September was earnestly working towards an exhibition in a recognized venue.

7. This is a remarkably clear statement of belief in Vincent's talent. It equals the belief expressed by Boch (French 18) and Van Rappard (Dutch 11); and leaves one full of admiration for the perspicacity and prophetic powers of the writer.

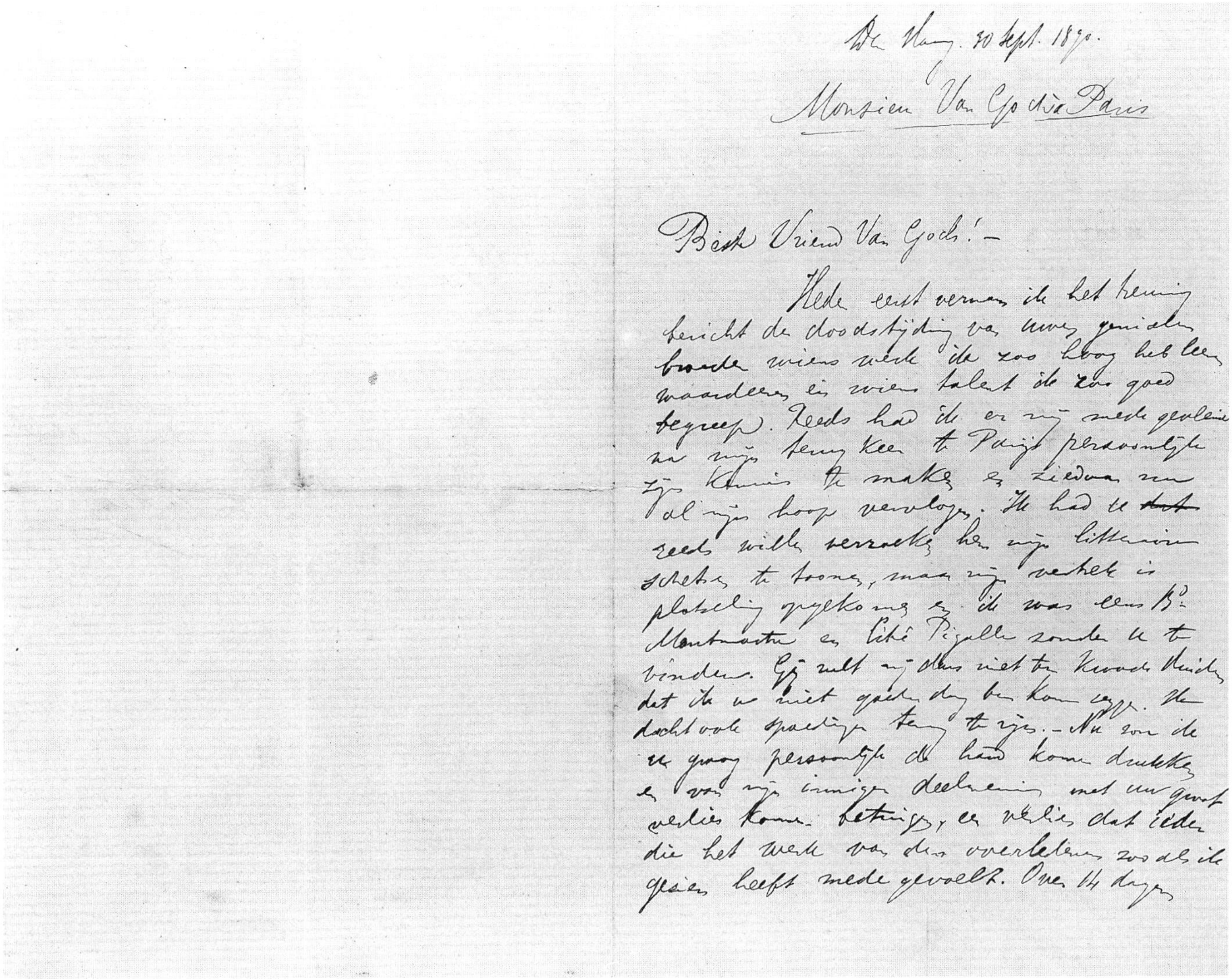

Den Haag. 30 Sept. 1890.

Monsieur Van Gogh à Paris

Beste Vriend Van Gogh!–

Hede eerst vernam ik het treurig bericht der doodstijding van uwen genialen broeder wiens werk ik zoo hoog heb leeren waardeeren en wiens talent ik zoo goed begreep. Reeds had ik er mij mede gevleid na mijn terugkeer te Parijs persoonlijk zijn kennis te maken en zie daar nu val mijn hoop vervlogen. Ik had u ~~dat~~ reeds willen verzoeken hem mijn litterarie schetsen te toonen, maar mijn vertrek is plotseling opgekomen en ik was eens B. Montmartre en Cité Pigalle zonder u te vinden. Gij zult mij dus niet ten kwade duiden dat ik u niet goeden dag ben komen zeggen. Ik dacht voor spoedig terug te zijn.– Nu zou ik u gaarne persoonlijk de hand komen drukken en van mijn innige deelneming met uw groot verlies komen betuigen, een verlies dat ieder die het werk van den overledene zoo als ik gezien heeft mede gevoelt. Over 14 dagen

DUTCH 10

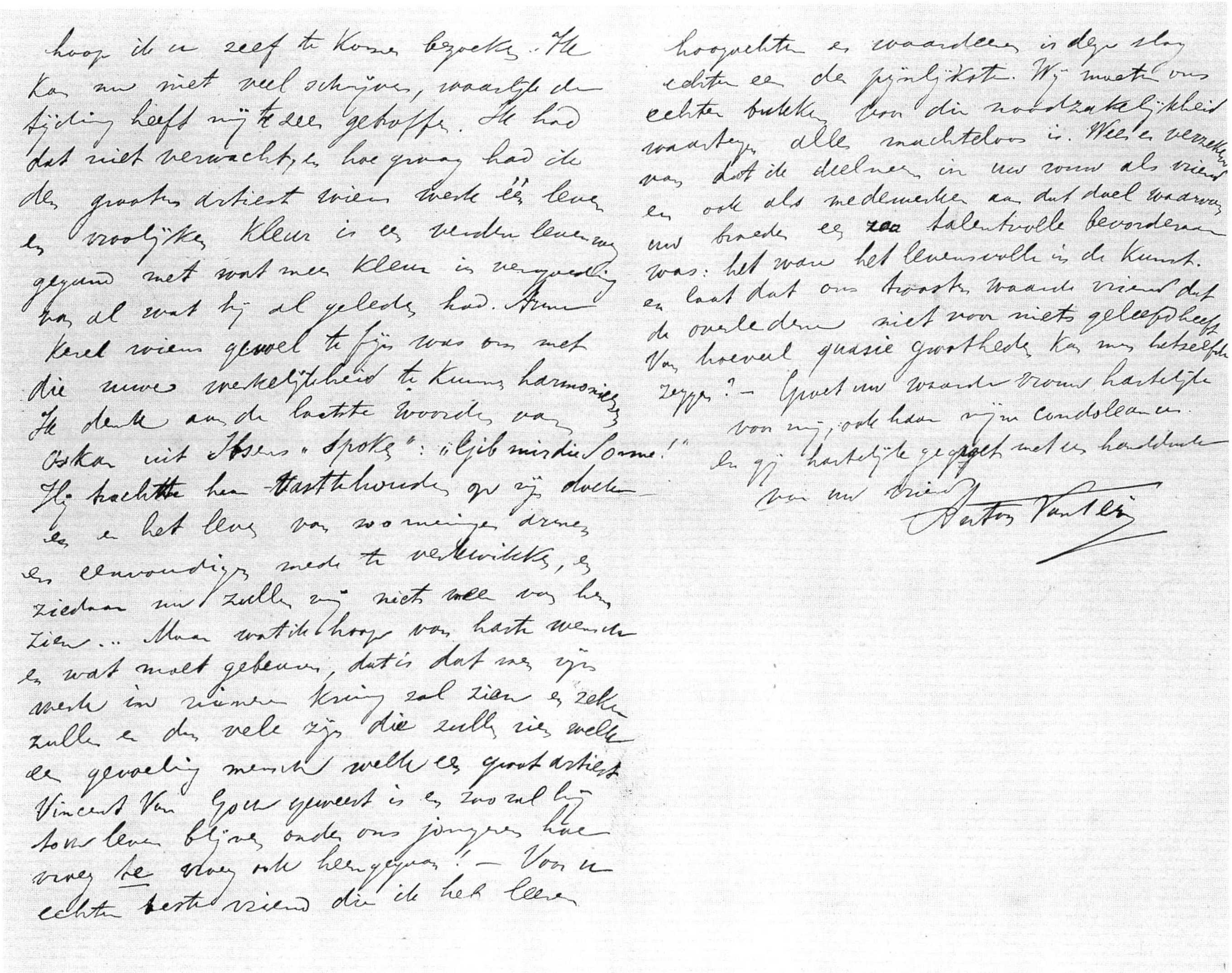
hoop ik u zelf te komen bezoeken. Ik
kan nu niet veel schrijven, waarlijk de
tijding heeft mij te zeer getroffen. Ik had
dat niet verwacht, en hoe graag had ik
den grooten artiest wiens werk een leven
en vroolijken kleur is en verder leven van
geven met wat meer kleur in vergoeding
van al wat hij al geleden had. Arme
kerel wiens gevoel te fijn was om met
die ruwe werkelijkheid te kunnen harmonieeren
Ik denk aan de laatste woorden van
Oskar uit Ibsens „Spoken": „Gib mir die Sonne!"
Hij trachtte een vasthouden op zijn doelen
en het leven van zoo menigen armen
en eenvoudigen mede te ontwikkelen, en
zie daar nu zullen wij niets meer van hem
zien... Maar wat ik hoop van harte wensch
en wat moet gebeuren, dat is dat men zijn
werk in ruimeren kring zal zien en zeker
zullen er dan vele zijn die zullen zien welk
een gevoelig mensch welk een groot artiest
Vincent Van Gogh geweest is en zoo zal hij
voortleven blijven onder ons jongeren hoe
vroeg te vroeg ook heengegaan! — Voor u
echter beste vriend die ik het leven

hoogachten en waardeeren is deze slag
echter een der pijnlijkste. Wij moeten ons
echter buigen voor die noodzakelijkheid
waartegen alles machteloos is. Wees er verzekerd
van dat ik deelneem in uw rouw als vriend
en ook als medewerker aan dat doel waarvan
uw broeder een zoo talentvolle bevorderaar
was: het ware het levensvolle in de Kunst.
En laat dat ons troosten waarde vriend dat
de overledene niet voor niets geleefd heeft
Van hoeveel quasie grootheden kan men hetzelfde
zeggen? — Groet uw waarde vrouw hartelijk
voor mij, ook haar mijn condoleances.
En gij hartelijk gegroet met een handdruk
van uw vriend
Anton [illegible]

Alsof het gisteren gebeurde staat onze kennismaking te Brussel mij nog voor den geest, toen hij 's morgens om 9 uur op mijn kamer kwam; hoe we het in 't eerst niet goed vinden konden; maar later wel, toen we een paar maal samen gewerkt hadden. [...] Wie, die dit zwoegende, strijdende en lijdende bestaan gezien heeft, zou geen sympathie gevoelen voor den man, die zóóveel van zich zelf vergde dat èn lichaam èn geest er door te gronde gingen. Hij behoorde tot het ras waar de groote artisten uit geboren worden. [...] Al waren Vincent en ik in de laatste jaren van elkander verwijderd geraakt door een misverstand dat ik dikwijls betreurd heb – ik heb toch niet anders dan met zeer veel vriendschap aan hem en aan onzen omgang gedacht. [...] Als ik voortaan aan dien tijd zal denken – en is me altijd een genot me in 't verledene te begeven – dan zal de karakteristieke figuur van Vincent mij in zulk een weemoedig maar toch helder licht verschijnen: die zwoegende en strijdende, fanatiek-sombere Vincent, die zoo dikwijls op kon bruisen en heftig zijn, maar die toch ook altijd door zijn edel gemoed en zijn hooge artistieke eigenschappen vriendschap en bewondering verdiende.

I remember, as though it were yesterday, our first meeting in Brussels, when he came to my room at nine o'clock in the morning;[1] how at first we did not get on very well; although we did later, after having worked together a few times. [...] Who, having witnessed this wrestling, struggling and sorrowful existence, could not but feel sympathy for the man who made such demands of himself that he destroyed both body and spirit. He was of the breed from which great artists are born.[2] [...] Though Vincent and I had grown apart in recent years through a misunderstanding I have often regretted – I have thought of him and of our association only with the greatest cordiality. [...] From now on, when I recall those times – and I always enjoy straying back to the past – Vincent's distinctive figure will appear to me in a melancholy though bright light: that fighting, struggling, fervent, sombre Vincent, so often volatile and so impassioned, yet, for his noble mind and artistic qualities, always worthy of friendship and admiration.

Anthon Gerard Alexander Ridder van Rappard to Mother van Gogh, date unknown.
Partly published by Johanna van Gogh-Bonger in the 1914 Introduction in three separate excerpts. The original letter, clearly accessible to Jo, is apparently lost; and its date is unknown.

Of all Vincent's friendships with Dutch artists, that with Anthon Gerard Alexander Ridder van Rappard (1858-1892) was the longest, most influential, and most rewarding. Its beginnings were not all that auspicious; its course was never even; its ending, after five years, was sad. The two artists spurred each other on. They shared a passion for English and French illustrators, endlessly discussing their merits, exchanging sheets, building op their collections. Van Rappard introduced him to, and lent him, books and manuals on art that became bibles for Vincent. Above all, they exchanged many letters. Fifty-eight of Vincent's survive: an indispensable source of information for his Dutch period (1881-1885).

1. This first meeting must have taken place in October 1880. Vincent mentioned it in a letter of 1 November (LT 138): 'I have also been to see Mr van Rappard, who now lives at Rue Raversiere 6a, and had a talk with him. He is a fine-looking man [...] he impressed me as one who takes things seriously.'

[...] En mijn logeeren in Etten! Ik zie U [Vincents moeder] nog bij 't raam zitten, toen ik binnenkwam, [...] ik geniet nog van die heerlijk wandeling die we dien eersten avond met ons allen maakten langs allerlei paadjes en velden! [...] En onze tochten naar Seppen, Passievaart, Liesbosch – ik kijk er mijn schetsboeken nog menigmaal op na. [...] Nog zóó dikwijls dacht ik aan al de studies van wevers die hij te Nuenen gemaakt heeft, met welk een innigheid had hij hun leven opgevat en weergegeven, welk een aangrijpende zwaarmoedigheid sprak daaruit, hoe onbeholpen van uitvoering zijn werk toen ook moge geweest zijn. [...] En wat had hij niet mooie studies van dien ouden toren op het kerkhof gemaakt, altijd is mij een maneschijn daarvan bijgebleven, die mij indertijd zoo bizonder trof. [..] De gedachte aan die studies in die twee kamers bij de kerk wekt weer zeer veel herinneringen bij mij op, brengt mij de geheele omgeving weer voor den geest, de vriendelijke gastvrije pastorie met haar mooien tuin, de familie Begemann, onze wandelingen naar wevers en boeren, wat heb ik daar veel genoten.

[...] And my visit to Etten![3] I can still see you [Vincent's mother] sitting at the window when I entered... I still feel the enjoyment of that wonderful walk we all took the first evening, along the little paths through the fields! [...] And our excursions to Seppen, Passievaart, Liesbosch – I often turn to them in my sketchbooks.[4] [...] How often I thought of the studies of the weavers which he made in Nuenen and the intensity of the feeling with which he depicted their lives;[5] what deep melancholy pervaded his work, however clumsy its execution may have been. [...] And what beautiful studies he made of the old church tower in the churchyard, I always remember a moonlight effect of it which particularly struck me at that time.[6] [...] Thinking of those studies in the two rooms near the church conjures up so many memories,[7] and I am reminded of all the surroundings, the cheerful, hospitable vicarage with its beautiful garden, the Begemann family,[8] our visits to the weavers and peasants, how I did enjoy it all.

2. A challenging judgement, not made by any ather well-known Dutch artist, neither Breitner, nor Koning, nor Israëls. Van Teijn's is the only comparable one (Dutch 11).
3. Van Rappard's first visit to Etten was in June 1881. He drew the vicarage, dating the drawing '14 June '81' (misattributed to Van Gogh by Tralbaut, it was rightly given back to Van Rappard in exhib. cat. *Anthon van Rappard: companion and correspondent of Vincent van Gogh*, Amsterdam (Rijksmuseum Vincent van Gogh) 1974, no. 58).

4. Vincent reported to Theo on Van Rappard's stay at Etten in June 1881. 'You must know that Rappard has been here for about twelve days, and now he has gone. [...] We have taken many long walks together have been, for instance, several times to the heath, near Seppe, to the so-called Passievaart, a big swamp. There Rappard painted a large study (1 meter by 50 cm.); it was not bad. Besides that, he did about 10 small sepias, also in the Liesbosch (LT 146)'. Two drawings which must surely be dismembered pages from one of the sketchbooks mentioned by Van Rappard show the Passievaart near Seppe (dated 13 June '81) and a landscape near Seppe (dated 14 June), both now in the Centraal Museum, Utrecht (see ibid., nos. 56-57).

5. Van Gogh did a whole series of weavers - drawings and gouaches as well as paintings – in 1883. And Van Rappard himself also depicted weavers (see ibid., p. 87 and no. 109; Richard Bionda *et al.*, exhib. cat. *The Age of Van Gogh. Dutch Painting 1880-1895*, Glasgow (The Burrell Collection) 1990, no. 69 and idem, exhib. cat. *De tachtigers. Nederlandse schilderkunst 1880-1895*, Amsterdam (Rijksmuseum Vincent van Gogh) 1991, no. 106. The reference is to F 40. Compare Theo's sister Lies's comments on the painting of the same old tower, but under snow (F 87) in her letter of 2 August (Fall).

7. Van Rappard is referring to the studio that Vincent rented in May 1884 from the Catholic verger: 'a spacious new studio [...] Two rooms – a big one, and a smaller one adjoining (LT 368).' Shortly afterwards, Van Rappard spent ten days with Vincent, so he was very familiar with this studio (see LT 369). He visited Nuenen again in October 1884.

8. The Begemann family lived in the house next door to the Nuenen parsonage. Vincent's affair with Margot Begemann reached an alarming climax in June 1884, when Margot tried to poison herself (see LT 375).

French and others

This final section consists of twenty-six letters. The majority (19) are French – eleven artists, three young art critics, two prominent collectors and a legendary art dealer. These are supplemented by seven others of various nationalities: Belgian, Italian, Danish, Australian and English, five of whom were artists, two friends of Theo's, and one an English art dealer. Only, the last, Charles Obach, goes back to the 1870s; and apart from Martin, Vignon and the Italian Corcos, who met Theo in the early 1880s, the rest became known to the Van Gogh brothers after Vincent's arrival in 1886. This wide circle of friends once again belies the easy assumption that Vincent died unappreciated, unrecognized, and virtually friendless.

Even though only fifteen of these twenty-six correspondents actually knew Vincent, it is made abundantly clear what those who did not meet him thought of his achievement as an artist. Among these were Monet and Carrière, Corcos and Hayet, the art critics Fénéon and Lecomte, and the distinguished collectors Comte Doria and Henri Rouart. That some of these thought particularly highly of Vincent's paintings is made manifest in their letters. Take those of Monet, Carrière, Gausson and Corcos. Each was vastly different from the other in artistic beliefs and practice, yet all were united in their high opinion of Vincent's artistic stature. Monet assured Theo, 'I have already told you of my feelings for your brother' – and indeed, he had, calling Vincent's ten paintings at the spring 1890 Salon des Indépendants 'the best of all in the exhibition' (T 32). Carrière spoke of 'this premature death of an artist who was so young and so full of talent'. Corcos recalled the works from Nuenen that Theo had shown him, 'which I thought showed an extremely well observed and intensely felt vision of nature that was executed with that inner conviction of the artist that makes no concessions to the profane public'. Gausson, Neo-Impressionist and fellow exhibitor at the Indépendants, often used to go to Tanguy's shop especially to see Vincent's works, and even suggested to Tanguy 'that he should ask this painter whom I loved without knowing him, whether he would agree to exchange a picture of his for one of mine'.

From those who had known Vincent came warm expressions of their deep appreciation of his friendship. Toulouse-Lautrec expressed it in lapidary form: 'You know what a friend he was to me and how eager he was to demonstrate his affection'.

The Australian John Russell, another artist whom Vincent met in Paris and who painted his portrait, assured Theo, 'He was a very good friend to me [...]. He had the rare quality of never forgetting a friend'.

Quost, the flower-painter whose work Vincent so admired, was in turn highly appreciative of 'your brother [who] had a warm heart and was a sincere artist'. The legendary Parisian art dealer, 'Père' Martin, who showed Vincent's work in 1886, described him as 'this brave man who was all too much an artist and for whom I felt a great affection'.

And the Dane Mourier Petersen, who spent much time with Vincent in Arles in the spring of 1888, affirmed to Theo: 'We got on so well together during our brief acquaintance, and he showed me a very sincere and very unselfish friendship'. And Mourier Petersen went on to admit that Vincent's 'opinions on art and life have had an unquestionable influence on my development'.

Camille Pissarro, composing his note of condolence in haste, touched on the question of achievement: 'I really felt a great affinity for your brother who had the spirit of an artist, and whose loss will be deeply felt by the younger generation!' While for Gauguin, better acquainted with Vincent than any of his contemporaries, he was not only a 'sincere friend', but also 'an *artist* a rare thing in our epoch'. And Gauguin recalled how Vincent would often say: 'Stone will perish, the word will remain' – his work would live.

Of the three young and committedly avant-garde art critics, Aurier, Fénéon and Lecomte, only Aurier actually met Vincent. Aurier has secured his place in the Van Gogh pantheon with his contribution to the first number of the *Mercure de France* of January 1890, the only long article devoted to Vincent during his lifetime. There cannot be complete certainty as to when they met, but it seems more likely to have been during Vincent's three-day stay in Paris in mid-May 1890, rather than on his day visit in 6 July, as Jo suggested. Such would seem to be implied from Theo's letter to Vincent of 5 June (T 36). Aurier's letter of condolence is relatively short, but doubly reassuring: 'I do not need to tell you – you must be aware of it – how great an admiration I felt for the artistic qualities of the man whom you are mourning today. I will therefore only add one word: men like him do not die entirely. He leaves behind a body of work which is a part of himself and which, one day, you and I can be sure, will make his name live again and for eternity'.

Lecomte probably never met Vincent, even though he was one of the few critics to say something of the paintings at the Salon des Indépendants of spring 1890. The mercurial Fénéon, by contrast, says categorically that he never met Vincent. Without this explicit testimony, it would be difficult to believe this. Fénéon certainly knew Theo, and Theo's gallery, which he began frequenting and writing about from December 1887, while Vincent was still in Paris. The assumption, made in the 1950s, that Fénéon, in top hat, sits next to Vincent in Lucien Pissarro's double-portrait drawing has to be abandoned. The likeness, in any case, was never very close, and the identification never totally convincing. As to Vincent's work, Fénéon had wrapped his idiosyncratic language around *Irises* (F 608) and *Starry Night on the Rhône* (F 474) when they were shown at the Indépendants in autumn 1889. So he can now assure Theo of 'the great and new talent of your brother'.

Lautrec, Mourier Petersen and Gauguin all worked with Vincent at various times. So did Eugène Boch, the Belgian artist whom he knew in Arles in the summer of 1888. His letter of condolence is one of the shortest; but in it Boch asserted: 'a great artist is dead'.

Not all artists were so revealing or prophetic. Just as Breitner and Koning were not terribly forthcoming in their letters to Theo, so neither were Guillaumin and Vignon. Both spent more time regretting their inability to be at the funeral than expressing their thoughts about Vincent, whether as friend or as artist. The Italian Zandomeneghi sent his name-card and was as succinct as his fellow country man Corcos was verbose.

Theo's standing as an art dealer of flair, imagination and tenacity, is borne out by the card and letter he received from Comte Doria and Henri Rouart. These were undoubtedly two of the greater collectors of French nineteenth-century painting. Rouart must surely have visited Theo's gallery, if only to see the works on show there by his great friend Degas. And it was Theo who was the moving spirit behind the publication by Boussod Valadon of fifteen lithographs after Degas's works in 1889: eleven of these came from the magnificent collection built up by Henri Rouart.

Theo often showed Degas's work, and handled some twenty of his works between April 1887 and October 1890. It is unlikely that Vincent met Degas. But Theo kept Degas informed of what was going on in Arles, especially once Gauguin arrived. The want of a letter of condolence from Degas to Theo is easily explained: he was taking a cure at Cauterets in the Pyrénées, and it is unlikely that Theo's card announcing Vincent's death ever reached him. Other artists whose work was handled or exhibited by Theo who appear not to have responded to Vincent's death include Raffaelli (Theo had just given him a one-man show in May-June), Schuffenecker, Redon and Rodin.

But these lacunae are more than made up for by Dr Gachet's letter of mid-August: a quite astonishing document. It is true that Jo quoted a chunk from this letter in her 1914 Introduction: 'The more I think of it, the more I regard Vincent as *a giant*. Not a day goes by without my looking at his canvases. I always find a new idea in them, something different from the day before, and I return by the mental phenomenon of thought to the man himself whom I think of as a Colossus... He was, moreover, a philosopher [...]. The word *love* of art is not right – *Faith* is the proper word. Faith to the point of martyrdom!!!'

But this has never really been commented upon, merely re-quoted by a few later authors. And, of course, its context has remained obscure. Giant – colossus – philosopher – martyr. Is all this exaggerated, a piece of psychotherapy designed to give Theo solace and hope? Surely it was genuine and heartfelt: Gachet was not dissimulating. But what follows this passage is also remarkable: the reason that Gachet seeks for Vincent's suicide. (In itself, the letter is unique: the only one that even mentions suicide, let alone the reasons for Vincent deciding to take his own life.) Hitherto, there has been virtually nothing to go on in trying to determine the reason for Dr Gachet's actions and to gain some idea of his opinions. Gachet gives us the first known medical interpretation of Van Gogh's suicide: the first, indeed, of many – far too many, some would argue.

The other revealing element in Gachet's letter is the promise that he would write something on Vincent for publication – 'a complete biography – of an extraordinary man'. Although Theo pressed him at the time to complete something, even an article for Antoine's *Art et Critique*, Gachet never did. The manuscript must have remained in the drawer – or in Gachet's head. Perhaps he sensed this himself, insisting to Theo in his postscript: 'keep this letter', already knowing that he would not manage anything of greater length. Nonetheless, the legend persisted that he was preparing something on Vincent. In 1904, Julius

Meier-Graefe, the prominent German art critic, visited Gachet at Auvers, and added, as a footnote, to his chapter on Van Gogh in *The Development of Modern Art* (published in 1904, translated in 1908): 'Dr Gachet is at work on a monograph of Van Gogh, to be illustrated with etchings from the artist's pictures'. And at Gachet's death in 1909, Johanna Van Gogh-Bonger concluded her brief obituary notice in the *Nieuwe Rotterdamsche Courant*: 'The book that he was engaged on writing on Vincent and which was to have been illustrated with etchings after his paintings has not been finished'.

Gachet's letter to Theo of mid-August 1890 therefore becomes his sole testimony, reading like a written embellishment of his graveside eulogy (as described briefly by Emile Bernard) or a peroration to a long obituary notice. How Gachet envisaged the transformation of all his embryonic ideas into a 'complete biography' remains obscure. As a unique document, its rediscovery and publication are all the more precious.

Eragny par Gisors
(Eure)

Mon cher Van Gogh.

Ce matin nous avons reçu la lamentable nouvelle de la mort de votre pauvre frère; mon fils Lucien n'a eu que quelques minutes pour prendre le train, avec l'espoir d'assister à l'enterrement, j'aurai bien voulu en faire autant, mais je ne pouvais être prêt à temps. C'est à mon grand regret, car j'avais vraiment une grande sympathie pour cet âme d'artiste qu'était votre frère, et qui laissera, un grand vide parmi les jeunes !..

je vous plains mon cher ami et vous serres sympathiques les mains

votre dévoué
C. Pissarro.

Eragny near Gisors
(Eure)

My dear Van Gogh.

This morning we received the shocking news of the death of your poor brother; my son Lucien only had a few minutes to catch the train, in the hope of attending the funeral.[1] I very much wanted to go too, but was unable to get there on time. I regret this very much, for I really felt a great affinity for your brother who had the spirit of an artist, and whose loss will be deeply felt by the younger generation!..[2]

I feel really sad for you, my dear friend, and you have my heartfelt sympathy

yours ever
C. Pissarro.

Camille Pissarro to Theo, Wednesday 30 July 1890.
Inv. no. b 818 v/1962
First published, with an English translation, in Lili Jampoller, 'Theo van Gogh and Camille Pissarro: correspondence and an exhibition', *Simiolus* 16 (1986), pp. 53-54, note 27. It was published there with its faults of orthography and loose punctuation. In Janine Bailly-Herzberg, *Correspondence de Camille Pissarro*, 3 vols., Paris 1980-88, vol. 2: 1886-1890, no. 592, pp. 354-55, these faults were silently corrected, and the punctuation improved. The letter was written in haste, presumably to answer Theo immediately, and to excuse Pissarro's inability to be present at the funeral. It was surely handed to Theo in Auvers by Pissarro's eldest son Lucien (1863-1944), who acted as his father's representative – and, of course, attended in his own right as a friend of Vincent's.

1. Lucien Pissarro (1863-1944), eldest son of Camille Pissarro (1830-1903), met Vincent in Paris in the autumn of 1887, when the two artists exchanged works, a still life of apples, dedicated to Lucien (F 378) against a set of some twenty wood-engravings (now in the Van Gogh Museum). Lucien's presence at the funeral was confirmed by Bernard's letter to Aurier of 31 July 1890 (see Prologue 3).

2. Camille Pissarro's 'great affinity' for Vincent was expressed on several occasions to Theo. For instance, he admired *La Mousmé* (F 531) when it arrived in Paris from Arles. Vincent was always anxious to hear Pissarro's response to the batches of work he sent Theo from both Arles and Saint-Rémy. In August 1890, some three weeks after Vincent's death, Pissarro offered Theo an exchange of paintings that involved *The Mulberry Tree* (F 637). 'Pissarro is in town and he saw the latest paintings and was full of admiration; he immediately wanted to make an exchange against a painting that pleased him. I don't know if you remember, Wil. A mulberry tree golden yellow in the autumn against a blue sky' (Theo to Wil, 24 August 1890; Van Gogh Museum, inv. no. b 936 v/1962). As to leaving a great gap among the young, Pissarro had often joined in the discussions regarding the Grand et Petit Boulevard with Vincent, Theo, and Guillaumin in January-February 1888, and therefore knew of Vincent's strong orientation toward the younger artists of the Petit Boulevard – Gauguin, Bernard, Lautrec, Anquetin, Seurat, Signac, Lucien, Lucien Pissarro, and Koning. Hence, the loss will be felt by these artists, believes Pissarro. For the materialization of this sentiment, Gausson's letter to Theo acts as a most outstanding example; but the letters from Boch, Hayet and Mourier Petersen also reflect it (see French 14, 18, 24, 26 respectively).

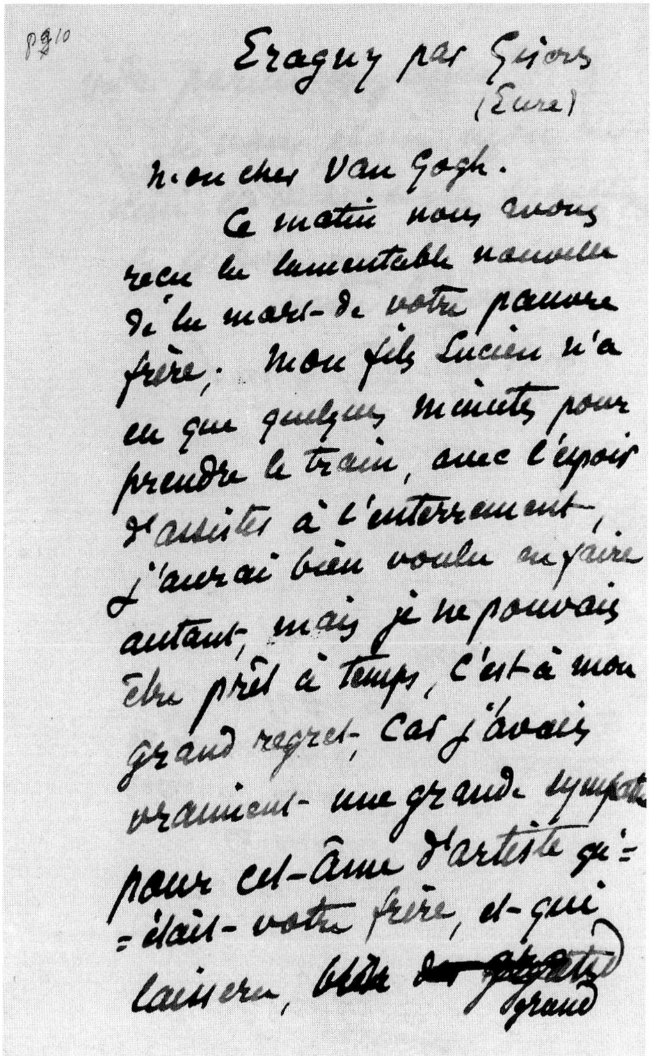

Eragny par Gisors
(Eure)

Mon cher Van Gogh.

Ce matin nous avons reçu la lamentable nouvelle de la mort de votre pauvre frère; mon fils Lucien n'a eu que quelques minutes pour prendre le train, avec l'espoir d'assister à l'enterrement, j'aurai bien voulu en faire autant, mais je ne pouvais être prêt à temps, c'est à mon grand regret, car j'avais vraiment une grande sympathie pour cet âme d'artiste qui était votre frère, et qui laissera, ~~[illegible]~~ grand

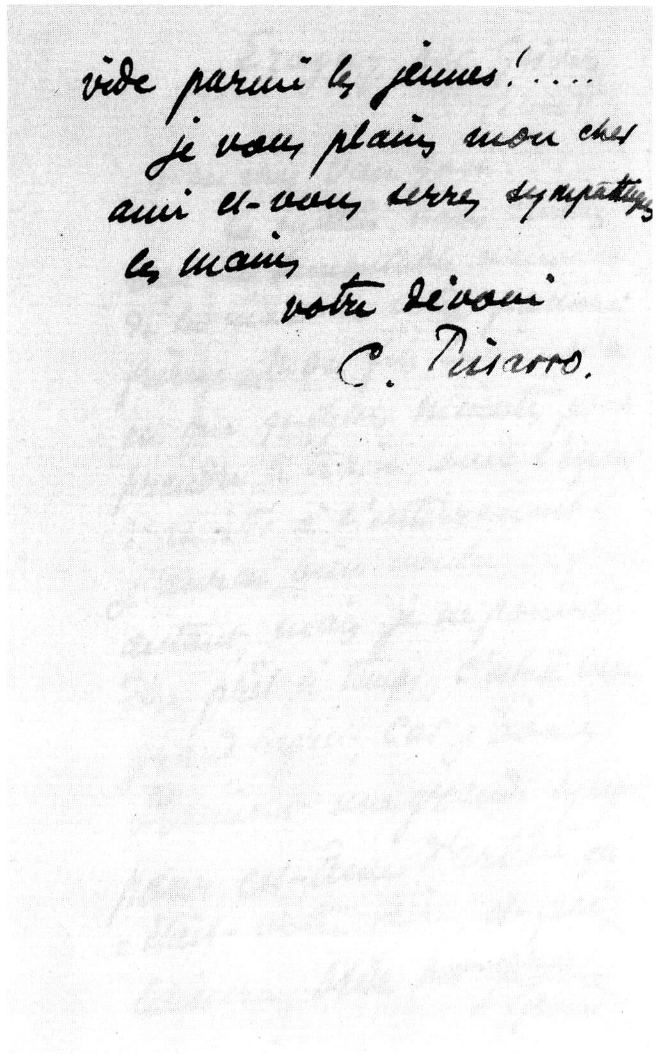

vide parmi les jeunes!....

Je vous plains mon cher ami et vous serre sympathiquement les mains

votre dévoué

C. Pissarro.

FRENCH I

Cher Mr. Van Gohh.

J'ai été douloureusement surpris par la nouvelle de la mort de votre cher frère. Je me rappelle ce que vous m'en disiez il y a peu de jours, et je pense que rien ne faisait prévoir un pareil malheur. Je n'ai trouvé qu'à mon retour à Paris le faire part. Je le regrette beaucoup, car la sympathie grande que j'ai pour vous et l'estime que les oeuvres de votre frère m'avait inspiré m'auraien fait un devoir de vous donner un témoignage plus complet de mes sentiments. Croyez cher Mr. Van Gohh que je prends la plus grande part à votre chagrin et que cette mort prématurée d'un artiste si jeune et si plein de talent m'a profondément attristé. Je sais par expérience que pour les grandes douleurs il n'y a pas de consolation, permettez moi donc cher monsieur de vous exprimer ma plus vive sympathie et la part que je prends vivement au malheur qui vous frappe.

Bien à vous cher Monsieur Van Gohh et croyez moi votre bien devoué

Eugène Carrière
30 Juillet 90.

Dear Mr. Van Gohh.

I was painfully surprised by the news of the death of your dear brother. I remember what you told me about him only a few days ago, and I think that nothing could have led one to foresee such a calamity.[1] I only found the announcement of his death on my return to Paris. I regret this very much, for the great affection that I have for you and the admiration that your brother's works had inspired in me would have compelled me to give you a more adequate expression of my feelings. Believe me dear Mr. Van Gohh that I share fully in your grief and that this premature death of an artist who was so young and so full of talent has profoundly saddened me. I know from experience that there is no consolation for great sorrows, allow me then, dear Sir, to express my deepest sympathy and to offer my heartfelt condolences for the tragedy that has struck you.

Every good wish to you Monsieur Van Gohh and believe me, ever yours

Eugène Carrière
30 July 90.

Eugène Carrière to Theo, Wednesday 30 July 1890.
Inv. no. b 1020 v/1962

1. Hitherto, there has been little indication of Eugène Carrière (1849-1906) being known to the Van Gogh brothers. On Vincent's side, there is no published evidence that he ever met Carrière, or even saw his work, since Carrière is never mentioned in his correspondence. Nor, on Theo's side, is there any evidence of Carrière's work being handled by Boussod Valadon, to judge from the surviving stockbooks; and none of his works figure in Theo's own collection. The first indication that Theo may have known him was not published until 1988: Carrière's name appears in Theo's address book (Pabst no. 51). However, the existence of a brief note to Theo, written on his name-card, suggests that Carrière already knew Theo quite well by 1888. This concerned Jean Dolent's book, *Amoureux d'art* (Paris 1888), sent to Theo by Carrière with a dedication from the author. (The volume still exists in the library of the Van Gogh Museum.)

Carrière's letter of condolence is surprising in several regards. Clearly, he had met Theo recently; clearly he had seen Vincent's paintings – chez Tanguy, at the Salon des Indépendants, and even, perhaps at Theo's apartment. Moreover, he found Vincent 'so full of talent' and 'admired' his work. And he would have liked to have been present at the funeral – like Pissarro, Toulouse-Lautrec, Guillaumin and Vignon (see French 1, 3, 4 and 13). Who, without this letter, would have predicted that Carrière, whose vision and style seem to be at the opposite pole to Vincent's (subdued, restrained, near-monochromatic), would have expressed such admiration for his work? A final irony: in April-May 1891, three months after Theo's death, an exhibition of fifty works by Carrière was mounted at Boussod Valadon, 19 Boulevard Montmartre, by Theo's successor, Maurice Joyant. Félix Fénéon wrote a review for *Le Chat Noir*, 2 May 1891; see also FF Oeuvres, p. 189.

Cher Mr Van Gogh.

J'ai été douloureusement surpris par la nouvelle de la mort de votre cher frère. Je me rappelle ce que vous m'en disiez il y a peu de jours. et je pense que rien ne faisait prévoir un pareil malheur. Je n'ai trouvé qu'à mon retour à Paris le faire part. Je le regrette beaucoup. car la sympathie grande que j'ai pour vous et l'estime que les oeuvres de votre frère m'avaient inspiré m'auraient fait un devoir de vous donner un témoignage plus complet de mes sentiments.

Croyez cher Mr Van Gogh que je prends la plus grande part à votre chagrin et que cette mort prématurée d'un artiste si jeune et si plein de talent m'a profondément attristé. Je sais par expérience que pour les grandes douleurs il n'y a pas de consolation. permettez moi donc cher Monsieur de vous exprimer ma plus vive sympathie et la part que je prends vivement au malheur qui vous frappe.

Bien à vous chère Madame Van Gogh et croyez moi votre bien dévoué

Eugène Carrière

30 Juillet 90.

FRENCH 2

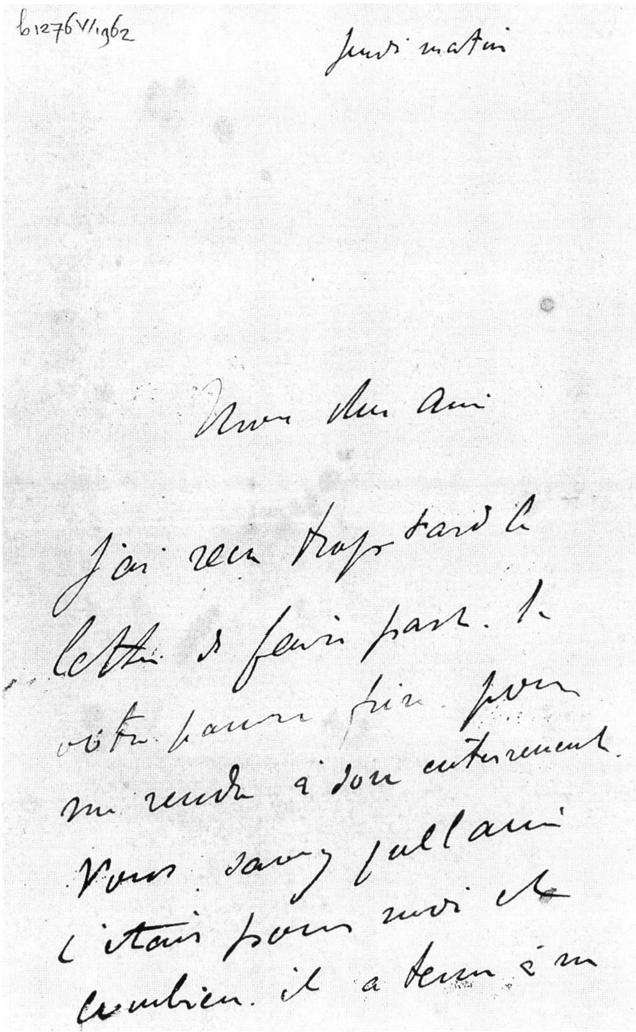

b1276V/1962

Jeudi matin

Mon cher ami

J'ai reçu trop tard la lettre de faire part de votre pauvre frère pour me rendre à son enterrement. Vous savez quel ami c'était pour moi et combien il a tenu à me

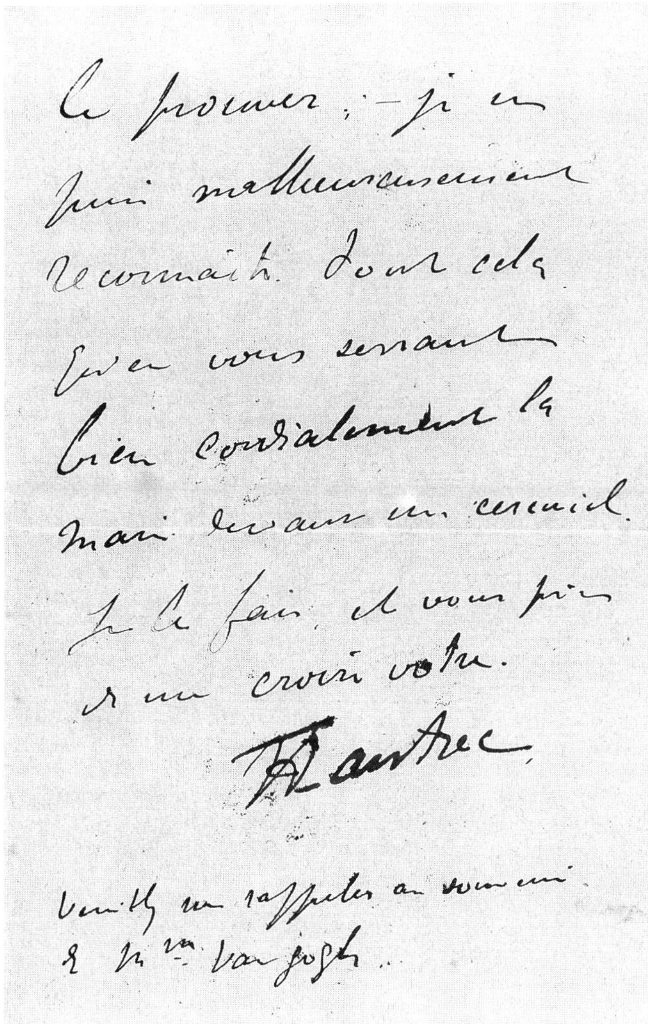

le prouver ; — je ne puis malheureusement reconnaître tout cela qu'en vous serrant bien cordialement la main devant un cercueil. Je le fais et vous prie de me croire votre.

HLautrec

Veuillez me rappeler au souvenir de Mme Van Gogh..

FRENCH 3

Jeudi matin

Mon cher ami

J'ai reçu trop tard la lettre de faire part de votre pauvre frère pour me rendre à son enterrement. Vous savez quel ami c'était pour moi et combien il a tenu à me le prouver. – je ne puis malheureusement reconnaître tout cela qu'en vous serrant bien cordialement la main devant un cercueil. Je le fais et vous prie de me croire votre.

HT Lautrec.

Veuillez me rappeler au souvenir de Mme Van Gogh.

Thursday morning

My dear friend

I received the letter announcing the death of your poor brother too late for me to be present at his funeral.[1] You know what a friend he was to me and how eager he was to demonstrate his affection. – unhappily, I am only able to tell you all this by clasping your hand very warmly but in the presence of a coffin. This is what I am doing with this letter, believe me yours.

HT Lautrec.

Please remember me to Mme Van Gogh.

Henri de Toulouse-Lautrec to Theo, Thursday 31 July 1890.
Inv. no. b 1276 v/1962
First published in Herbert D. Schimmel (ed.), *The Letters of Henry de Toulouse-Lautrec*, Oxford 1991, no. 176.

1. The friendship of Henri-Marie-Raymond de Toulouse-Lautrec (1864-1901) and Vincent van Gogh is well known, but surprisingly little documented. Their paths must surely have crossed at Cormon's studio, where Lautrec studied, somewhat intermittently, from December 1882 to spring 1887, and where Vincent spent only two brief months, almost certainly from March to May 1886. (Photographs of Lautrec and others at Cormon's studio predate Vincent's presence there). In the summer of 1886, they became fairly close neighbours in Montmartre – the Van Gogh brothers at 54 rue Lepic, Lautrec in his studio at 27 rue Caulaincourt (at the corner with 7 rue Tourlaque). Yet Theo, as art dealer, did not exhibit Lautrec's works in 1887 or 1888, and it wasn't until October 1888 that he bought his first and only Lautrec for Boussod Valadon. On the other hand, he certainly acquired a Lautrec for his own collection on 12 January 1888, the superb *Poudre de riz*, for which the receipt survives (Herbert D. Schimmel, op. cit., no. 160). Lautrec's three brief letters to Theo are all undated (ibid., nos. 139, 156, 167). Only his letter of condolence is dated.

By contrast, no letters to Vincent survive, while Vincent's one known letter to Lautrec (of 18 March 1888 from Arles) is lost. And Lautrec only refers to Vincent once in his surviving correspondence between 1886 and 1890: he visited Van Gogh's studio in early January 1888 – that is, a few weeks before Vincent left Paris for Arles (ibid., no. 158). Yet the two were close: Vincent exchanged his view from the rue Lepic (F 341a) with Lautrec's pastel portrait of himself (now in the Van Gogh Museum). And during his stay in Provence, Vincent was kept informed by Theo of Lautrec's progress. In January 1890, it was Lautrec who challenged the Belgian painter Charles de Groux (1867-1930) to a duel because of his antagonistic remarks on Vincent's paintings then being shown at Les XX in Brussels. The two artists last met at Theo's apartment, Cité Pigalle, on 6 July 1890, three weeks before Vincent shot himself. Toulouse-Lautrec stayed for lunch and made many jokes with Vincent about a pallbearer they had met on the stairs, Jo remembered in 1914. And on his return to Auvers, Vincent wrote: 'Lautrec's picture, portrait of a musician, is amazing, I saw it with emotion' (LT 649). The painting is the *Portrait of Mlle Dihau au piano* (Musée d'Albi).

Jeudi 31 Juillet,

Mon cher Van-gogh,

je n'ai reçu que hier Mercredi la triste nouvelle que votre lettre m'annonçait. Comme je vous l'avais dit, je suis parti pour la campagne Lundi soir. Vous m'excuserez donc de ne pas avoir assister au service de votre frère, et je vous prie de croire que je participe à tout le chagrin que vous devez éprouver.

en attendant je vous serre la main

Guillaumin

à Breuillet
par St-Chéron
Seine & Oise

Thursday 31 July,

My dear Van-gogh

I only received your letter with its sad news on Wednesday, yesterday, that is. As I told you, I left for the country on Monday evening.[1] You will excuse me then for not having been present at your brother's funeral service, and I would like you to know that my thoughts are with you in all the grief you must be feeling.

in the meantime I send you my heartfelt regards

Guillaumin

Breuillet[2]
near St-Chéron
Seine & Oise

Jean-Baptiste Armand Guillaumin to Theo, Thursday 31 July 1890.
Inv. no. b 1274 V/1962

1. Van Gogh met Armand Guillaumin (1841-1927) in Paris in the autumn of 1887 - at much the same time that he met Gauguin. According to Coquiot (*Vincent van Gogh*, Paris 1923, p. 136), it was the art dealer Arsène Portier (1841-1902) who took Guillaumin to the Van Gogh's apartment at 54 rue Lepic, where he saw Vincent at work on his *Romans Parisiens* (F 359). And Vincent visited Guillaumin's studio at 13 quai d'Anjou on the Ile Saint-Louis, formerly Daubigny's studio. He not only mentioned such a visit to Bernard (B 1), but also recalled in Arles the effect of so many paintings reflecting Guillaumin's productivity.
It was probably Vincent's prompting that pushed Theo into acquiring works by Guilaumin for his own collection. Two paintings (cat. Amsterdam 1987, nos. 1.267-268) and one pastel (ibid., no. 2.708) were bought. In addition, Theo exhibited Guillaumin's paintings at Boussod Valadon from as early as December 1887, as well as buying three of them for the gallery. On his last visit to Paris on Sunday 6 July, Vincent had hoped to meet Guillaumin once again, but was forced to leave before his friend arrived (LT 649). Guillaumin admired Vincent's paintings, especially the ten exhibited at the Salon des Indépendants in spring 1890. Theo wrote on 5 June (T 36) 'Guillaumin has placed at your disposal a magnificent picture which he had at Tanguy's, a Sunset'. But the proposed exchange evidently did not take place.

2. Guillaumin left for Breuillet, a small hamlet near Saint-Chéron, some 50 kilometers south-west of Paris, en route to Chartres, on Monday 28 July. He often painted there between 1889 and 1893.

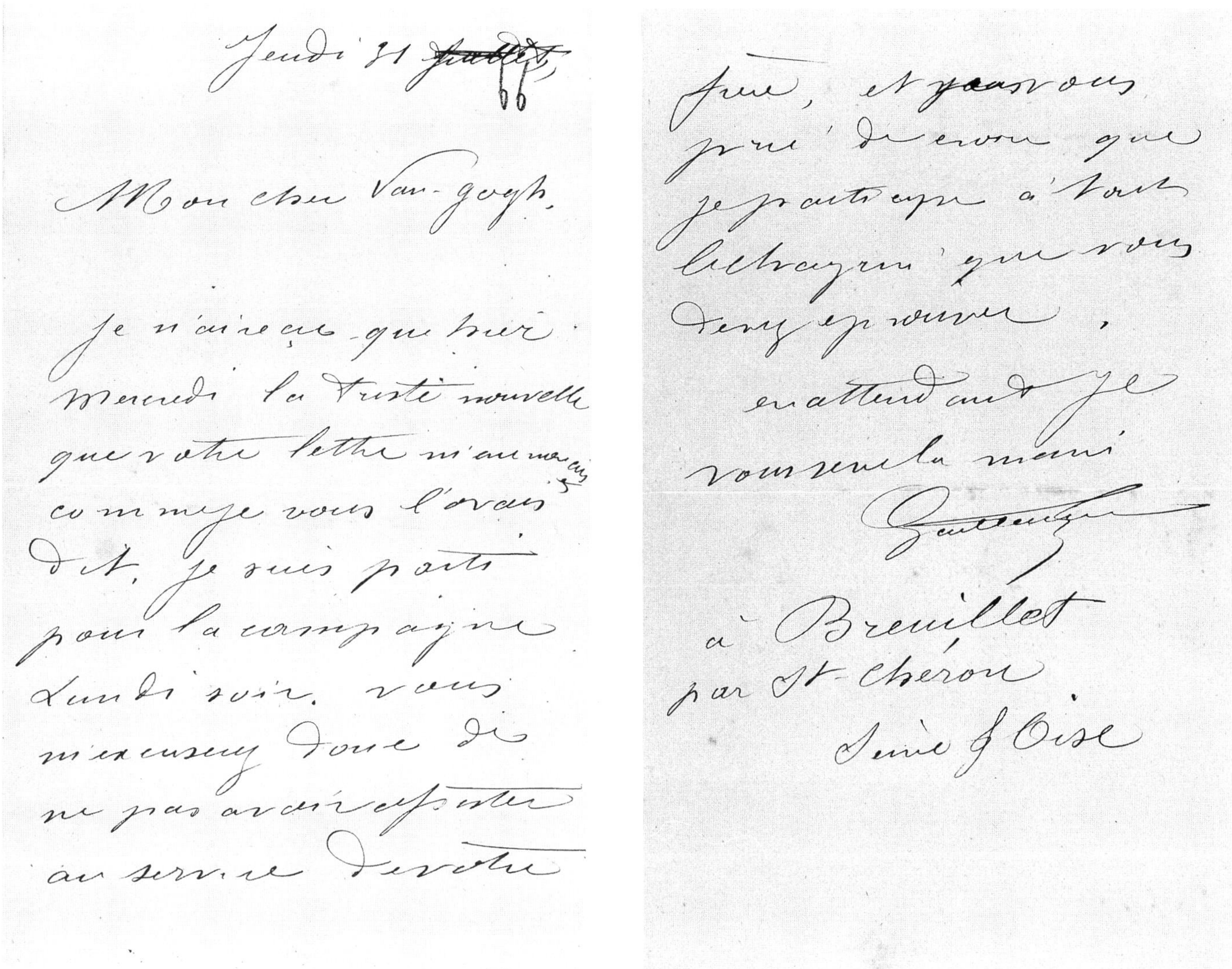
Jeudi 31 ~~juillet~~ 66

Mon cher Van-Gogh.

Je n'ai reçu que hier mercredi la triste nouvelle que votre lettre m'annonçait comme je vous l'avais dit, je suis parti pour la campagne Lundi soir. vous m'excusez donc de ne pas avoir assisté au service de votre frère, et je vous prie de croire que je partage à toute la douleur que vous devez éprouver.

en attendant je vous serre la main

Guillaumin

à Breuillet
par St-Chéron
Seine & Oise

FRENCH 4

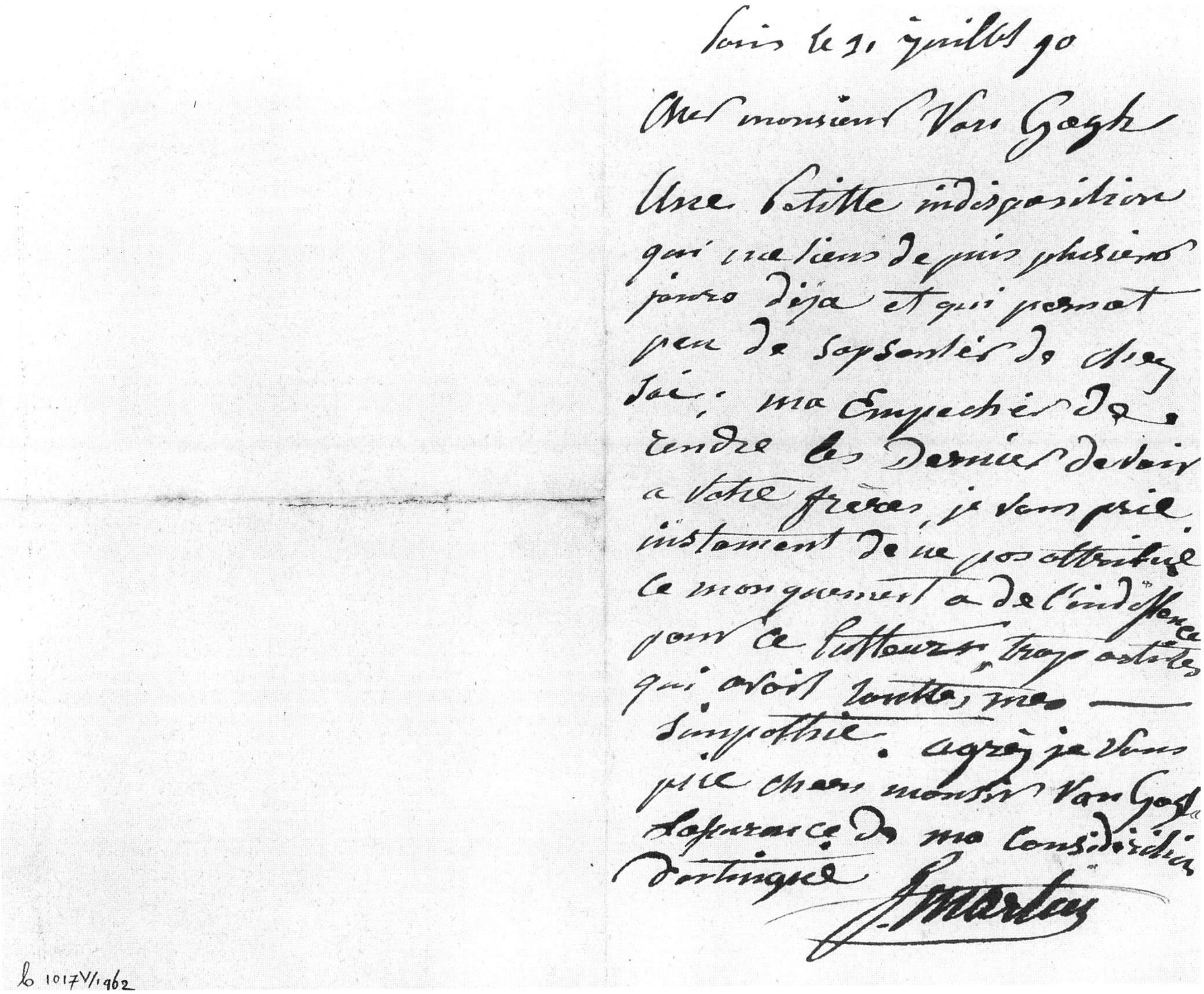

Paris le 31 juillet 90

Cher monsieur Van Gogh

Une petitte indisposition qui me tiens depuis plusieurs jours déja et qui permet peu de sopsentir de chez moi ; ma empechér de rendre les dernier devoir a votre frères, je vous prie instament de ne pas attribué ce manquement a de l'indifference pour ce peintre, trop artiste qui avoit toutes mes simpathie. agréé je vous prie cher monsieur Van Gogh l'assurance de ma considération distinguée

J Martin

b 1017V/1962

FRENCH 5

Paris le 31 juillet 90

Cher monsieur Van Gogh

Une pettite indisposition qui me tiens depuis plusieurs jours déja et qui permet peu de sapsentér de chez soi ma Empecher de rendre les Dernier devoir a votre frères, je vous prie instament de ne pas attribué ce manquement a de l'indifference pour ce lutteur trop artistes qui avait toutes mes simpathie. Agrèz je vous prie cher monsieur Van Gogh lassurance de ma considération distingué

P. Martin

Paris 31 july 90

Dear monsieur Van Gogh,

A slight indisposition which I have had for several days now and which hardly allows me to leave the house has prevented me from paying my last respects to your brother, I beg you not to attribute my absence to any lack of feeling towards this brave man who was all too much an artist and for whom I felt a great affection.[1] I am, dear monsieur Van Gogh, yours very truly

P. Martin

Pierre-Firmin Martin to Theo, Thursday 31 July 1890.
Inv. no. b 1017 v/1962

1. Pierre-Firmin Martin (1817-1891) was an important art dealer in Paris from the 1850s onwards. He handled the works of Boudin, Corot, Diaz, Jongkind and Cals (who painted his portrait in 1878, see exhib. cat. Paris 1988, p. 341); later, his artists included Pissarro, Guillaumin, Degas, Sisley and Vignon, and his name figures among the lenders to the Impressionist exhibitions of 1874, 1876 and 1880. Among his distinguished clients were Comte Doria (see French 12) and Henri Rouart (see French 16).

Vincent met him in Paris, probably as early as 1886. He recalled from Arles exhibiting canvases at three Parisian dealers, one of whom was Martin. And in 1887 he painted a portrait of Martin's niece, Léonie Rosie Davy (F 369), long known as *Woman by a cradle* (now in the Van Gogh Museum). After Martin's death, she continued to deal in a small way.

31 juillet 90

Cher Monsieur,

Bien que je n'eusse pas l'honneur de connaître personnellement Vincent, cette nouvelle très triste m'a fait beaucoup beaucoup de peine, à cause de vous et à cause du très haut et neuf talent de votre frère.

Veuillez, cher Monsieur van Gogh, agréer mes hommages les plus sympathiques

féliporph.fenéon

31 july 90

Dear Sir,

Although I did not have the honour of knowing Vincent personally,[1] this very sad news has caused me profound sadness, both for your sake[2] and because of your brother's exceptionally original talent.[3]

Dear Monsieur van Gogh, please accept my heartfelt sympathy

féliporph.fenéon[4]

Félix Fénéon to Theo, Thursday 31 July 1890.
Inv. no. b 1021 V/1962
Published in exhib. cat. Paris 1988, p. 262, omitting 'très' before 'triste' and misreading the signature as 'Feliorph Fénéon'. Translated into English by J. Halperin, *Félix Fénéon; Aesthete and Anarchist in Fin-de-Siècle Paris*, New Haven & London, 1988, pp. 208, 391, note 8.

1. Louis-Félix-Jule-Alexandre Fénéon (1861-1944), generally known as Félix or F.F, was an early friend and protagonist of the Neo-Impressionist painters and Symbolist poets. He was painted and drawn by many artists, notably Signac (1890), Toulouse-Lautrec, Vallotton, and Van Dongen. However, his testimony that he never knew Vincent removes any possibility that he is to be seen next to Vincent in Lucien Pissarro's double-portrait drawing (see K.T. Parker, 'Van Gogh and Fénéon: a Conversation Piece', in: *Festschrift Friedrich Winkler*, Berlin 1959, pp. 351-356; and exhib. cat. Paris 1988, no. 100, p. 262, where the identification was also rejected).

2. Fénéon must have met Theo by December 1887, when he wrote his first of several monthly exhibition notices in the *Revue Indépendante*, where he often described works on show at the Van Gogh gallery (how that must have angered Boussod and Valadon!). Without his precious references, we should never know that Theo showed works of Schuffenecker and Zandomeneghi (see French 9) as well as Chéret's posters. Yet, this letter of condolence is Fénéon's only (surviving) letter to Theo.

3. Fénéon was one of the few critics to notice Vincent's two paintings at the 5th Salon des Indépendants (3 September-4 October 1889). See FF Oeuvres, p. 168, and Halperin, op.cit., p. 208.

4. Read as Féliorph Fénéon in exhib. cat. Paris 1988, p. 262, the signature is more likely to be Féliporph. Fénéon. The allusion seems to be to Orpheus, the paragon of grief, as Halperin has suggested (op.cit., p. 208). See also Halperin, p. 155 for Fénéon's fondness for facetious signatures.

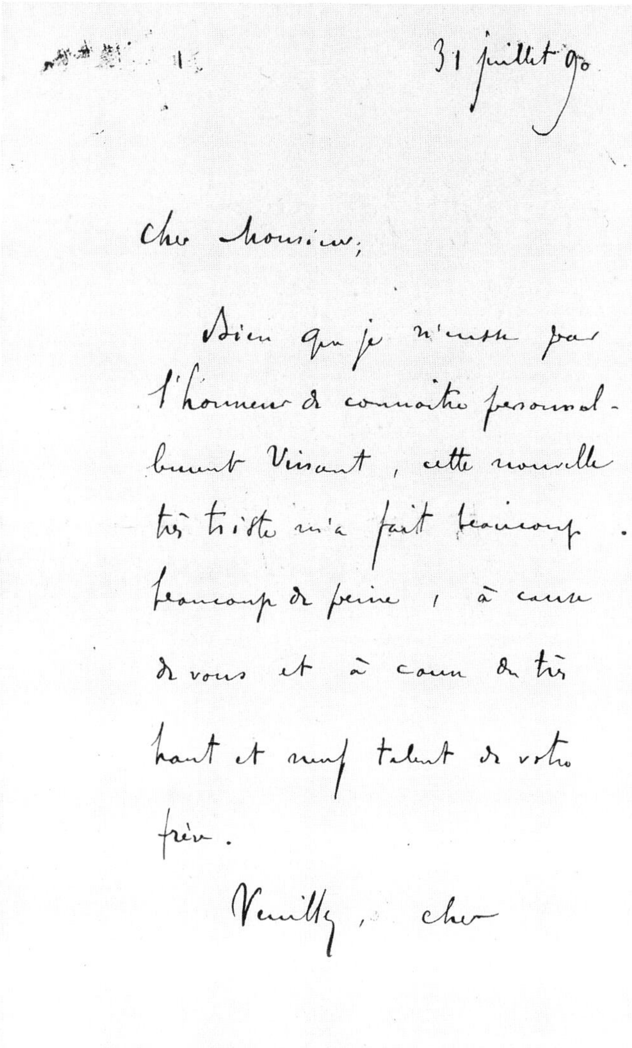

31 juillet 90

Cher Monsieur,

Bien que je n'eusse pas l'honneur de connaître personnellement Vincent, cette nouvelle très triste m'a fait beaucoup, beaucoup de peine, à cause de vous et à cause du très haut et neuf talent de votre frère.

Veuillez, cher

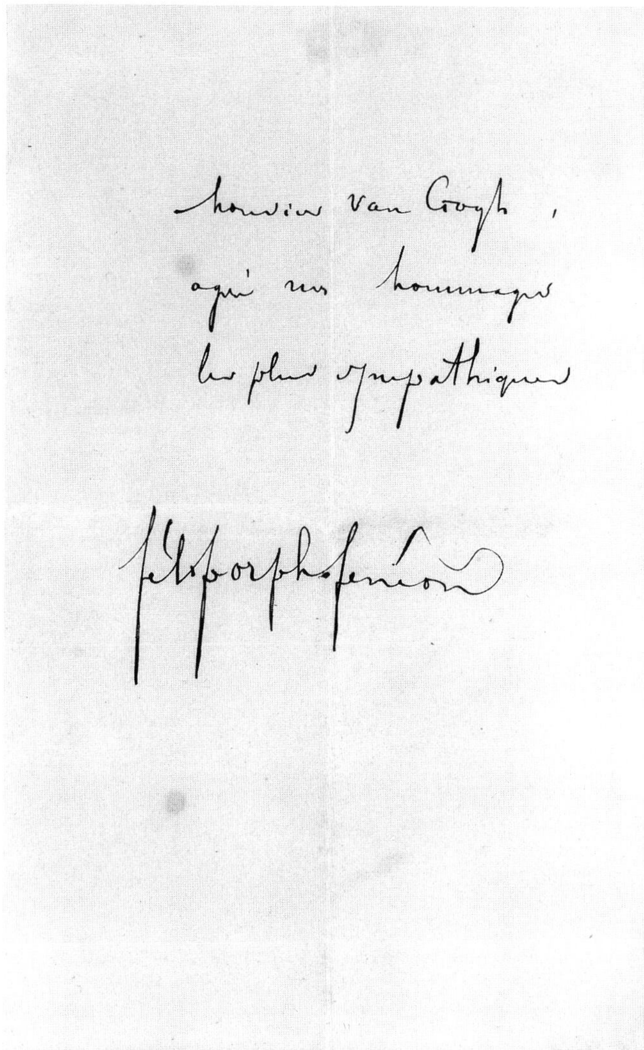

Monsieur van Gogh, agréer mes hommages les plus sympathiques

félixfénéon

FRENCH 6

Cher Monsieur —

J'apprends à l'instant, par un billet de faire-part qu'on me fait suivre ici, l'affreux et si inattendu malheur qui vient de vous frapper. Je tiens à vous témoigner combien profondément je m'associe à votre douleur.

Je n'ai point besoin de vous dire — vous le savez, n'est-ce pas? — en quelle haute estime artistique je tenais Celui que vous pleurez aujourd'hui. Je n'ajouterai donc qu'un mot: Des hommes tels que lui ne meurent point tout entiers. Il laisse une oeuvre qui est une partie de lui-même et qui, un jour, nous en sommes sûrs, vous et moi, fera revivre son nom et pour éternellement. Faible consolation, sans doute, pour votre affection de frère, mais consolation pourtant et dont beaucoup sont privés devant cet irréparable.

Veuillez agréer, Cher Monsieur, l'expression de mes plus cordiales condoléances

1r Août 1890 G Albert Aurier

Châteauroux (Indre) rue du pressoir 19

b 1277 V/1962

FRENCH 7

Cher Monsieur –

J'apprends à l'instant, par un billet de faire-part qu'on me fait suivre ici, l'affreux et si inattendu malheur qui vient de vous frapper. Je tiens à vous témoigner combien profondément je m'associe à votre douleur.

Je n'ai point besoin de vous dire – vous le savez, n'est-ce pas? – en quelle haute estime artistique je tenais celui que vous pleurez aujourd'hui. Je n'ajouterai donc qu'un mot: Des hommes tels que lui ne meurent point tout entiers. Il laisse une oeuvre qui est une partie de lui-même et qui, un jour, nous en sommes surs, vous et moi, fera revivre son nom et pour éternellement. Faible consolation, sans doute, pour votre affection de frère, mais consolation pourtant, et dont beaucoup sont privés devant cet irréparable

Veuillez agréer, Cher Monsieur, l'expression de mes plus cordiales condoléances

1: Aout 1890 *G Albert Aurier*

Châteauroux (Indre) rue du pressoir 19

Dear Sir –

I have just learnt from a bereavement notice that was forwarded to me here of the terrible and quite unexpected calamity that has just struck you.[1] I want to tell you how deeply I feel for you in your grief.

I do not need to tell you – you must be aware of it – how great an admiration I felt for the artistic qualities of the man whom you are mourning today.[2] I will therefore only add one word: men like him do not die entirely. He leaves behind a body of work which is a part of himself and which, one day, you and I can be sure, will make his name live again and for eternity. This will no doubt be poor consolation for you who felt a brother's love for him but it is consolation all the same, and something that many people faced with the irreparable [fact of death] do not have.

Please accept, dear Sir, my heartfelt condolences[3]

1: August 1890 G Albert Aurier

Châteauroux (Indre) rue du pressoir 19

Gustave-Albert Aurier to Theo, Friday 1 August 1890.
Inv. no. b 1277 V/1962
First published in the 1952-1953 centenary edition of the Letters, as T 54, p. 316.

1. Gustave-Albert Aurier (1865-1892), poet, novelist, editor (of the short-lived *Le Moderniste*, April-September, 1889) and art critic, has the distinction of having written the only long article on Vincent to have been published during the artist's lifetime. This was 'Les Isolés, Vincent van Gogh' that appeared in the first number of the *Mercure de France* in January 1890, pp. 24-29. It became a point of reference and source of quotation in the writings of other critics in the 1890s. Aurier died at the age of 27: his article was reprinted (with some minor modifications) in his *Oeuvres posthumes*, Paris 1893, pp. 257-268. Aurier – like many others – had left Paris in late July 1890, spending the month of August in his birthplace, Châteauroux, some 280 kilometres south of Paris. As well as receiving Theo's announcement card of Vincent's death, he must have received Bernard's letter of 31 July (see Prologue 3) on the same day that he sent his condolences to Theo.

2. A reference to his article in the *Mercure de France*. Aurier probably met Vincent in Paris between 17 and 19 May, rather than on 6 July, as Jo suggested. The evidence is conflicting. According to Aurier's friend, Julien Leclercq (1865-1901), who wrote the introduction to the catalogue of Van Gogh's exhibition at Bernheim-Jeune in March 1901: 'It was at Aurier's that I met Vincent for a moment'.

3. Theo responded to Aurier's letter on 27 August 1890 (see T 55). Translated in Stein 1986, p. 234.

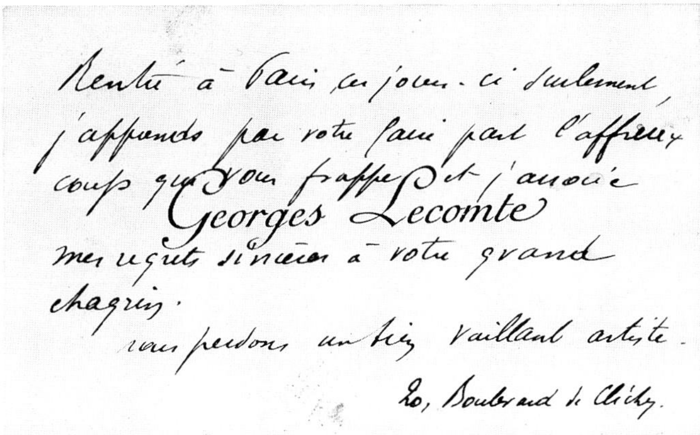

FRENCH 8

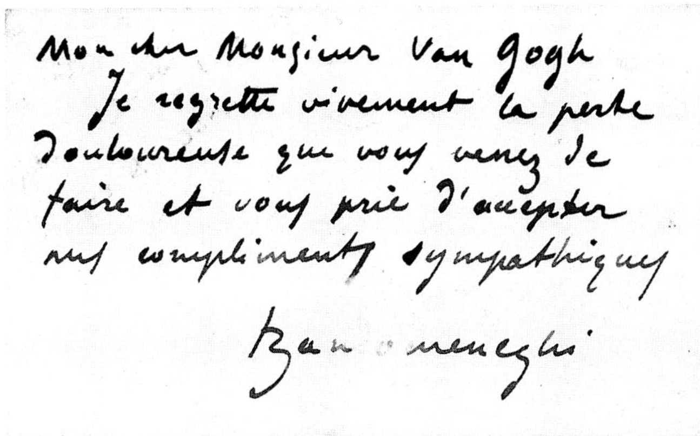

FRENCH 9

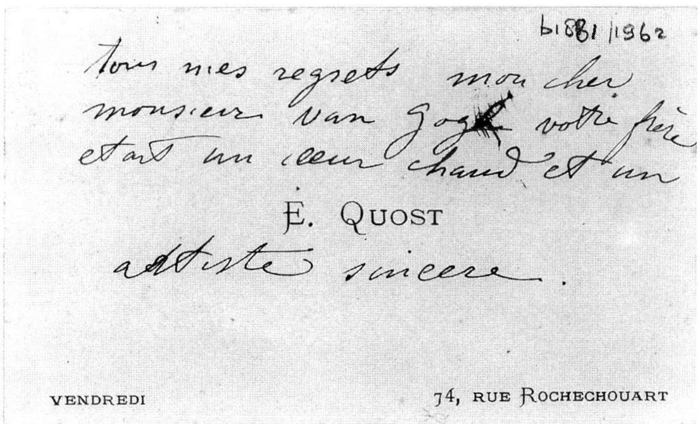

b1881/1962
Tous mes regrets mon cher
monsieur Van Gogh votre frère
était un cœur chaud et un
E. Quost
artiste sincère.
VENDREDI
74, RUE ROCHECHOUART

FRENCH 10

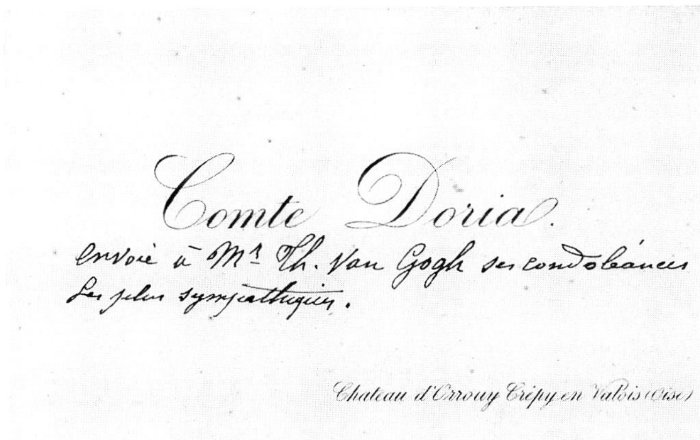

Comte Doria.
Envoie à Mr Th. Van Gogh ses condoléances
les plus sympathiques.
Chateau d'Orrouy Crépy en Valois (Oise)

FRENCH 12

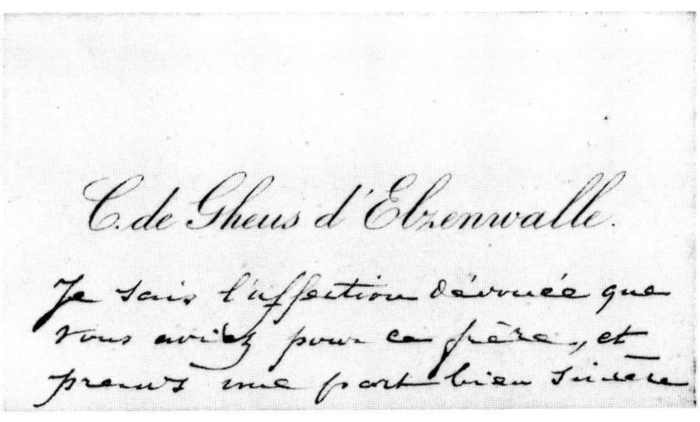

C. de Gheus d'Elzenwalle.
Je sais l'affection dévouée que
vous aviez pour ce frère, et
prends une part bien sincère

FRENCH 11

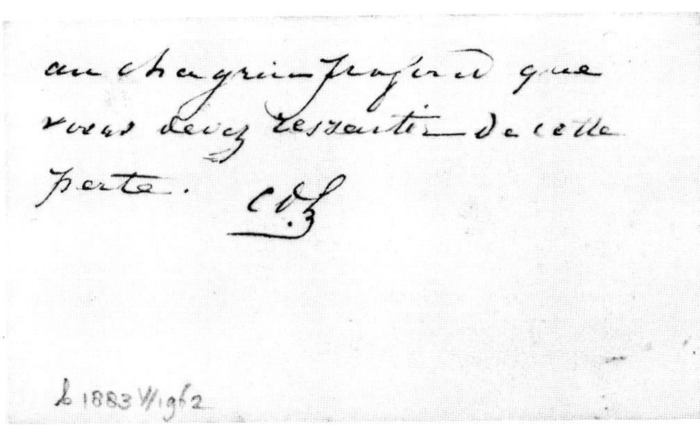

FRENCH 11

Georges Lecomte

Rentré à Paris ces jours-ci seulement, j'apprends par votre faire part l'affreux coup qui vous frappe et j'associe mes regrets sincères à votre grand chagrin.

nous perdons un bien vaillant artiste.

20, Boulevard de Clichy.

Georges Lecomte

I have only just returned to Paris to learn from your bereavement notice of the frightful blow that has struck you, and I want to tell you how sad I feel for you in your profound grief.[1]

we have lost a very courageous artist.[2]

20, Boulevard de Clichy.

Georges-Charles Lecomte to Theo, circa Friday 1 August 1890.
Inv. no. b 1880 V/1962
Visiting card with the name Georges Lecomte printed on it. First published (illustrated) in exhib. cat. Paris 1988, p. 362, fig. 154.

1. Georges-Charles Lecomte (1867-1958) was the third art critic to write a note of condolence to Theo. He was a close friend of Fénéon's, being part of the Symbolist circle that hovered, in literary terms, between the periodicals *La Revue Indépendante, La Cravache*, and *Art et Critique*. In particular, Lecomte edited *La Cravache* after his return from his year's military service in November 1889. He was then living at 54 rue Blanche, but shortly afterwards Lecomte moved to 20 Boulevard de Clichy, his address in Theo's address book (Pabst no. 154) and on the name-card he used as his condolence letter. From his windows he overlooked the studio of Puvis de Chavannes (1824-1898).

2. If Fénéon was apparently silent on the 6th exhibition of the Indépendants (20 March-27 April 1890), his friend Lecomte did review it. Writing in *Art et Critique* of 29 March 1890, p. 203, he noted: 'Monsieur Vincent van Gogh's ferocious impasto and his exclusive use of colours that harmonize easily result in powerful effects: the violet background of *Cypresses* and the symphony of green in a landscape make a vivid impression'. Lecomte is referring to F 613 and almost certainly F 737 (numbers 823 and 839 in the 1890 exhibition).

Mon cher Monsieur Van Gogh

Je regrette vivement la perte douloureuse que vous venez de faire et vous prie d'accepter mes compliments sympathiques

FZandomeneghi

My dear Monsieur Van Gogh

I deeply regret the distressing loss that you have just experienced, and beg you to accept my heartfelt condolences[1]

FZandomeneghi

Federico Zandomeneghi to Theo, circa Friday 1 Augustus 1890.
Inv. no. b 1879 V/1962
Visiting card with the name Federico Zandomeneghi printed on the reverse.

1. The Italian artist, Federico Zandomeneghi (1841-1917) is never mentioned by Van Gogh in his letters. Yet it seems possible that the two artists met, since Zandomeneghi was a friend of Toulouse-Lautrec, and had a studio in the same building at 7 rue Tourlaque, very close to the Van Gogh's apartment at 54 rue Lepic. But Theo certainly knew Zandomeneghi. Another name-card, probably dating from 1888, attests to Theo's handling of his pictures (exhib. cat. Paris 1988, p. 369). On two occasions in 1888, Fénéon referred to works by Zandomeneghi being shown at Theo's gallery at 19 Boulevard Montmartre in his *Calendrier* of April and again of September (FF Oeuvres, pp. 111 and 119), finding them 'vulgar'. Theo's business relationship with Zandomeneghi was by no means as close and continuous as that between him and Degas, or Monet, or Pissarro. And he did not acquire any examples of the Venetian artist's work for his own collection.

E. Quost

Tous mes regrets mon cher monsieur van Gogh votre frère etait un coeur chaud et un artiste sincere.

Vendredi *74, rue Rochechouart*

E. Quost

All my regrets my dear monsieur van Gogh your brother had a warm heart and was a sincere artist.[1]

Friday 74, rue Rochechouart

Ernest Quost to Theo, circa Friday 1 August 1890.
Inv. no. b 1881 V/1962
Visiting card with the name, day and address printed on it.

1. The artist Ernest Quost (1844-1931) was greatly admired by Vincent, who met him in Paris, probably in the summer of 1886. Quost had a flower garden in Montmartre, from where Vincent must often have obtained blooms for the long series of flower still lifes he painted in Paris. Quost's own flower still lifes were often alluded to by Vincent. In particular, Vincent saw Quost as the painter of 'magnificent and perfect hollyhocks' in his famous letter to Aurier of February 1890 (LT 626a). Quost figures in Theo's address book at the same address from where he sent his brief note of condolence (Pabst no. 188). While Quost was not handled by Boussod Valadon, Theo did acquire one of his drawings for his own collection (cat. Amsterdam 1987, no. 2.750).

FRENCH 11

C. de Gheus d'Elzenwalle to Theo

C. de Gheus d'Elzenwalle.

Je sais l'affection dévouée que vous aviez pour ce frère, et prends une part bien sincère au chagrin profond que vous deviez ressentir de cette perte.

C d G

C. de Gheus d'Elzenwalle.

I know how much devotion and affection you had for your brother, and I send you my sincere condolences in the deep grief you must be feeling for his loss.[1]

C d G

C. de Gheus d'Elzenwalle to Theo, circa Friday 1 August 1890.
Inv. no. b 1883 V/1962
Visiting card with the name printed. Published in part (illustrated one side of name card only) in exhib. cat. Paris 1988, p. 357, no. 81.

1. This mysterious figure, with a Huysmanesque name, lived at 56 rue de Florence in the 19th arrondissement. Theo listed him under 'G' in his address book as 'Gheus (C. de)' (Pabst no. 81); and, indeed, on his note of condolence, the signature is made of the initials C d G. He was clearly more than a passing acquaintance to Theo, even though it seems unlikely that he ever met Vincent.

Comte Doria.
envoie à Mr Th. Van Gogh ses condoléances les plus sympathiques.

Château d'Orrouy Crépy en Valois (Oise)

Comte Doria.
sends Mr Th. van Gogh his heartfelt condolences.[1]

Château d'Orrouy Crépy en Valois (Oise)

Comte Armand Doria to Theo, circa Friday 1 August 1890.
Inv. no. b 1884 V/1962
Visiting card with the name and address printed. Published (illustrated) in exhib. cat. Paris 1988, p. 357, no. 68.

1. Comte Armand Doria (1824-1896) was descended from the Genoese family immortalized by Van Dyck in the early 17th century. He became one of the most assiduous and far-seeing collectors of nineteenth century French art, with a decided propensity for the masters of romantism, realism, naturalism, and impressionism. Many paintings were acquired from Père Martin (see French 5). Comte Doria must have visited the gallery of Boussod Valadon and admired Theo's courage, taste and flair. As for Vincent, he referred to Comte Doria once only, in connection with the series of painted 'transpositions' he was doing of Millet. Writing to Theo in November 1889 (LT 611), he likened his special collection of copies after Millet to 'the works of Prévost who copied the Goyas and Velasquezes for M. Doria'. Whether Comte Doria ever saw works by Vincent remains conjectural. But his small name-card, with its brief message, speaks a great deal for Theo's moral standing among important French collectors.

Mon Cher Van Gogh

Je n'ai pu à mon très grand regret aller accompagner votre frère à sa dernière demeure car, au moment de partir, il m'est arrivé une lettre et une visite qui m'ont forcé de rester chez moi.

Hier, je suis allé à Paris, et j'espérais, de vive-voix, vous dire la part que je prends à votre douleur que je sais très grande, et qui doit aussi bien toucher votre dame, mais le temps m'a absolument manqué, C'est pourquoi vous ne vous étonnerez pas de recevoir seulement aujourd'hui cette triste missive.

Bien sympathiquement et à bientot j'espère, et courage.

V^or Vignon

My dear Van Gogh

To my great regret, I was not able to accompany your brother to his last resting place, for just as I was leaving, a letter and a visitor arrived that obliged me to stay at home.[1]

I went to Paris yesterday, and I was hoping to be able to tell you in person how much I feel for you in your grief which I am sure is very great, and which must also greatly affect your wife, but I had no time at all to do so. You will, I hope, then appreciate that it is only today that you will receive this letter of condolence.

Please accept my heartfelt sympathy, I hope to see you soon, and I wish you courage.

V^or Vignon

Victor Alfred Paul Vignon to Theo, circa Saturday 2 Augustus 1890.
Inv. no. b 1023 V/1962

1. Victor Alfred Paul Vignon (1847-1909) exhibited with the Impressionists at their last four exhibitions of 1880, 1881, 1882 and 1886. His work was also bought by the art dealer 'Père' Martin (see French 5). That Theo knew him by 1884 is confirmed by a letter of 26 July 1884 from Vignon. And three of his landscape paintings were acquired by Theo for his own collection (cat. Amsterdam 1987, nos. 1.337-339).
Vincent possibly met him during his two-year stay in Paris, since he proposed sharing a studio with Vignon on his return to the North from Saint-Rémy (LT 605). Theo did not respond to this suggestion and the possibility never materialized. It seems unlikely that they met during Vincent's last weeks in Paris and Auvers-sur-Oise.

Mon Cher Van Gogh

Je n'ai pu à mon très grand regret aller accompagner votre frère à sa dernière demeure, car, au moment de partir, il m'est arrivé une lettre et une visite qui m'ont forcé de rester chez moi.

Hier, je suis allé à Paris, et j'espérais; de vive. voix, vous dire la part que je prends à votre douleur que ~~jai sais~~ très grande, et qui doit aussi bien toucher votre dame, mais le temps m'a absolument manqué, C'est pourquoi vous ne vous étonnerez pas de recevoir seulement aujourd'hui cette triste missive.

Bien Sympathiquement et à bientôt j'espère, et Courage.

V. Vignon

FRENCH 13

Lagny août 1890

Cher Monsieur Van gogh,

Je reçois la triste nouvelle du malheur qui vient de vous affliger, et croyez bien que je prends sincèrement part à votre douleur.

Votre frère vient de mourrir dans toute la force de la jeunesse, je n'ai pas eu le plaisir de le connaître personnellement quoique j'en eusse le plus grand désir, une vive sympathie m'attirait vers lui.

J'allais souvent chez ce bon Mr Tanguy spécialement pour voir ses travaux, peu de peintres peut-être avaient su comprendre et deviner quelle véritable âme d'artiste fut votre frère. Ne me trouvant pas en situation d'acheter, j'avais même dit à Mr Tanguy qu'il voulut bien demander à ce peintre que j'aimais tant sans le connaître, s'il consentirait à échanger un tableau contre un des miens. Si mon désir ne vous paraissait pas trop indiscret, j'oserais vous renouveler cette demande. En art, on a souvent ainsi des amis inconnus, ce sont aussi les plus sincères, car aucun intérêt ne commande leur sympathie faite exclusivement d'attirance, d'affinités intellectuelles.

Enfin, Monsieur, si je suis indiscret, vous me pardonnerez et je n'en garderai pas moins un pieux souvenir de Vincent Van gogh.

Veuillez agréer, cher Monsieur, avec mes sincères condoléances, mes salutations empressées,

Leo Gausson

Leo Gausson
3 rue St Paul. Lagny s/marne.

Lagny august 1890

Dear Monsieur Van gogh,

I received the sad news of the calamity you have just suffered, and believe me I sincerely share in your grief.[1]

Your brother died in the full power of his youth, I had not the pleasure of having made his acquaintance personally though I very much wanted to do so, I felt drawn to him by a great sense of affinity.

I often used to visit Mr Tanguy's especially to see his works, few artists perhaps were able to guess or appreciate what a true artist your brother was. Not being in a situation where I could afford to buy any of his works, I even suggested to Mr Tanguy that he should ask this painter whom I loved without knowing him, whether he would agree to exchange a picture of his for one of mine.[2] If you do not think that my request is too indiscreet, I would be so bold as to make it again. In art, one often has friends whom one does not know, who are also the most sincere, for no selfish interest governs their affection which is made up exclusively of intellectual attractions and affinities.[3]

Well, Sir, if I am indiscreet, I am sure that you will excuse me, and I will continue to feel the same devotion to the memory of Vincent Van gogh.

Dear Sir, please accept my sincere condolences, yours truly,

Leo Gausson

Leo Gausson
3 rue St Paul. Lagny s/Marne.

Louis-Léon Gausson to Theo, circa Saturday 2 August 1890.
Inv. no. b 1275 v/1962
Published (illustrated) in exhib. cat. *Neo-impressionisten*, Amsterdam (Rijksmuseum Vincent van Gogh) 1988, p. 76. Partly published by Lili Jampoller, 'Theo and Vincent as art collectors', cat. Amsterdam 1987, pp. 34 and note 25 on p. 88.

1. Louis-Léon Gausson (1860-1944), known as Léo, was born at Lagny-sur-Marne, some 40 kilometres east of Paris, where he continued to live and work during his twenty years as an artist. By 1887, he had become a neo-impressionist, exhibiting paintings at the Salon des Indépendants, where Vincent showed in 1888, 1889 and 1890.

2. Already by early June 1890, he had clearly spoken to Theo about his admiration. 'Gausson will make an exchange with you, anything you would like to have from him against anything you would like to give him'. (T 36). The exchange was presumably effected in August, when Gausson's painting, *The Church of Bussy-Saint-Georges* (cat. Amsterdam 1987, 1.55) was exchanged against an unidentified and probably lost painting by Vincent.

3. Fénéon, perceptive as ever, noted the influence of Vincent on Gausson's painting as early as 1891, when reviewing the Salon des Indépendants: 'Artistes indépendants: stenographié par Willy', in *Le Chat Noir* of 21 March 1891, (FF Oeuvres, p. 182).

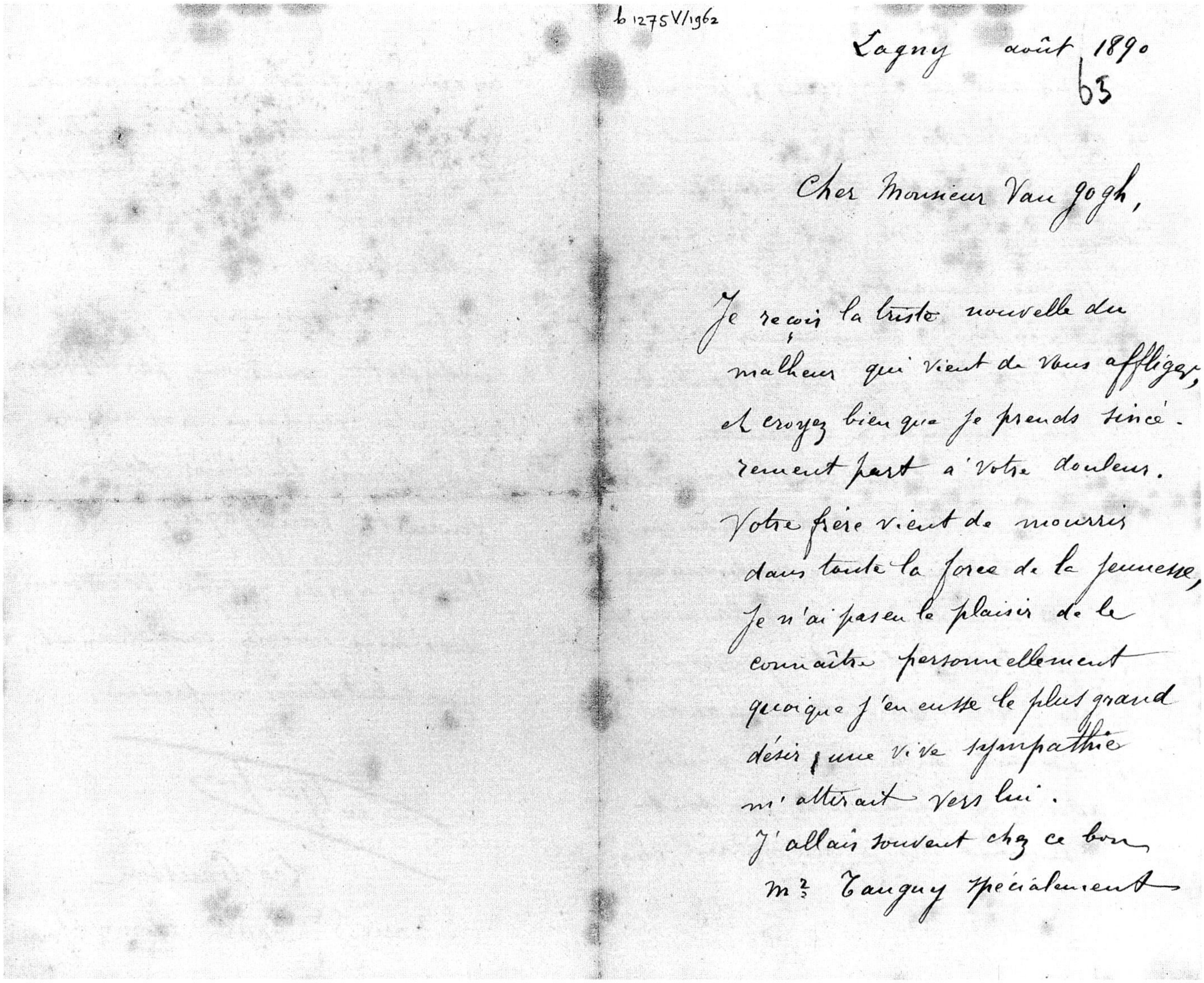
b 1275 V/1962

Lagny août 1890
63

Cher Monsieur Van Gogh,

Je reçois la triste nouvelle du
malheur qui vient de vous affliger,
et croyez bien que je prends sincèrement part à votre douleur.
Votre frère vient de mourir
dans toute la force de la jeunesse,
je n'ai pas eu le plaisir de le
connaître personnellement
quoique j'en eusse le plus grand
désir, une vive sympathie
m'attirait vers lui.
J'allais souvent chez ce bon
Mr Tanguy spécialement

FRENCH 14

pour voir ses travaux, peu
de peintres peut-être avaient
su comprendre et deviner quelle
véritable âme d'artiste fut votre frère.
Ne me trouvant pas en situation
d'acheter, j'avais même dit
à Mr. Tanguy qu'il voulut
bien demander à ce peintre que
j'aimais tant sans le connaître,
s'il consentirait à échanger
un tableau contre un des miens.
Si mon désir ne vous paraissait
pas trop indiscret, j'oserais
vous renouveler cette demande.
En art, on a souvent ainsi
des amis inconnus, ce sont
~~souvent~~ aussi les plus sincères, car
aucun intérêt ne commande
leur sympathie faite exclusivement
d'attirances, d'affinités
intellectuelles.
Enfin, Monsieur, si je suis
indiscret, vous me pardonnerez
et je n'en garderai pas moins
un pieux souvenir de
Vincent Van Gogh.
Veuillez agréer, cher Monsieur,
avec mes sincères condoléances,
mes salutations empressées.

Leo Gausson

Leo Gausson
3 rue Ste Paul. Lagny S/marne

FRENCH 14

Mon cher Van Gogh

Nous venons de recevoir la
triste nouvelle qui nous afflige.
En cette circonstance je ne
veux pas vous faire des phrases
de condoléance. Vous savez
qu'il était pour moi un
ami sincère; et qu'il était
un <u>artiste</u> chose rare à notre
époque. Vous continuerez à le voir
en ses oeuvres. Comme Vincent
le disait souvent – (La pierre
périra la parole restera –
Et pour moi je le verrai
mes yeux et mon coeur dans
ses oeuvres –
Cordialement à vous
P Gauguin

FRENCH 15

Mon cher Van Gogh

Nous venons de recevoir la triste nouvelle qui nous afflige.

En cette circonstance je ne veux pas vous faire des phrases de condoléance – vous savez qu'il était pour moi un ami sincère; et qu'il était un artiste *chose rare à notre époque. Vous continuerez à les voir en ses oeuvres. Comme Vincent le disait souvent – (La pierre périra, la parole restera.*

Et pour moi je le verrai mes yeux et mon coeur dans ses oeuvres.

Cordialement tav
P Gauguin

My dear Van Gogh

We have just received your sad news which greatly distresses us.[1]

In these circumstances, I don't want to write the usual phrases of condolence – you know that for me he was a sincere friend; and that he was an *artist* a rare thing in our epoch. You will continue to see him in his works. As Vincent used often to say – Stone will perish, the word will remain.[2]

As for me, I shall see him with my eyes and with my heart in his works.

Cordially, ever yours
P Gauguin

Paul Gauguin to Theo, circa Saturday 2 August 1890.
Inv. no. b 1481 V/1962
First published, in an English translation, by John Rewald, *Post-Impressionism. From Van Gogh to Gauguin*, New York 1956, p. 412; first published fully in French in Cooper 1983, no. 26; translated in Stein 1986, p. 231.

1. The relations between Eugène-Henri-Paul Gauguin (1848-1903) and Van Gogh are too well-known to need repeating here. Suffice it to say that Gauguin was living in Le Pouldu, Brittany, with the Dutch artist Meijer de Haan (see Dutch 1), when Theo's announcement of Vincent's death arrived. They answered together, Gauguin in French on one side of the sheet, De Haan in Dutch on the other.

2. Vincent's phrase was surely used by him during Gauguin's two month stay in Arles in October-December 1888. Gauguin used it in a letter to Emile Bernard of November 1889 (see Maurice Malingue, *Lettres de Gauguin à sa femme et à ses amis*, Paris 1946 (rev. ed. 1949), no. CVI, p. 193; wrongly dated June 1890).

La Queue en Brie
(S et O)

3 aout 90

Votre triste faire part, m'arrive ici, mon cher van Gogh; je sais de quelle sollicitude vous entouriez votre frère. Je concois votre chagrin, et j'y compatis de tout coeur.

Bien à vous
Henri Rouart

La Queue en Brie
(S et O)

3 august 90

Your sad bereavement notice has been sent on to me here, my dear Van Gogh; I know how great your concern was for your brother's welfare.[1] I can easily imagine your grief, and I commiserate with you with all my heart.

Yours truly
Henri Rouart

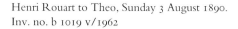

Henri Rouart to Theo, Sunday 3 August 1890.
Inv. no. b 1019 V/1962

1. Henri Rouart (1833-1912) was successful industrialist, ingenious inventor of refrigerators, great collector, and talented painter. Apart from some works by El Greco, Goya, Chardin and Fragonard, his collection was a celebration of nineteenth-century French painting, dominated by Delacroix, Corot, Daumier, Courbet and Millet on the one hand, and by Degas, Manet, Monet, Pissarro, Renoir and Cézanne on the other, with works by minor masters plentifully interspersed. Many acquisitions were made at Père Martin's (see French 5), often with Comte Doria (see French 12). His own paintings reflected more the influence of Corot than the more 'advanced' aspects of post-1860 painting. Rouart exhibited with the Impressionists in all but one – that of 1882 – of the Eight Impressionist exhibitions – exactly like his great friend Degas. It seems that Rouart got to know Theo through Degas. Theo had begun buying works by Degas from April 1887 and in the next three years more than twenty paintings and pastels passed through his hands. In 1888, fifteen of Degas's works were re-interpreted as lithographs by G.W. Thornley, and in April 1889 published by Boussod Valadon. Of these fifteen lithographs, eleven were based on works in the collection of Henri Rouart. Yet no letters were exchanged between Rouart and Theo, although he was listed in Theo's adress book at 34 rue de Lisbonne (Pabst no. 190). In fact, his letter of condolence, written from his country house at La Queue-en-Brie, is Rouart's only known correspondence with Theo.

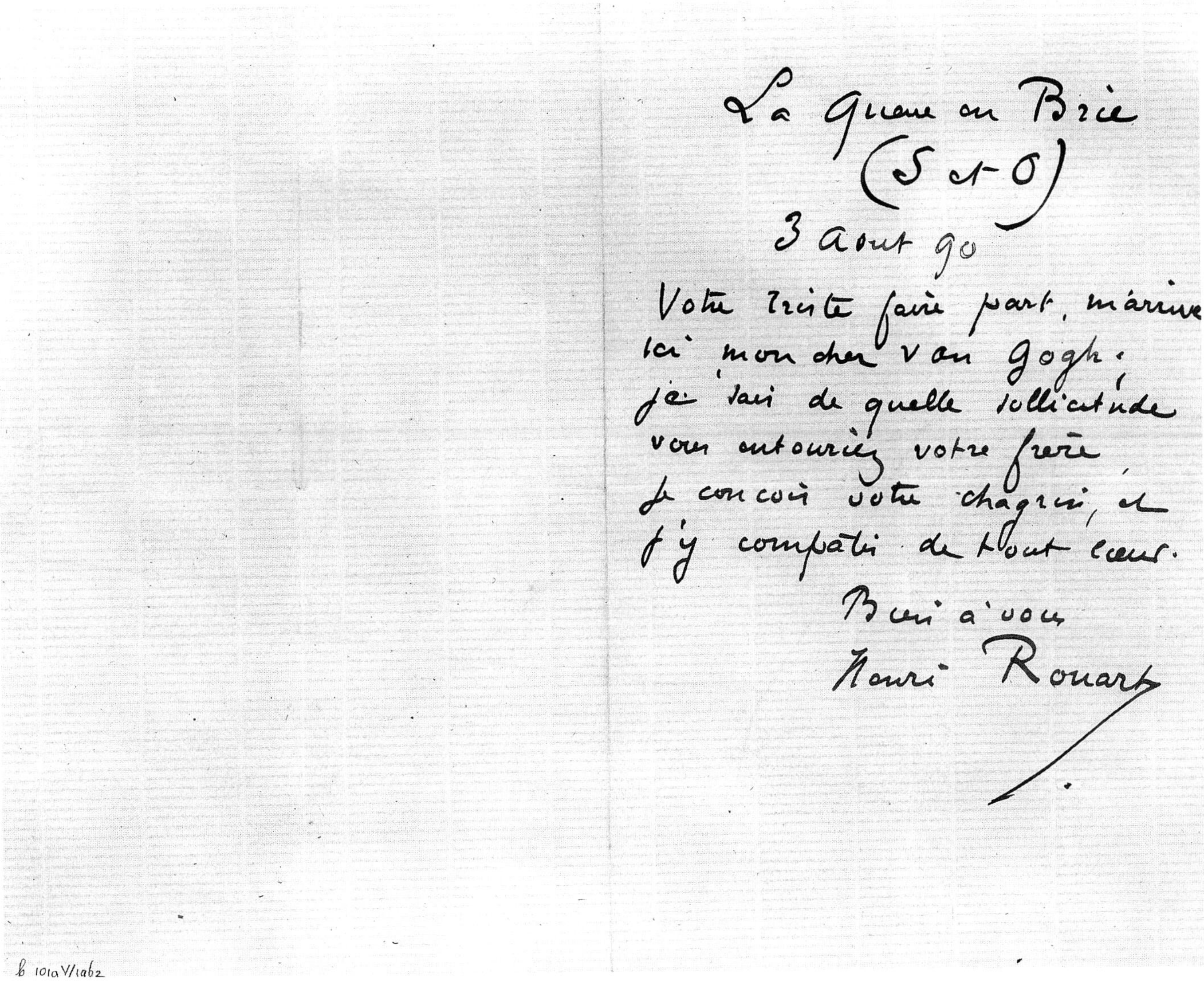

La Queue en Brie
(S et O)

3 Aout 90

Votre triste faire part m'arrive ici mon cher van Gogh. je sais de quelle sollicitude vous entouriez votre frère je conçois votre chagrin, et j'y compati de tout cœur.

Bien à vous

Henri Rouart

b 101a V/1962

FRENCH 16

Paris 4 Aug. 90
6 rue Paul Lelong

Amice!

Ontvang ook namens mijn vrouw onze welgemeende condoléances ter gelegenheid van het overlijden van je broer.

Ik vernam heden B^d Montmartre dat je in Holland zijt. Hoe maakt het de kleine Vincent. Als de Hollandsche lucht hem evenveel goed doet als de lucht van Neuilly aan onzen Rene zal het al een flinke jongen zijn.

De eerste tant van mijn jongen begint te komen en daarom waarschijnlijk wordt ZEd [zijne edele] 's morgens om vijf uur wakker. Gelukkig dat het zomer is!

Mijn respectes aan je vrouw en een fermen handdruk van

tàt
L Meganck

Paris 4 Aug. 90
6 rue Paul Lelong

My dear friend!

Please accept my wife's and my heartfelt condolences on the occasion of the death of your brother.[1]

Today I heard at B^d Montmartre that you were in Holland. How is little Vincent? If the Dutch air is as good for him as the Neuilly air is for our René he must be quite a strapping lad.[2]

My son is starting to cut his first tooth, which is probably why he wakes up at five o'clock in the morning. How fortunate that it is summer!

My respects to your wife and a firm handshake from

yours truly
L Meganck

L. Meganck to Theo, Monday 4 August 1890.
Inv. no. b 1010 V/1962

1. L. Meganck was employed by the insurance company Daverveldt & Co., whose Paris offices were at 6 rue Paul Lelong, not far from the Bourse. He is listed in Theo's address book (Pabst no. 165) at this address, rather than in Neuilly where he lived. His surname is Belgian rather than Dutch; but he has so far eluded attempts to identify him.

2. Meganck sent his felicitations to Theo and Jo on the birth of their son Vincent Willem (letter of 2 February 1890). His own son René was presumably born in late 1889.

Portsalio 4 Août 90.

Cher Monsieur van Gogh.

J'ai été très peiné en apprenant la mort de Monsieur Vincent votre frère; un grand artiste est mort.
Je m'associe à votre grande douleur et reste

Votre dévoué.
E. Boch

Portsalio 4 August 90.

Dear Monsieur van Gogh.

I was very distressed to learn of the death of your brother Monsieur Vincent; a great artist is dead.[1]
I sympathize with you in your profound grief and remain

Ever yours.
E. Boch

Eugène-Guillaume Boch to Theo, Monday 4 August 1890.
Inv. no. b 1016 V/1962

1. Eugène-Guillaume Boch (1855-1941), a Belgian artist, two years younger than Vincent, was one of three friends Vincent had in Arles before Gauguin's arrival in October 1888. The others were the Dane Mourier Petersen (see French 26) and the American Dodge Macknight (1860-1950). They often met during that hot summer, either in Arles or in the nearby village of Fontvieille where Boch stayed with Macknight. Vincent liked Boch: 'A face like a razor blade, green eyes and a touch of distinction' (LT 505); 'a head rather like a Flemish gentleman of the time of the Compromise of the Nobles, William the Silent's time and Marnix's. A decent fellow, I should think' (LT 506). Vincent thought of using Boch as his model for *The Poet*, but it was only in early September, just before Boch left Arles, that he was able to paint 'a first sketch [...] of the poet' (LT 531). From Arles, Boch went to the Belgian coalmining district of the Borinage, where Vincent had lived in 1879-1880. And it was one of these Borinage paintings, *The Crachet-Pecry Mine* (cat. Amsterdam 1987, no. 1.25) that Boch exchanged with Theo for Vincent's *Mountains at Saint-Rémy* (F 622). That was on Sunday 22 June 1890, when Boch visited the Salon with Theo, lunched at 8 Cité Pigalle, and then looked at Vincent's pictures (T 38). Boch did not see Vincent during his last weeks in Paris and Auvers. He returned to Belle-Ile, the island off the coast of Brittany where Russell (see French 19) had a house. It was from there that he sent his brief, heartfelt and prophetic letter of condolence: 'a great artist is dead'.

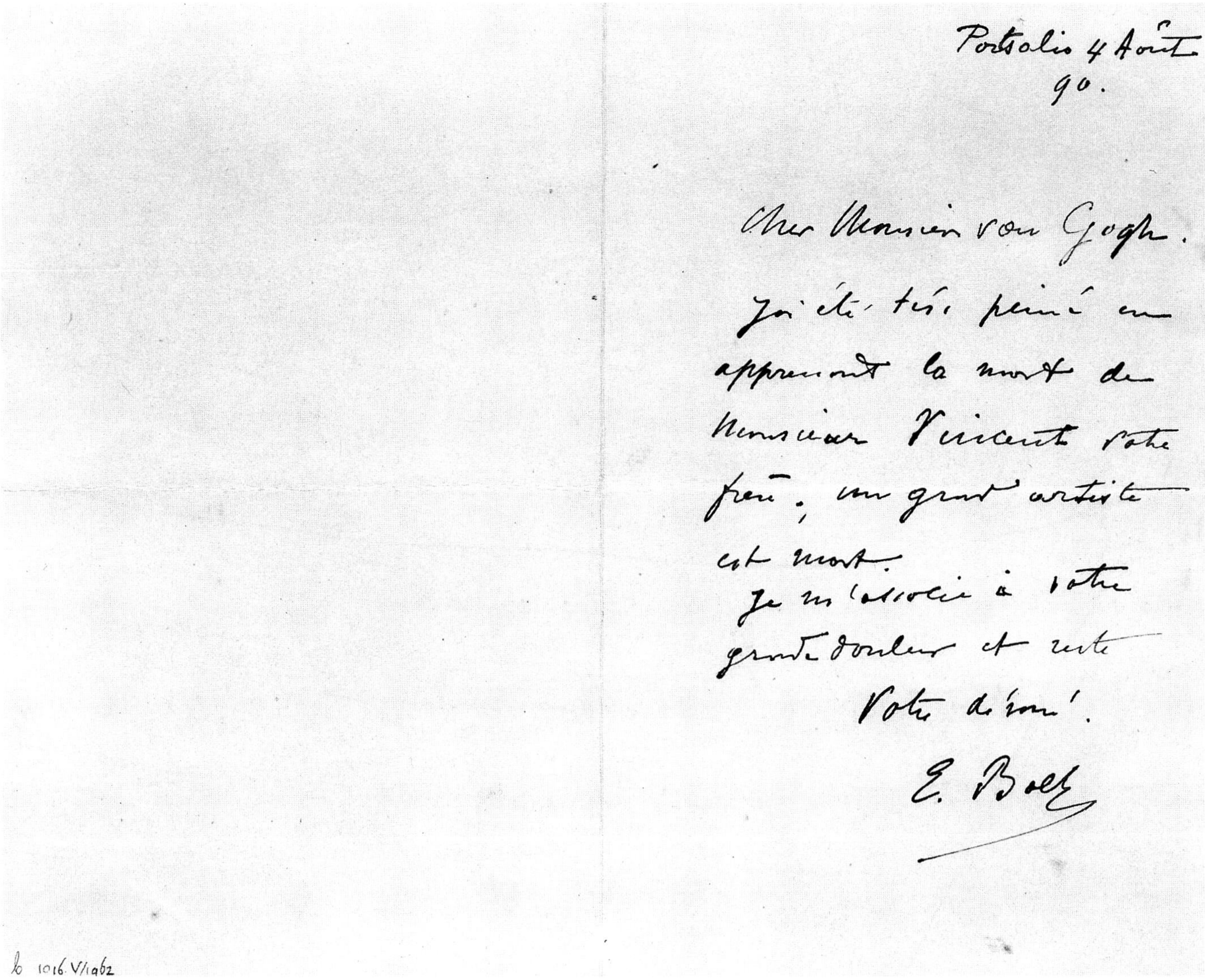

Portsolis 4 Août
90.

Cher Monsieur van Gogh.

J'ai été très peiné en apprenant la mort de Monsieur Vincent votre frère; un grand artiste est mort.

Je m'associe à votre grande douleur et reste

Votre dévoué.

E. Boch

b 1016 V/1962

FRENCH 18

Belle-Ile
Morbihan,

Dear Sir,

I am very sincerely grieved to hear of your brother's death. He was a very good friend to me.[1] *I was looking forward to meeting him soon thoroughly restored to health, for a short time ago he wrote to me an interesting letter writing hopefully of the future.*[2] *He had the rare quality of never forgetting a friend. I look forward with much interest to an exhibition of his work. He wrote me very often describing his work in the Midi.*[3] *Your brother was most original in his work. Unfortunately he has been taken just as he was feeling his power.*

With deep sympathy for you I am

faithfully yrs,
John P Russell.

John Peter Russell to Theo, August 1890.
Inv. no. b 1323 V/1962

1. John Peter Russell (1858-1931), Australian-born of Scottish ancestry, studied art in London and Paris (where, from December 1884 to early 1888, he attended Cormon's studio). He probably met Vincent at Cormon's in spring 1886; his famous portrait of Vincent is dated 1886(Van Gogh Museum). He lived quite close to Vincent on the boulevard de Clichy, with his studio at the impasse Hélène. Vincent admired his work, especially his pictures of Sicilian trees in blossom, painted during a six-months' stay in Italy in 1886-87. Once in Arles, Vincent kept up his friendship with Russell by a fairly frequent exchange of letters. He also sent him a suit of twelve drawings done specifically after some recently completed paintings (see Ronald Pickvance, exhib. cat. *Van Gogh in Arles*, New York (The Metropolitan Museum of Art) 1984, pp. 124-127 and nos. 73-81).

2. Vincent wrote to Russell in early February 1890 (LT 623 a). Russell replied (see LT 628), and it is probably Vincent's reply, sent in late April, that Russell is referring to. Unfortunately, these last two letters are lost.

3. Van Gogh wrote some seven letters to Russell from Arles, of which only two survive (LT 477a and LT 501a). Just a fragment of one of Russell's replies has been preserved (LT 501b). Vincent wrote in English.

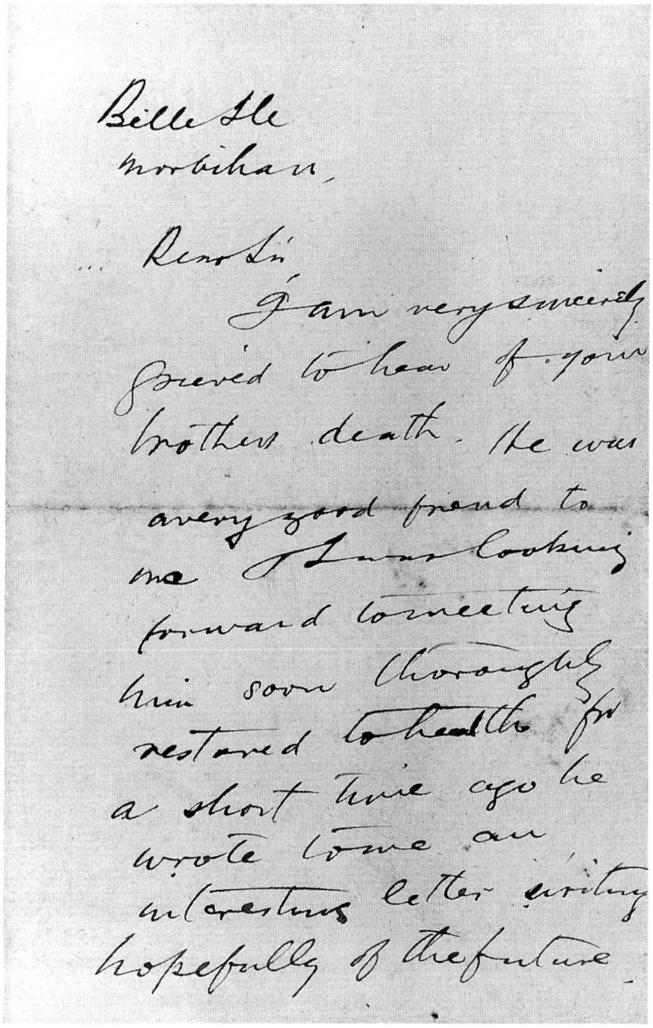

Belle Ile
Morbihan,

Dear Sir,
I am very sincerely grieved to hear of your brothers death. He was a very good friend to me. I was looking forward to meeting him soon thoroughly restored to health for a short time ago he wrote to me an interesting letter writing hopefully of the future.

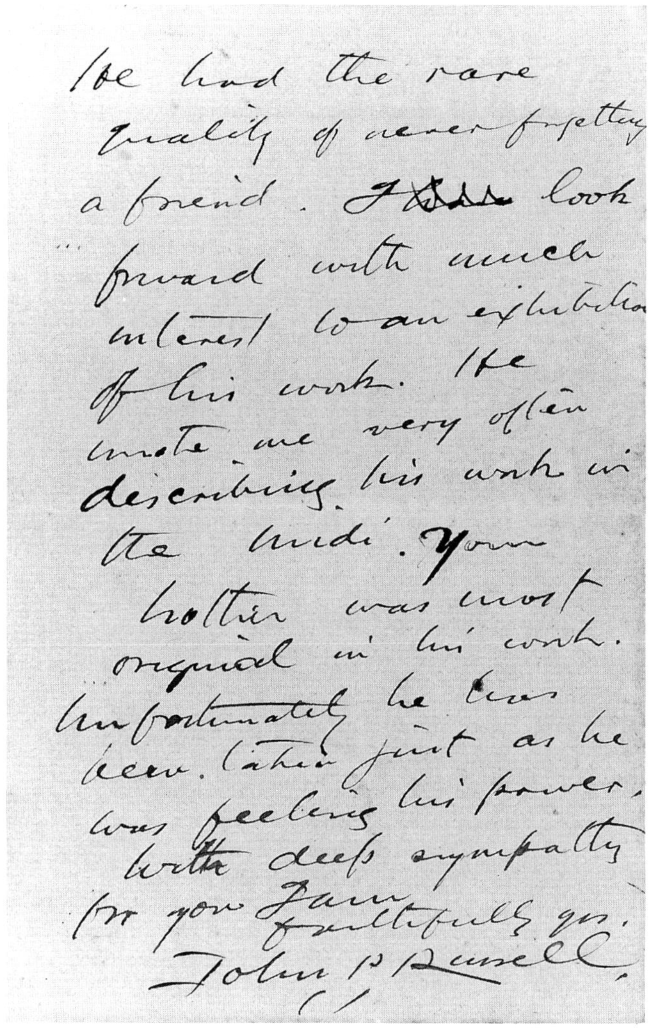

He had the rare quality of never forgetting a friend. I shall look forward with much interest to an exhibition of his work. He wrote me very often describing his work in the Midi. Your brother was most original in his work. Unfortunately he has been taken just as he was feeling his power.
With deep sympathy for you I am faithfully yrs.
John P Russell.

FRENCH 19

Auvers 12 Aout 1890

Monsieur

En voyant votre malheureux frère, faire ce tableau qu'il a bien voulu me lèguer, j'étais loin de penser que j'en deviendrais la propriétaire. Je vous remercie Monsieur, et vous prie de croire que j'ai bien pris part à votre peine.

Recevez Monsieur l'expression de mes sentiments distingués

Veuve Daubigny

Auvers 12 August 1890

Sir

When I watched your unfortunate brother painting this picture that he intended to bequeath to me, I was far from imagining that I should become its owner.[1] I thank you Sir, and can assure you that you have all my sympathy in your grief.

Yours most respectfully

Veuve Daubigny

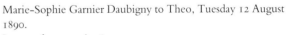

Marie-Sophie Garnier Daubigny to Theo, Tuesday 12 August 1890.
Inv. no. b 1014 V/1962

1. Madame Veuve Daubigny (1817-1890), born Marie-Sophie Garnier, married Charles-François Daubigny (1817-1878) in 1842. They had three children, a daughter Cécile-Jeanne Hélène (1843-1896) and two sons, the artist Karl (1846-1886) and the art dealer Bernard André (1853-1913). The day after his arrival in Auvers-sur-Oise, Vincent wrote to Theo: 'Mmes Daubigny and Daumier, they say, are still staying here, at least I am sure that the former is' (LT 636, 21 May). Madame Daubigny had accompanied her husband to Auvers in 1861 when he built a house with studio and large garden in the centre of the village known as Les Vallées (now 61 rue Daubigny). Just before his death in 1878, Daubigny had acquired another house in Auvers, situated opposite the railway-station. He never lived there himself; but it was there, in 1890, that his widow still lived. And it was the garden of his house that obsessed Vincent as artist: he eventually produced three paintings of the garden, with part of the house visible (F 765, 776 and 777). In the latter two a woman's figure is present. This is Mme Daubigny, who, after Vincent's death, was offered the painting by Theo – presumably at Vincent's suggestion. The version given to Mme Daubigny is that now in Hiroshima (F 776). Unfortunately, Mme Daubigny did not enjoy her gift for long. She died on Christmas Day, 1890.

Amsterdam, le 12 aout 1890.

Mon Cher Docteur,

Mon intention était de vous écrire il y a déjà plusieurs jours, mais probablement par réaction des jours trés agités, je me sentais tellement las que cela m'était complètement impossible.

Cependant d'étre avec ma mére et de causer avec elle de mon frère dont elle m'a encore raconté des quantités de petites choses qui complètent l'histoire d'un homme, m'a fait du bien. Aussi, avons-nous retrouvé un paquet de lettres qu'il m'a adressées de 1873 à 1877 et dont j'en ai lu quelques-unes qui m'ont encore une fois touché.

A cette époque-là, lui, il était dans sa période de préoccupations religieuses et me communiquait ce qui se passait en lui.

Ces lettres pourront nous servir énormément si nous voulons décrire comment on devient artiste peintre et comment se développe l'idée que l'on ne peut pas faire autrement de suivre son chemin dans ce sens.

Elles sont pour la plupart écrites en hollandais, mais je vous en traduirai quelques-unes pour que vous en connaissiez le contenu. Dans ces lettres, je trouverai beaucoup de curieux détails sur sa vie à Paris et qui vous intéresseront aussi.

Aussitôt que je serai de retour j'ai l'intention d'aller voir Durand-Ruel pour voir avec lui s'il y aura moyen de faire son exposition dans l'une de ses salles.

Aussitôt de retour d'Auvers, j'ai donné des ordres pour faire monter les toiles afin que je puisse déjà les faire voir à de certains qui pourraient s'y intéresser.

J'ai reçu de nombreuses marques de sympathie pour le talent de mon frère et plusieurs me parlent qu'ils avaient le sentiment qu'il avait quelque chose d'absolument génial.

Amsterdam, 12 August 1980

My dear Doctor,

I have been meaning to write to you for several days now, but I have felt so weary that I have been completely incapable of doing so, probably as a result of these days of great stress.[1]

However, it has done me good to be with my mother and to talk with her about my brother, about whom she has told me countless of those little things that go to make up the life story of a man. Also we have found a packet of letters that he sent me from 1873 to 1877, some of which I read and which moved me once again.[2]

At that time he was going through his period of religious preoccupations and he wrote to me about his experiences.

These letters could be enormously useful, if we wanted to describe how one becomes a painter and how the idea takes root that one cannot do anything else but follow this path.

Most of these letters are written in Dutch, but I will translate a few so that you may know their contents. In them I found many fascinating details of his life in Paris which should also interest you.

As soon as I get back, I intend to visit Durand-Ruel to see if it is possible to hold an exhibition in one of his rooms.[3]

As soon as I returned from Auvers, I had the canvases stretched so that I am already able to show them to some people who might be interested.

I have received numerous tokens of appreciation of my brother's talent, and several people have told me that they felt that he had something of absolute genius about him.[4]

Theo to Dr Paul-Fernand Gachet, Tuesday 12 August 1890. First published in Paul Gachet, *Deux amis des impressionnistes: le Docteur Gachet et Murer*, Paris 1956, pp. 122-23; and in idem, *Lettres impressionnistes au Dr Gachet et à Murer*, [Paris] 1957, pp. 150-52. The present whereabouts of the letter are unknown. The French text cited here is from the former publication.

1. Theo arrived in Leiden on Sunday 3 August. He and Jo probably spent a week there, before joining Jo's parents in Amsterdam, from where he wrote this letter to Dr Gachet.
2. These are the earliest surviving letters from Vincent to Theo, actually beginning in August 1872, rather than 1873. See LT 1-94 and 1990 Letters nos. 1-113 (that is excluding any from Amsterdam from May 1877 onwards)

3. Such an idea was already in Theo's mind by 5 August when he wrote to his sister Lies (French 11a). Here, however, he names the most important dealer in Impressionist painting in Paris, Paul Durand-Ruel (1831-1922): he could hardly have aimed higher.

4. Theo is referring to letters of condolence he has already received, several of which must have been sent on to him in Holland. At this point – 12 August – he had already received

Je suis tout spécialement chargé par ma mère de vous exprimer tous ses sentiments de gratitude, qu'elle peut exprimer difficilement elle-même en français, pour tout ce que vous avez fait pour son pauvre fils, avec tant de dévouement, tant d'affection comme si vous étiez un membre de notre famille.

Quand je lui ai raconté la suite des événements, et le dernier jour quand l'enterrement a eu lieu, elle s'est sentie très émue de toutes les marques de sympathie que vous m'avez données.

Je me joins à elle pour vous dire encore une fois que je n'avais jamais osé espérer de trouver tant de bonté et d'amitié.

Croyez-moi, mon Cher Docteur, que nos paroles ne peuvent pas rendre entièrement mes sentiments, mais que je n'oublierai jamais ce que vous avez fait pour moi. Je ne sais pas ce que j'aurais fait si je ne vous avais pas eu. Ma femme me prie aussi de vous faire bien ses compliments. Elle et le bébé se portent assez bien mais elle n'est pas encore forte. Elle a dû cesser de nourrir le bébé, le lait faisant défaut. Depuis, elle se porte beaucoup mieux.

Il faut encore que je vous dise qu'il a fait énormément plaisir à ma mére de voir le dessin que vous avez fait du cher Vincent.

Plusieurs personnes qui l'ont vu l'ont trouvé admirable.

Nous comptons retourner à Paris à la fin de cette semaine et si par hasard vous avez un soir de la semaine suivante pour venir dîner chez nous, vous nous ferez infiniment plaisir.

Un petit mot pour fixer le jour si vous voulez bien et nous vous attendrons avec infiniment de plaisir.

Veuillez je vous prie, me rappeler au bon souvenir de votre famille et agréer mes sentiments d'affection et de respect.

T. Van Gogh.

My mother has particularly asked me to tell you of her deep gratitude – which she herself has difficulty in expressing in French – for all that you have done for her poor son whom you have shown as much devotion and affection as if you were a member of the family.

When I described to her all that had happened and the events of the final day when the burial took place, she was very moved by all the kindness you have shown me.

I join her in telling you once again that the warmth and friendship that you offered me were beyond anything I could have hoped for.[5]

Dear Doctor, I can assure you that words are quite inadequate to convey my feelings, but I will never forget what you have done for me. I don't know what I would have done without you. My wife also asks me to send you her kind regards. She and the baby are fairly well, but she has not yet regained her strength. She had to stop feeding the baby for lack of milk. Since then, she has been feeling much better.[6]

I must also tell you that it gave my mother immense pleasure to see the drawing you have made of our dear Vincent.[7]

A number of people have seen and admired it.

We are planning to return to Paris at the end of this week, and if you happen to be free to dine with us one evening next week, we should be really delighted.[8]

Send us a note, if it suits you, stating on what day you can come, and we shall look forward to seeing you with the greatest pleasure.[9]

Please remember me to your family. With much affection and respect, I remain yours truly

T. van Gogh.

some 25 letters from Dutch and French sources, and 10 from members of the family.

5. These expressions of gratitude to Dr Gachet are particularly moving in their absolute sincerity. Both Mother and Wil conveyed their gratitude to Dr Gachet in letters to Theo (French 2).

6. Gachet had written on 27 July: 'I would advise you to take the greatest precautions with your wife who is still breast feeding' (Prologue 1). And Jo had had trouble feeding her baby at the end of June, when, for a time at least, ass's milk was prescribed. See also Anna's letter to Jo (French 4).

7. Gachet's drawing of Vincent on his deathbed, now at the Van Gogh Museum, cat. Amsterdam 1987, no. 2.766.

8. Theo, Jo and the baby must have returned to Paris on either Saturday 16 August, or Sunday 17 August. Certainly, Theo was back in his office at Boussod Valadon by Monday 18 August (see his letter to Mother and Wil, 24 August).

9. Gachet's letter responding to this letter of Theo accepted the invitation to dinner (French 21).

Mon cher ami

C'est désormais ainsi que je vous appelerai si vous le voulez bien. Il y a entre nous le trait d'union de Vincent. Cela ne peut être autrement…

Votre lettre m'a fait grand bien. Il faut vous dire que depuis le tragique événement, je ne suis pas bien portant, une vilaine laryngite qui m'a pris le lendemain de l'enterrement me fait horriblement tousser la nuit surtout. De plus la pensée de votre frère me suit partout… j'ai profité de cette pensée pour commencer à écrire ce que je vous avais dit – j'ai tout un plan d'idées que je vous communiquerai à notre prochaine entrevue que je désire ardement quoique pas bien d'aplomb.

Je suis heureux de savoir que vous avez dès maintenant tous les renseignements complémentaires pour faire non pas un catalogue mais une biographie complete – à un homme extraordinair, *il ne faut pas une chose ordinaire…*

Plus j'y pense, plus je trouve Vincent un géant. *Il n'est pas de jour que je me mis en face de ses toiles. Toujours j'y trouve une idée nouvelle autre chose que la veille et par le phenomène cérebral de la pensée je reviens à l'homme que je trouve un Colosse…*

C'était en outre un philosophe à la façon de Sénèque.

Ce souverain mépris qu'il avait de la vie émanation certaine de son violent amour *de l'art, est une connexion extraordinaire. C'est à mon avis une sorte de transposition cérébrale où le coté Religiosité avait une grande part.*

My dear friend

This is how I will refer to you from now on, with your permission. Vincent has brought us together. It has to be so…[1]

Your letter has done me a great deal of good.[2] I must tell you that my health has not been too good since the tragic event, the day after the funeral I caught an unpleasant bout of laryngitis which makes me cough terribly, especially at night. Not only that but I have been thinking about your brother the whole time… I have turned this train of thought to advantage and started writing down the things I told you about[3] – I have a whole series of ideas that I shall tell you about at our next meeting, a meeting that I am eagerly looking forward to, even though I am feeling rather poorly.

I am glad to hear that you now have all the additional information you need to make, not a catalogue but a complete biography – for a man who was so *exceptional* something commonplace would be inappropriate…[4]

The more I think of it, the more I regard Vincent as *a giant.* Not a day goes by without my looking at his canvases. I always find a new idea in them, something different from the day before, and I return by the mental phenomenon of thought to the man himself whom I think of as a Colossus…

He was, moreover, a philosopher of the same type as Seneca.

This sovereign disdain that he felt for life which was surely a product of his passionate *love* for art, is extraordinarily suggestive. In my view, it was a sort of mental transposition in which the religious side of his character played an important role.

Dr Paul-Ferdinand Gachet to Theo, circa Friday 15 August 1890. Inv. no. b 3266 V/1966
Letterhead: 'Le Docteur P.F. Gachet / Médecin Consultant / Paris'. Largely unpublished: just a few sentences were used by Johanna van Gogh-Bonger in her 1914 Inroduction and by a few subsequent writers (see note 5 below). The letter was apparently lost by Theo's mother after he sent it to her in Leiden on 8 September 1890 (see note 7 below). It continued to be 'lost' until I discovered it in 1988 (along with Prologue 1) in a grey folder among the uncatalogued Gustave Coquiot archive in the Van Gogh Museum.

1. Compare the more formal usage in Gachet's letter of 27 July (Prologue 1)

2. Gachet's undated letter is in reply to Theo's letter of 12 August (French 21a). This letter must date from circa Friday 15 August.

3. That is during the discussions they must have had in Auvers-sur-Oise from Monday to Wednesday, 28-30 July. The two had not met since then; Theo left Paris for Holland on Sunday 3 August.

4. This is in response to Theo's disclosure in his letter of 12 August (French 21a) that he had discovered at his mother's a bundle of Vincent's early letters from 1873 to 1877. See French 21a, note 2.

5. Several sentences from this passage were quoted by Johanna van Gogh-Bonger in her 1914 Indroduction. Parts or the whole of them were later used by Gustave Coquiot, *Vincent*

Le mot amour *de l'art n'est pas juste c'est* Croyance *qu'il faut dire. Croyance jusqu'au martyr !!!!*

Il m'est venu une idée étrange que je vous communique avec tous ses points d'interrogation.

Vincent Vivant c'était encore des années et des années pour le triomphe de l'art humain. *Lui mort, il y a une sorte de consécration, résultat de la lutte de deux principes opposés, la lumière et l'obscurité, la vie et la mort.*

Je ne dis pas qu'il ait eu la conception de son suicide par ce coté et en vertu de cela, mais certainement, lui qui connaissait les hommes et ce qu'ils valent, a du par moments entrevoir cette idée de néant non pour s'y arrêter à cet endroit précis, mais au moins pour la caresser avec énergie comme une certitude posthume...

Tout cela est tellement drôle que je m'arrête sur cette pente où certainement en pensant à lui, (Vincent) il m'attire...

au revoir mon cher ami, toutes nos amitiés de toute la maison, à vous votre femme à Bébé

à vous
Dr Gachet

PS. *jeudi prochain 21 Aout de 7 hr a 7 ½ à moins de circonstances Extraordinaires j'irai diner avec vous*

PS. *Conserver cette lettre.*

The word *love* of art is not right – *Faith* is the proper word. Faith to the point of martyrdom!!!![5]

A strange idea has occurred to me that I will tell you of while putting a question mark after it.

Had Vincent lived, it would still be years and years before the triumph of the *art of humanity*. His death however means a kind of consecration that results from the struggle between two opposing principles, light and darkness, life and death.

I don't mean that he got the idea for his suicide from this or because of it, but he knew mankind and what man is worth and he must certainly have had moments when he glimpsed this idea of the void not in order to stay put in that place, but at least to entertain it energetically as offering some sort of certainty beyond death...

All this is so bizarre that I have to pull myself up short on this slope down which when I think of him (Vincent), he surely lures me...

Good-bye my dear friend, fondest regards from all the family, to you, your wife and baby

Yours
Dr Gachet

PS. Barring anything unexpected I will come to dinner with you next Thursday, 21 August, between 7 and 7.30.[6]

PS. Keep this letter.[7]

van Gogh, Paris 1923, p. 299; Louis Piérard, *La vie tragique de Vincent van Gogh*, Bruxelles 1924, p. 186; and J.B. de la Faille, *L'époque française de Van Gogh*, Paris 1927, p. 70. Compare Bernard's comments on Gachet's graveside oration which contained sentiments close to those expressed here (Prologue 3, note 16).

6. It appears, from Theo's letter to his sister Wil of 24 August, that Gachet dined at 8 Cité Pigalle on Wednesday 20 August, rather than the following day, as proposed by Gachet.

7. This request turned out to be full of irony. Theo wrote to Wil on 24 August: 'I will send you a letter one of these days which you should read to see something of what he [Dr Gachet] thinks of him [Vincent]. After the funeral he has been ill from emotion [...] While he was ill he wrote about Vincent and he will let it appear sometime in a magazine. It may be good'. Eventually, on 8 September, writing to his Mother, Theo enclosed a few letters 'which will certainly do you good. The one by Dr Gachet I think is the most remarkable'. Unfortunately, Mother and Wil misplaced Gachet's letter and were unable to find it. Theo tried to reassure them on 16 September: 'But I am sorry that you were worried about Dr Gachet's letter. It is nothing, you know. I read the letter many times and know what is in it and he will write again sometime. It doesn't matter at all and please do not look for it any more for it is nothing when it is not found, really *nothing*'. The letter hibernated, as it were, until I came across it in 1988. As for Theo, he wrote again to Dr Gachet on 12 September, not having seen his friend since their dinner on 20 August. The letter was first published in Paul Gachet, *Deux amis des impressionnistes: le Docteur Gachet et Murer*, [Paris] 1956, pp. 124-25; and in idem, *Lettres impressionnistes au Dr Gachet et à Murer*, [Paris] 1957, pp. 153-55. It was translated in Stein 1986, pp. 235-236.

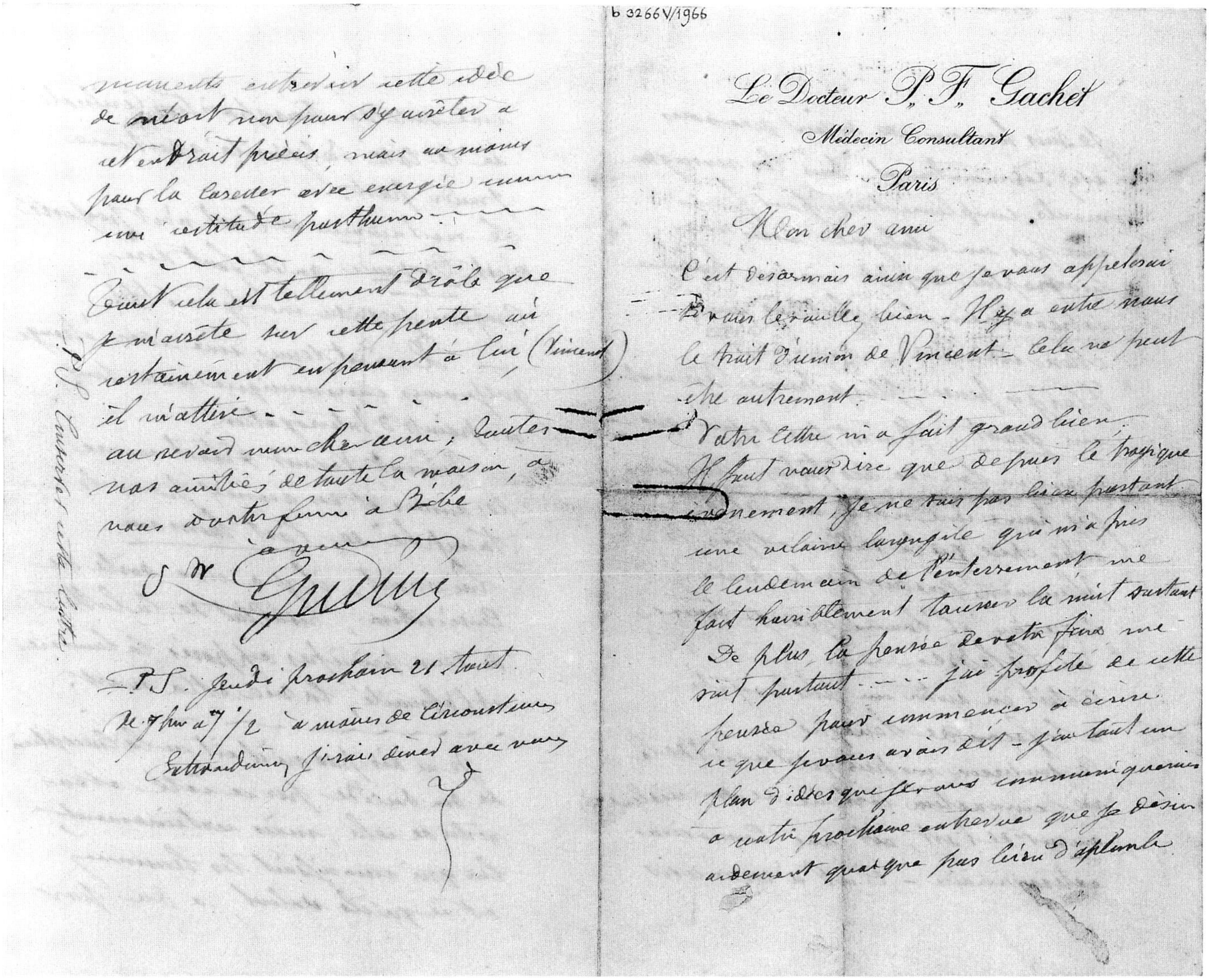
b 3266V/1966
moments entrevoir cette idée
de mort non pour s'y arrêter à
cet extrait précis, mais au moins
pour la considérer avec énergie comme
une certitude posthume - - -
Tout cela est tellement drôle que
je m'arrête sur cette pente où
certainement en pensant à lui (Vincent)
il m'attire - - -
au revoir mon cher ami; toutes
nos amitiés de toute la maison, à
vous votre femme à Bébé
à vous
Dr Gachet
P.S. Jeudi prochain 21 Aout
de 7 h à 7 1/2 à moins de circonstance
extraordinaire j'irai dîner avec vous
P.S. Excusez cette lettre.
Le Docteur P. F. Gachet
Médecin Consultant
Paris
Mon cher ami
C'est désormais ainsi que je vous appelerai
avec le vieille lien - Il y a entre nous
le trait d'union de Vincent - cela ne peut
être autrement -
Votre lettre m'a fait grand bien.
Il faut vous dire que depuis le tragique
événement je ne suis pas bien portant
une vilaine laryngite qui m'a pris
le lendemain de l'enterrement me
fait horriblement tousser la nuit surtout
De plus la pensée de votre frère me
suit partout ... j'ai profité de cette
pensée pour commencer à écrire
ce que je vous avais dit - j'ai tout un
plan d'idées que je vous communiquerai
à votre prochaine entrevue que je désire
ardemment quoique pas bien d'aplomb

4 I

FRENCH 21

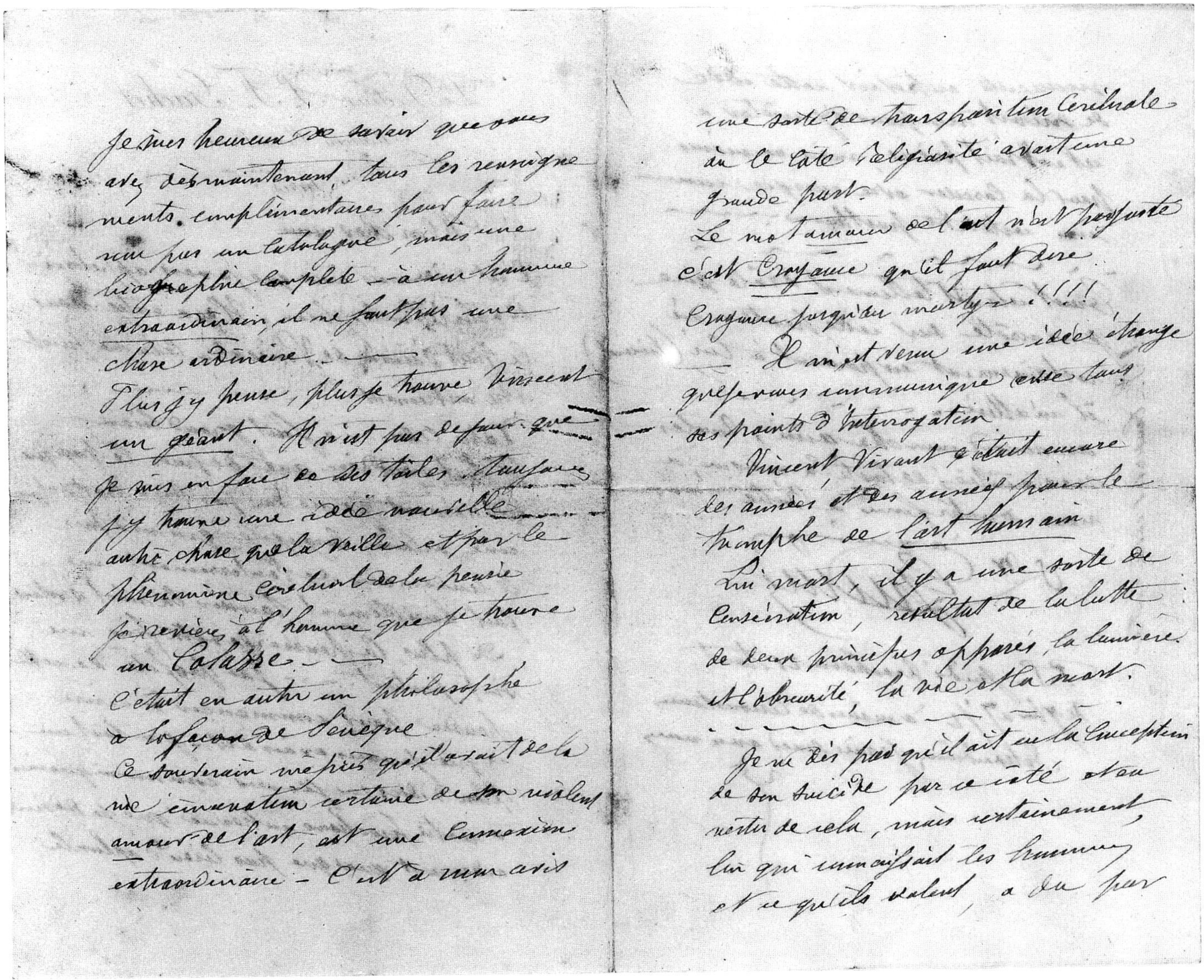

Je suis heureux de savoir que vous
avez dès maintenant tous les renseigne
ments complémentaires pour faire
non pas un catalogue, mais une
biographie complète — à un homme
extraordinaire, il ne faut pas une
chose ordinaire. —
Plus j'y pense, plus je trouve Vincent
un géant. Il n'est pas de jour que
je suis en face de ses toiles toujours
j'y trouve une idée nouvelle
autre chose que la veille et par le
phénomène cérébral de la pensée
je reviens, à l'homme que je trouve
un Colosse. —
C'était en outre un philosophe
à la façon de Sénèque
Ce souverain mépris qu'il avait de la
vie émanation certaine de son violent
amour de l'art, est une Connexion
extraordinaire — C'est à mon avis

une sorte de transposition cérébrale
où le côté religieux avait une
grande part.
Le mot amour de l'art n'est pas juste
c'est Croyance qu'il faut dire
Croyance jusqu'au martyre !!!
Il m'est venu une idée étrange
que je vous communique avec tous
ses points d'interrogation
Vincent Vivant c'était encore
des années et des années pour le
triomphe de l'art humain
Lui mort, il y a une sorte de
consécration, résultat de la lutte
de deux principes opposés, la lumière
et l'obscurité, la vie et la mort.

Je ne dis pas qu'il ait eu la conception
de son suicide par ce côté et au
vu de cela, mais certainement,
lui qui connaissait les hommes
et ce qu'ils valent, a dû par

2 3

FRENCH 21

Kurort Stoos, Suisse
14 Aug 1890

Cher Monsieur.

A l'instant M. Velten de Londres me fait part de la triste perte que vous venez d'éprouver par la mort de votre cher frere Vincent et je m'empresse de vous exprimer notre profonde condoléance à ce douloureux evénement. Agréez cher Monsieur mes très sincères salutations.

C. Obach

Kurort Stoos, Switzerland
14 Aug 1890

Dear Sir,

I have just this moment heard from Mr Velten of London of the sad loss that you have experienced with the death of your dear brother Vincent and I am writing to send you our heartfelt condolences on this distressing occasion.[1]
Yours very sincerely.

C. Obach

Charles Obach to Theo, Thursday 14 August 1890.
Inv. no. b 1887 V/1962
Postcard addressed to: 'Monsieur / Van Gogh / Messrs Boussod Valadon C. / Paris / 19 Boulevard Montmartre'.

1. Charles Obach was the director of Goupil's gallery in London, and therefore Vincent's boss during his stay in London from 1873 to May 1875 (with a three months' break in Paris from October 1874). Obach invited him to his house in Clapham; and took him on a Sunday visit to Box Hill, a beauty spot near Dorking in Surrey. Vincent never describes Obach, either physically or character-wise. When Vincent returned to London in the latter half of 1876, he occasionally visited the Goupil Gallery, and once visited Obach's house (LT 82) where he saw the study for Boughton's *God Speed! Pilgrims Setting Out for Canterbury* (which Vincent erroneously referred to as *The Pilgrim's Progress*), an image that so fuelled his evangelist imagination that it became the focus of the sermon he delivered in November 1876.

Vincent last met Obach in the summer of 1881 in The Hague (LT 165). And when Theo himself visited London in August 1884, Vincent asked him to be remembered to Obach (LT 374). By that time, however, Obach was about to set up his own gallery, Obach and Co, at 20 Cockspur Street, Pall Mall, just off Trafalgar Square and two minutes' walk from the National Gallery. This was Obach's address in Theo's address book (Pabst no. 172). His partner was Hans Velten, who sent on the news of Vincent's death from London to the health resort ('Kurort') Stoos in Switzerland.

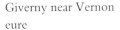

Giverny par Vernon
eure

15 Aout 90

Cher Monsieur Van Gogh.

Je vous prie de m'excuser. je voulais chaque jour vous adresser un mot de condoléances pour le malheur qui vous a frappé mais je suis dans un telle crise de travail, je suis dehors depuis 5 h^res du matin et ne rentrant que pour les repas, et si absorbé que j'oublie tout le reste.

Vous voudrez bien m'excuser n'est ce pas, et croire combien j'ai été touché pour vous d'une telle perte. je vous ai dit ce que je pensais de votre frère, c'est un double malheur pour vous.

recevez mes meilleurs compliments, et croyez moi tout à vous

Claude Monet.

Giverny near Vernon
eure

15 August 90

Dear Monsieur Van Gogh.

Please forgive me. Every day I have been meaning to write you a word of condolence for the tragedy that has struck you, but I am in the midst of a great work crisis, I am out of doors from 5 o'clock in the morning only returning for meals, and I am so absorbed that I forget everything else.[1]

I am sure you will be kind enough to forgive me, and that you will believe me when I say that I was greatly affected by your terrible loss.[2] I have already told you of my feelings for your brother,[3] for you it is a double tragedy.

I send you my warmest regards, believe me ever yours

Claude Monet.

Claude-Oscar Monet to Theo, Friday 15 August 1890.
Inv. no. b 1022 V/1962
Published in exhib. cat. *Monet in Holland*, Amsterdam (Rijksmuseum Vincent van Gogh) 1986, p. 93 (illustrated) and p. 184 (transcription).

1. Claude-Oscar Monet (1840-1926) first met Theo in the spring of 1887. For the next three years a constant stream of business transactions ensued. (See John Rewald, 'Theo van Gogh, Goupil and the Impressionists', *Gazette des Beaux Arts* 81 (1973), pp. 1-108 (also included in idem, *Studies in Post-Impressionism*, London 1986, pp. 7-115); and Ronald Pickvance, 'Monet and Theo van Gogh', in exhib. cat. *Monet in Holland*, op. cit., pp. 83-97). Some eight of Monet's letters to Theo survive (see ibid., pp. 183-184).

2. Monet had done very little painting in the early summer of 1890, most of his energies being devoted to ensuring that Manet's *Olympia* entered the Louvre. It was only in July and more so early August that he really got back to painting: hence, his tardiness in replying to Theo.

3. While it seems certain that Vincent never met Monet, we know that Monet greatly admired Vincent's paintings. Theo confided to Vincent on 23 April 1890 (T 32) that 'Monet said your pictures were the best of all in the exhibition [of the Indépendants]'. High praise indeed from the high priest of Impressionism! And Monet's high regard for Vincent's paintings continued after 1890. For instance, he greatly admired *Irises* (F 608), according to Léon Daudet, as well as the *Field of Poppies* (F 581) according to Meier-Graefe.

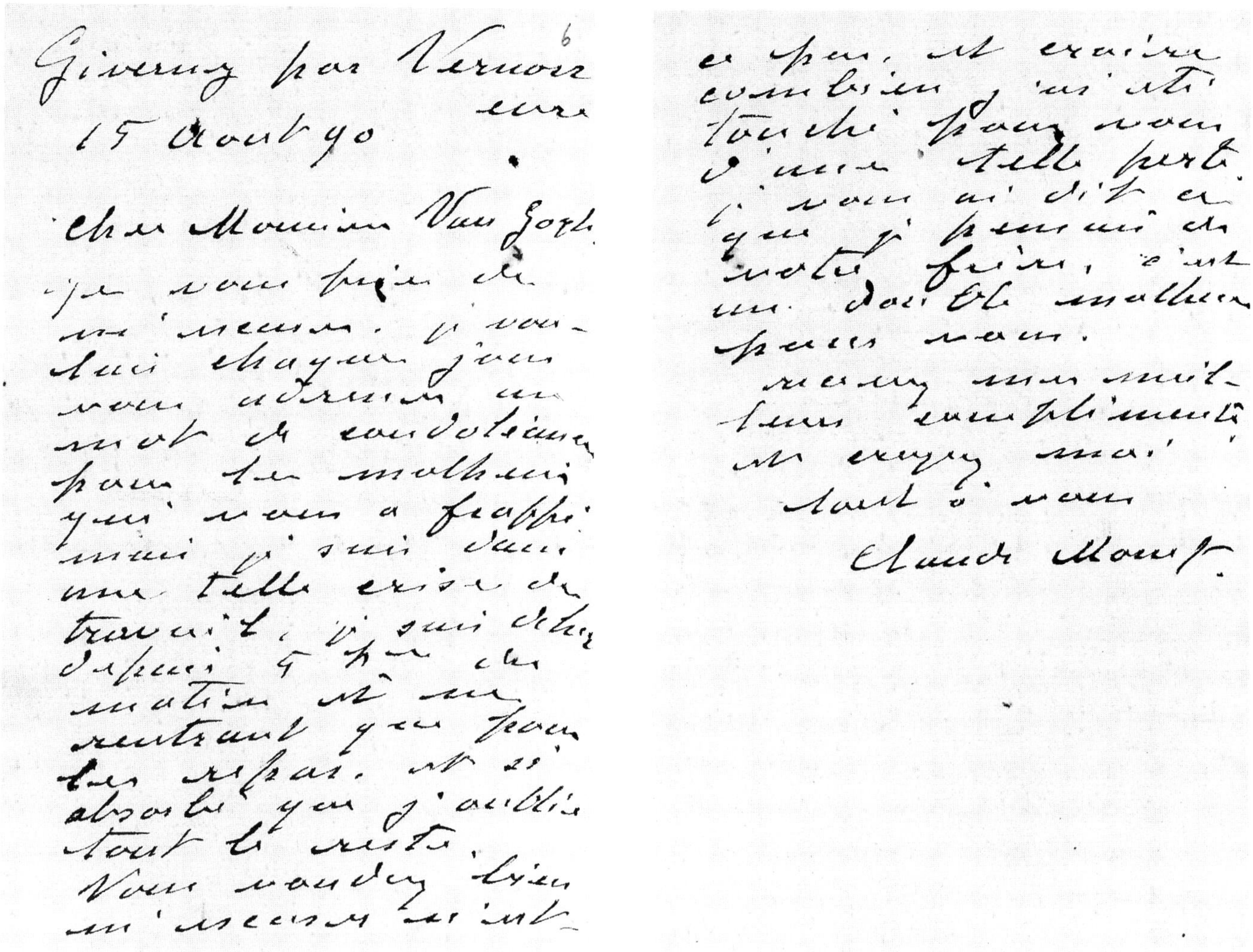
Giverny par Vernon
Eure
15 Août 90

Cher Monsieur Van Gogh,

Je vous prie de m'excuser. J'ai voulu chaque jour vous adresser un mot de condoléance pour le malheur qui vous a frappé mais je suis dans une telle crise de travail. Je suis dehors depuis 4 h. du matin et ne rentrant que pour les repas. Et si absorbé que j'oublie tout le reste.
Vous voudrez bien m'excuser si c'est ce peu. Et croire combien j'ai été touché pour vous d'une telle perte. Je vous ai dit ce que je pensais de votre frère, c'est un double malheur pour vous.

Recevez mes meilleurs compliments et croyez moi tout à vous

Claude Monet.

FRENCH 23

Aix-les-Bains

Monsieur Van Gogh

Une lettre de Paris m'apprend la peine qui vous frappe.
Votre frere avait toutes mes sympathies. Je partage votre douleur.

Votre

L Hayet

Aix-les-Bains

Monsieur Van Gogh

I have had a letter from Paris informing me of your bereavement.[1]
Your brother had all my affection. I share your grief.

Yours

L Hayet

Louis Hayet to Theo, Friday 22 August 1890.
Inv. no. b 1018 V/1962
The envelope is postmarked 22 August and addressed to: 'Monsieur / Van Gogh / 8 cité Pigalle / Montmartre. Paris'.

1. Louis Hayet (1868-1940), Neo-Impressionist painter, probably never met Vincent – though he was a close friend of Lucien Pissarro. And it is unlikely that he knew Theo well. Theo mentioned Hayet once only to Vincent, in a letter of 5 September 1889, praising a view of the Place de la Concorde at night exhibited at the Salon des Indépendants. It was clearly one of Hayet's friends, rather than Theo, who sent the news of Vincent's death to Aix-les-Bains where Hayet had chosen to paint some landscapes that summer.

(Toscane) *Empoli le 9 Septembre 1890*
Italie

Mon cher ami

Vous n'avez pas idée, mon pauvre Van-Gogh, de la part immense que je prends à votre malheur. Jamais j'aurais cru que votre silence devait s'atribuer à une telle catastrophe, et je n'ai pas assez de paroles pour vous exprimer ce que mon coeur voudrait vous dire en ce moment; ce serait l'expression sincère de mes sentiments envers vous, que la plume ne peut reproduire. Et si par hasard je me trouvais auprès de vous maintenant, il me serait impossible de pouvoir vous consoler, car, si pour un moment je songe au malheur qui vous frappe, et si un malheur pareil venait me frapper, aucune parole vaudrait à me faire oublier le pauvre mort, aucune expression servirait à effacer de ma mémoire et de mon coeur cette image cherie que jamais je en devrais revoir. Donc, Mon cher Van Gogh, contentez vous de savoir qu'un de vos meilleurs amis prend une part très vive à votre malheur et n'espérez pas de moi des paroles sans valeur, comme le mot: Courage qu'on vous aura répété cent fois ces jours-ci par des personnes, dont la plupart indifférentes à votre chagrin. Je mentirais aussi, si je vous disais de me rappeler très bien de votre frère, ce dont je conserve excellente mémoire ce sont quelques unes de ses oeuvres que vous m'avez montré maintes fois, que je trouvais extrèmement senties et vues sur nature avec l'intime persuasion d'un artiste qui ne fait aucune concession au public profane. Votre pauvre frère avait le vrai sentiment du plein air et

(Tuscany) Empoli 9 September 1890
Italy

My dear friend

You have no idea, my poor Van Gogh, how deeply I sympathize with you in your misfortune.[1] I never suspected that your silence was due to such a catastrophe, and I have no words to express everything that I have in my heart to tell you at this time; that would be a sincere expression of my feelings towards you that my pen is unable to record. And even if I happened to be close to you now, I still couldn't console you, because if I just imagine for a moment of the calamity that has struck you and that a similar calamity had just happened to me, no words could succeed in making me forget the poor deceased, no expression could help efface from my heart and memory the precious image of the person whom I would never see again. My dear Van Gogh be assured that one of your best friends feels for you acutely in your misfortune and please don't expect me to offer you useless expressions like the word courage that will have been repeated to you a hundred times during these days by people most of whom are indifferent to your sorrow. I would be lying as well if I told you that I remember your brother very clearly, what I do have an excellent memory of is of some of his works which you have shown me many times and which I thought showed an extremely well observed and intensely felt vision of nature that was executed with that inner conviction of the artist that makes no concessions to the profane public.[2] Your poor

Vittorio-Matteo Corcos to Theo, Monday 9 September 1890.
Inv. no. b 1144 V/1962

1. Vittorio-Matteo Corcos (1859-1933) was one of several *juste milieu* artists whom Theo befriended in the early 1880s before he discovered the Impressionists. Like many Italian artists, Corcos came to Paris to study, arriving in 1880 and remaining until 1886. As De Nittis had done in the 1870s, Corcos found an outlet for his work at Boussod Valadon. In 1884, he dedicated a small painting of a young woman to Theo (cat. Amsterdam 1987, no. 1.39). A letter from Corcos of 31 August 1886 gives a clear

possédait en haut lieu la facilité de le rendre, et une puissance de coloris qui impressionnait vivement un artiste, surtout moi, pauvre piocheur, condamné à faire un art contraire à mes sentiments, un art fardé et poudré qui je n'aime pas, et que je devrai faire. Dieu sait pour combien de temps encore!

Pensez un peu, mon cher ami, ce que vous seriez devenu, si la Providence ne vous avait pas embelli l'existence d'un enfant pour lequel vous devez de toute façon reconquerir votre tranquillité, et auquel vous devez consacrer votre existence entière? Pensez un peu, de ce que votre solitude aurait été immense maintenant, si vous n'aviez pas eu votre femme et votre fils pour vous donner la force de supporter votre malheur? Vous voyez bien que Dieu sait ce qu'il fait dans toute ses actions, et il faut toujours et docilement, se soumettre à ses volontés, contre lesquelles aucune puissance humaine peut lutter. C'est tout ce que je peux vous dire aujourd'hui, je mentirais si je parlais autrement.

Quant aux affaires, je vous en parlerai une autre fois quand vous serez plus tranquille. Il est même probable que j'aille à Paris vers Novembre, où naturellement j'irai tout de suite vous voir.

Quant à d'autres tableaux je ne vous en enverrai qu'au moment où vous m'écrirez de vous en expedier.

Dites à Mme Van Gogh mille choses sincères de ma part et de la part de ma femme. Embrassez l'enfant et n'oubliez pas votre ami dévoué

V. Corcos

brother had a genuine feeling for the outdoor world and he possessed a very great facility in rendering it, as well as a power of colouring that made a vivid impression on an artist, like myself, a poor plodder, condemned to produce an art that goes against my feelings, an art of rouge and powder that I feel no love for and which I will have to go on producing for God knows how long!

Just think for a moment, my dear friend, what would have become of you, if Providence had not enhanced your existence with a child for whose sake you must at all costs regain your peace of mind, and to whom must devote your entire life. Think for a moment how great your loneliness would be now, if you did not have your wife and your son to give you the strength to endure your misfortune. You understand that God knows what he is doing in all his ways, and one must always submit oneself obediently to his will, against which no human power can fight. That is all I can say to you today, I would be lying if I told you anything different.

As to our business affairs, I shall talk of them another time when things are easier for you. There is even a chance that I will be visiting Paris in November, in which case I will of course come and visit you straightway.

As to the other pictures, I won't send them until you write asking me to dispatch them.[3]

Please give Mme Van Gogh my warmest regards on behalf of my wife and myself. Give your child a kiss from me and don't forget your devoted friend

V. Corcos

indication of their friendship, as well as the saleability of his paintings (see Lili Jampoller, 'Vittorio Corcos', *Vincent: Bulletin van het Rijksmuseum Vincent van Gogh*, 4 (1975), no. 2, pp. 2–3).

2. Corcos did not meet Vincent – he left Paris in 1886, the year Vincent arrived. But he had clearly seen Vincent's paintings of the Dutch period, especially of Nuenen, and very much admired them.

3. Corcos continued to sell pictures to Boussod Valadon after his return to Italy in 1886.

si je parlais autrement.
Quant aux affaires je vous en parlerai une autre fois quand vous serez plus tranquille.
C'est même probable que j'aille à Paris vers Novembre, où naturellement j'irai tout de suite vous voir.
Quant à d'autres tableaux je ne vous en enverrai qu'au moment où vous m'écrirez de vous en expédier.
Dites à Mme Van Gogh mille choses sincères de ma part et de la part de ma femme. Embrassez l'enfant et n'oubliez pas votre ami dévoué
V. Cocoz

Pensez un peu, mon cher ami, ce que vous seriez devenu, si la Providence ne vous avait pas embelli l'existence d'un enfant pour lequel vous devez de toute façon reconquérir votre tranquillité, et auquel vous devez consacrer votre existence entière? Pensez un peu, de ce que votre solitude aurait été immense maintenant, si vous n'aviez pas eu votre femme et votre fils pour vous donner la force de supporter votre malheur? Vous voyez bien que Dieu sait ce qu'Il fait dans toutes ses actions, et il faut toujours et docilement, se soumettre à ses volontés, contre lesquelles aucune puissance humaine peut lutter. C'est tout ce que je peux vous dire aujourd'hui, je mentirais

4

b 1144 V/1962

(Toscane)
Italie

Empoli le 9 Septembre 1890

Mon cher ami

Vous n'avez pas idée mon pauvre Van-Gogh, de la part immense que je prends à votre malheur. Jamais j'aurais cru que votre silence devait s'attribuer à une telle catastrophe, et je n'ai pas assez de paroles pour vous exprimer ce que mon coeur voudrait vous dire en ce moment; ce serait l'expression sincère de mes sentiments envers vous, que la plume ne peut reproduire. Et si par hasard je me trouvais auprès de vous maintenant, il me serait impossible de pouvoir vous consoler, car, si pour un moment je songe au malheur qui vous frappe, et si un malheur pareil venait me

I

FRENCH 25

frapper, aucune parole vaudrait à me faire oublier le pauvre mort, aucune expression servirait à effacer de ma memoire et de mon coeur cette image cherie que jamais je ne devrais revoir. Donc, mon cher Van Gogh, contentez vous de savoir qu'un de vos meilleurs amis prend une part très vive à votre malheur et n'espérez pas de moi les paroles sans valeur, comme le mot: courage qu'on vous aura repeté cent fois ces jours-ci par des personnes, ~~dont~~ la plupart indifférente à votre chagrin. Je mentirais aussi, si je vous disais de me rappeler très bien de votre frère, ce dont je conserve excellente

2

memoire ce sont quelques unes de ses oeuvres que vous m'avez montré maintes fois, que je trouvais extrèmement senties et vues sur nature avec l'intime persuasion d'un artiste qui ne fait aucune concession au public profane. Votre pauvre frère avait le vrai sentiment du plein air et possedait en haut lieu la facilité de le rendre, et une puissance de coloris qui impressionait vivement un artiste, surtout moi, pauvre pécheur, condamné à faire un art contraire à mes sentiments, un art fardé et poudré que je n'aime pas, et que je devrai faire dieu sait pour combien de temps encore!

3

FRENCH 25

Holbakgaard. 25ième Nov 90.

Mon cher Monsieur van Gogh!

Permettez moi d'abord de vous exprimer combien je prends part à votre douleur et combien je regrets ce qui c'est passé. D'Arles on m'avait vaguement parlé de l'accident arrivé à votre frère pendant son séjour la bas, mais je n'y avait pas prêté loreille, croyant la nouvelle fausse ou éxagérée. D'autres lettres aussi la démentirent elles, et comme plusieurs de mes amis avaient vu des tableaux de Vincent à Paris, je croyais qu'il allait bien et j'avais la ferme éspoir de le revoir une fois. Ainsi la triste nouvelle de sa mort m'est elle venue à l'improviste et m'a fortement ému. Nous étions si bien ensemble pendant notre courte connaissançe, et il ma montré une amitié très sinçère et très desinteressée. Aussi ses opinions sur l'art et sur la vie ont elles été d'une influénce contestable sur mon developpement. –

Malheureusement je n'ai pu venir à Paris l'année de l'exposition ni plus tard. Toujours mon projet de voyage a dû être renvoyé plus loin, mais je viendrai certainement un

Holbakgaard. 25 Nov 90.

My dear Monsieur van Gogh!

Allow me to say first of all how much I mourn with you and how much I regret what has happened.[1] From Arles, people had written to me vaguely mentioning the accident that happened to your brother during his stay down there, but I paid little heed to it, believing the news to be false or exaggerated. Some other letters also contradicted it, and as several of my friends had seen some pictures of Vincent in Paris, I believed that he was well and I had the firm hope of seeing him once again.[2] The sad news of his death has come out of the blue therefore and has deeply moved me. We got on so well together during our brief acquaintance, and he showed me a very sincere and very unselfish friendship. Also his opinions on art and life have had an unquestionable influence on my development.[3] –

Unfortunately I was not able to come to Paris during the year of the exhibition, nor has it been possible since. My travel plans are constantly having to be postponed, but

jour et le temps me dure-t-il de voir ce qu'a fait dernièrement votre frère.

Hors votre lettre contient aussi une bonne nouvelle, celle de votre mariage, dont je vous féliçite de tout mon coeur, éspérant que la vie en famille vous rendra moins sensible la perte cruelle, que vous venez d'éprouver. –

Quand à moi je m'acharne toujours à faire des tableaux et depuis mon rétour de l'étranger j'ai exposé chaque année. La dernière fois j'ai eu un peu de succès et j'ai vendu une toile, mais du reste je ne suis pas trop content de mon progrés içi, et je voudrais bientôt aller à Paris m'y fixer définitivement. –

Je vous saurai graçe de me tenir au courant au sujet de l'exposition des oeuvres de Vinçent. Je trouverai moyen peut-être d'y aller. –

Je vous renouvelle l'assurance de mon amitié et vous serre bien la main.

Chr Mourier Petersen.
Frederiksholms Canal 24.
Copenhague. K

I shall certainly come one day and I am impatient to see your brother's last work.

Your letter also contains good news, that of your marriage, on which I congratulate you with all my heart, hoping that family life will soften the blow of the cruel loss that you have just suffered.[4] –

As for me, I am working constantly on my paintings, and since my return from abroad I have exhibited work of mine every year. Recently I had some success and sold a canvas, but otherwise I am not too happy with my progress here, and I should like to go to Paris soon and take up residence there permanently.[5] –

I shall be grateful if you will keep me informed on the subject of the exhibition of Vincent's work.[6] Maybe I will manage to get to it. –

Once again I assure you of my friendship and send you my warmest regards.

Chr Mourier Petersen.
Frederiksholms Canal 24.
Copenhagen. K

Christian Mourier Petersen to Theo, Tuesday 25 November 1890.
Inv. no. b 1329 v/1962
The front of the envelope was originally addressed to: 'Monsieur Th van Gogh. / 6 Cité Pigalle. / Paris. / Françe.' This was deleted and the following address was written on the back of the envelope: 'Chez Mr Bonger / Amsterdam / 121 Weteringschans / Hollande'.

1. Christian Mourier Petersen (1858-1945), Danish artist, met Vincent in Arles in March 1888 and the two saw a great deal of each other in the following two months. After leaving Arles, he spent some weeks in Paris, actually sharing Theo's apartment at 54 rue Lepic.

2. Mourier Petersen sent a long and friendly letter to Vincent on 25 January 1889 (see 1990 Letters, no. 746).

3. Mourier Petersen wrote 'contestable', but clearly meant 'incontestable'.

4. Theo's letter to Mourier Petersen has not come to light, but clearly Theo had not written to Petersen since well before his marriage (April 1889).

5. Mourier Petersen had written to Theo on 25 February 1890, a short letter that accompanied the gift of a painting, 'A field of tulips' – 'en souvenir de Christian Mourier Petersen'. The painting is now in the Van Gogh Museum (cat. Amsterdam 1987, no. 1.321).

6. Theo had clearly told Mourier Petersen of his plans for an exhibition of Vincent's work. Mourier Petersen's letter of condolence came too late for Theo to appreciate its warm and friendly tribute. Theo was taken ill on 9 October; Mourier Petersen's letter arrived in Amsterdam (after being sent there from Paris) on 29 November 1890 (see envelope).

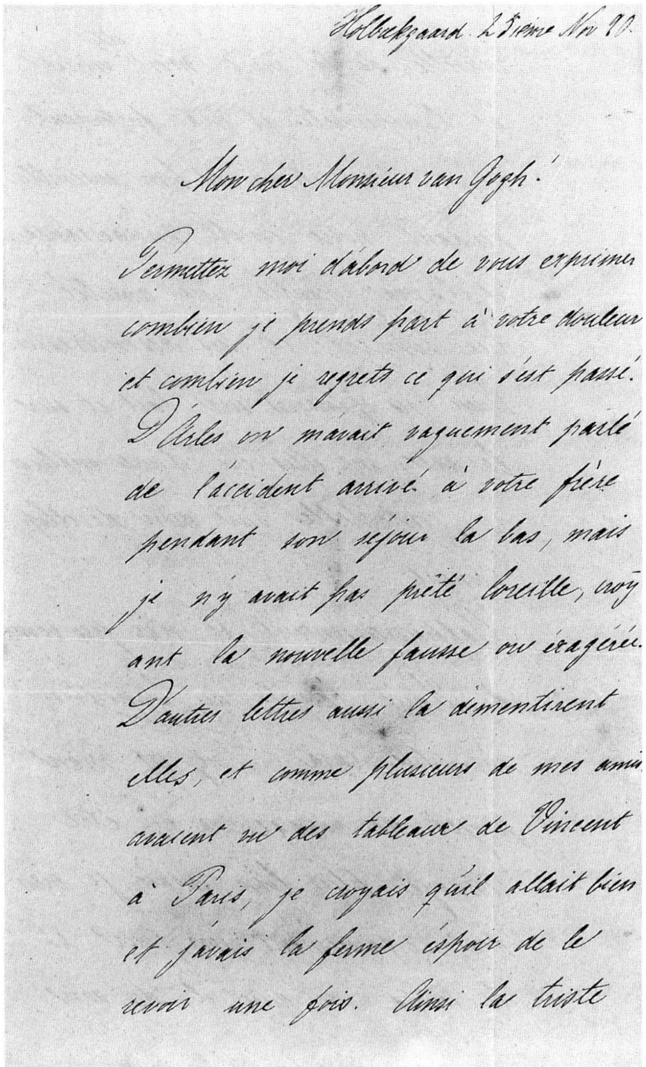

Holbekgaard 25ième Nov 90.

Mon cher Monsieur van Gogh.

Permettez moi d'abord de vous exprimer combien je prends part à votre douleur et combien je regrets ce qui s'est passé. D'Arles on m'avait vaguement parlé de l'accident arrivé à votre frère pendant son séjour là bas, mais je n'y avait pas prêté l'oreille, croyant la nouvelle fausse ou exagérée. D'autres lettres aussi la dementirent elles, et comme plusieurs de mes amis avaient vu des tableaux de Vincent à Paris, je croyais qu'il allait bien et j'avais la ferme espoir de le revoir une fois. Ainsi la triste

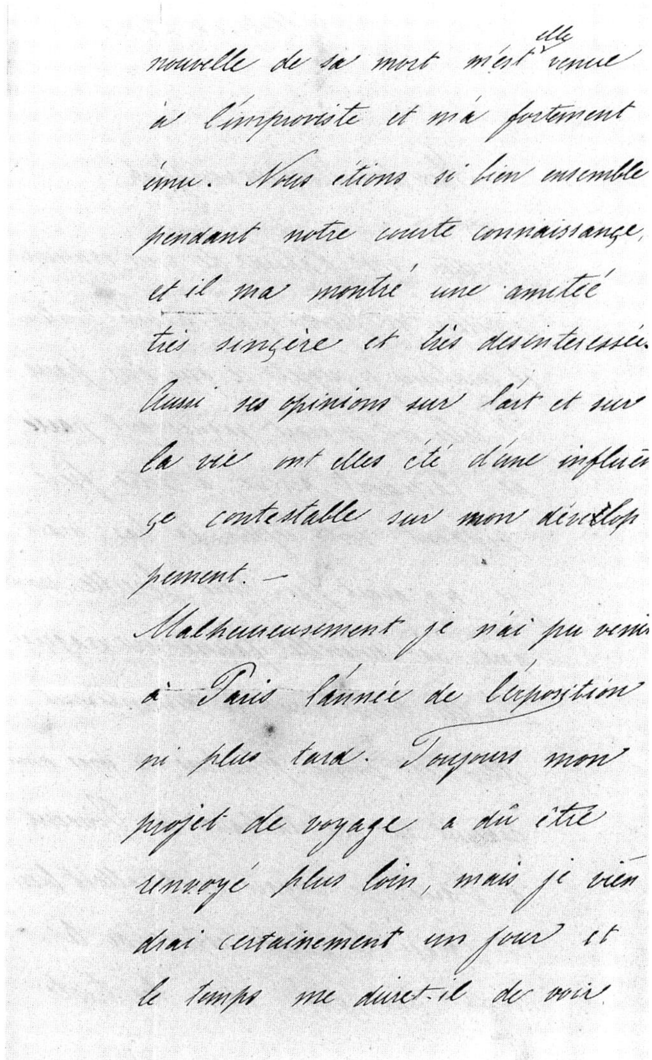

nouvelle de sa mort m'est elle venue à l'improviste et m'a fortement ému. Nous étions si bien ensemble pendant notre courte connaissance, et il m'a montré une amitié très sincère et très desinteressée. Aussi ses opinions sur l'art et sur la vie ont elles été d'une influence incontestable sur mon dévelop pement. —

Malheureusement je n'ai pu venir à Paris l'année de l'exposition ni plus tard. Toujours mon projet de voyage a dû être renvoyé plus loin, mais je viendrai certainement un jour et le temps me duret-il de voir

FRENCH 26

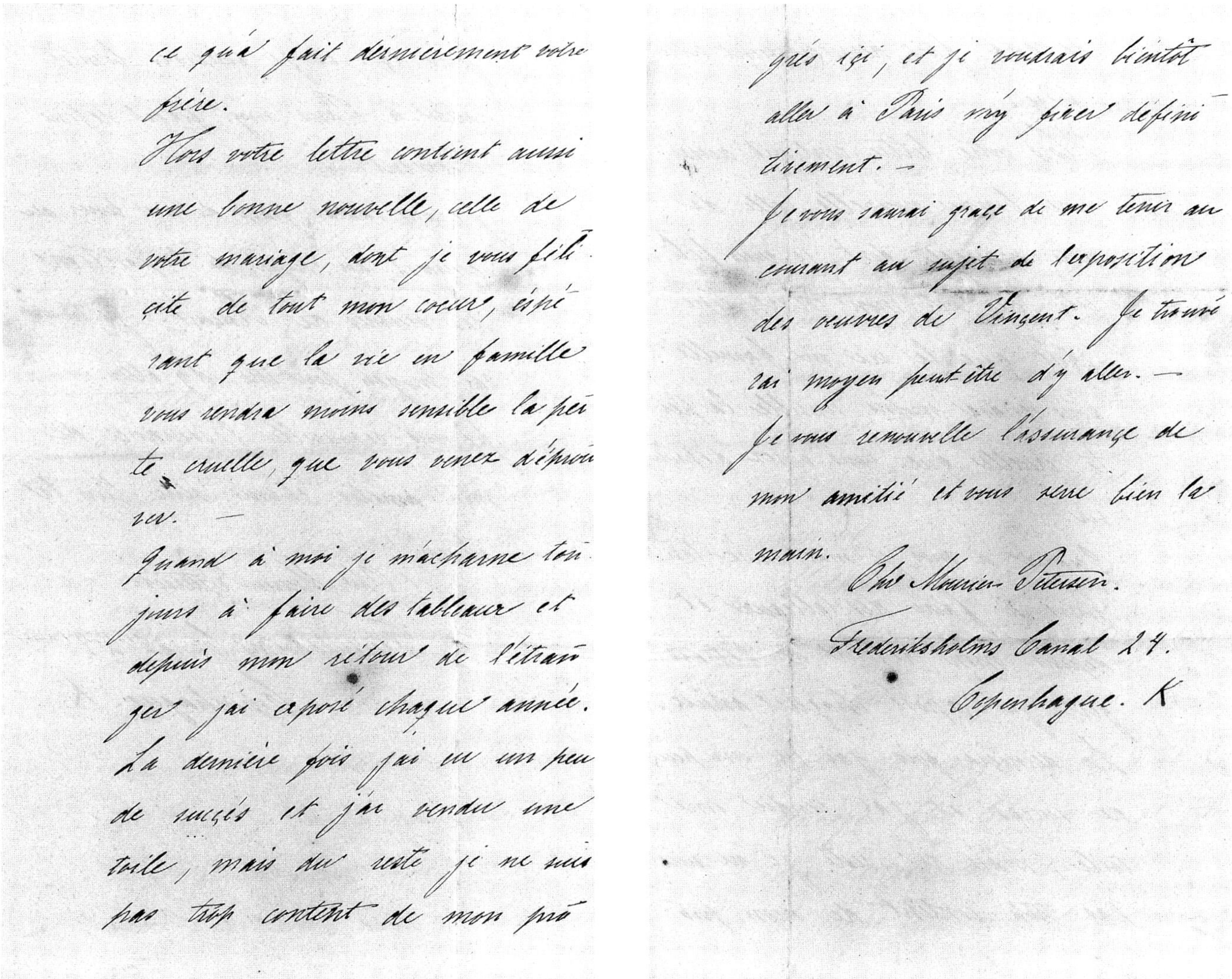

ce qu'a fait dernièrement votre
frère.
Hors votre lettre contient aussi
une bonne nouvelle, celle de
votre mariage, dont je vous féli
cite de tout mon coeur, espé
rant que la vie en famille
vous rendra moins sensible la per
te cruelle, que vous venez d'éprou
ver. —
Quand à moi je m'acharne tou
jours à faire des tableaux et
depuis mon retour de l'étran
ger j'ai exposé chaque année.
La dernière fois j'ai eu un peu
de succès et j'ai vendu une
toile, mais du reste je ne suis
pas trop content de mon pro

grès ici, et je voudrais bientôt
aller à Paris m'y fixer défini
tivement. —
Je vous saurai grace de me tenir au
courant au sujet de l'exposition
des oeuvres de Vincent. Je trouve
rai moyen peut-être d'y aller. —
Je vous renouvelle l'assurance de
mon amitié et vous serre bien la
main.

Chr. Mourier Petersen.
Frederiksholms Canal 24.
Copenhague. K

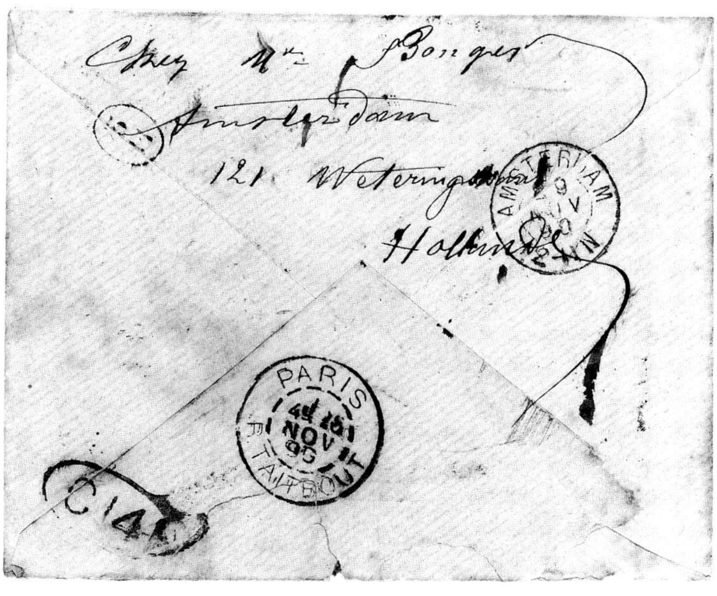

FRENCH 26

Photographs

The portrait photographs published with the letters are all from the photograph archive of the Van Gogh Museum, except for that of Mme Daubigny (French 20), which was kindly provided by Daniel Raskin. Unless otherwise stated, the drawings and painted portraits listed below are likewise from the Van Gogh Museum (Vincent van Gogh Foundation).

Dutch 1: Jozef J. Isaacson, *Portrait of Meijer de Haan.*

Dutch 7: Jan Veth, *Portrait of Sara de Swart*, photograph: the Netherlands Institute for Art History, The Hague.

Dutch 8: Isaac Lazarus Israëls, *Self-Portrait with Black Hat.*

Dutch 9: Jan Veth, *Portrait of George Hendrik Breitner*, photograph: the Netherlands Institute for Art History, The Hague.

French 1: Jozef J. Isaacson, *Portrait of Camille Pissarro.*

French 2: Eugène Carrière, *Self-Portrait*, circa 1890-1900, photograph: the Netherlands Institute for Art History, The Hague.

French 4: Armand Guillaumin, *Self-Portrait with Palette.*

French 5: A.F. Cals, *Portrait of Père Martin*, 1878, Musée Eugène Boudin, Honfleur.

French 6: Paul Signac, *Against the Enamel of a Background Rhythmic with Beats and Angles, Tones and Colours, Portrait of M. Félix Fénéon in 1890*, Emil Bührle Collection, Zürich.

French 14: Maximilien Luce, *Portrait of Léo Gausson*, private collection.

French 15: Paul Gauguin, *Self-Portrait with Portrait of Bernard, 'Les Misérables'.*

French 16: Edgar Degas, *Henri Rouart in front of his factory*, The Carnegie Institute, Pittsburgh.

French 18: Vincent van Gogh, *The Poet, Portrait of Eugène Boch*, Musée d'Orsay, Paris. Bequest of Eugène Boch, with the support of La Société des Amis du Louvre, 1941.

French 19: John Peter Russell, *Self-Portrait*, Musée Rodin, Paris.

Colophon

Editors
Sjraar van Heugten
Fieke Pabst

Translations from the Dutch
Yvette Rosenberg

Translations from the French
Ronald Pickvance
Donald Gardner

Design
Marjo Starink, Amsterdam

Technical Production
Waanders Printers, Zwolle

ISBN 90 6630 215 1

© Copyright 1992
Waanders Publishers, Zwolle
Rijksmuseum Vincent van Gogh, Amsterdam

All rights reserved. Nothing in this publication may be copied, stored in an automated database, or published in any manner or form, be it electronic, mechanical, by photocopying, recording or in any other way, without the express and prior written permission of Waanders Publishers and the Rijksmuseum Vincent van Gogh.